The First Hundred Years
AD 1-100

❁

The First Hundred Years
AD 1-100

Failures and Successes of Christianity's Beginning:
The Jesus Movement, Christian Anti-Semitism, Christian Sexism

by Daniel Walker, J.D.

Authors Choice Press
San Jose New York Lincoln Shanghai

The First Hundred Years AD 1-100
Failures and Successes of Christianity's Beginning: The Jesus Movement,
Christian Anti-Semitism, Christian Sexism

Authors Choice Press
an imprint of iUniverse.com, Inc.

For information address:
iUniverse.com, Inc.
5220 S 16th, Ste. 200
Lincoln, NE 68512
www.iuniverse.com

ISBN: 0-595-19634-9

Printed in the United States of America

To Roberta Marie

Contents

Preface

For centuries, the churches of Christianity have taught that the 1st Century A.D. began with the birth of Jesus and ended with Christianity as a matured religion separate from Judaism. The church teaching is said to be based on eyewitness writings embodied in the Gospels of Matthew, Mark, Luke and John. The new religion was unified and grew under bishops in Rome who directly succeeded the Apostle Peter who was commanded by Jesus to found his church.

The reality, most scholars say today, is quite different. The century did not begin with the birth of Jesus; he was about 5 years old. The Gospels of Matthew, Mark, Luke and John were almost completely unknown by Christians at the end of the century. Factually, there was no "chain of bishops" starting with Peter and it is extremely unlikely that Jesus even thought about starting a new religion.

At the end of the century, Christianity was far from being unified. It had separated from Judaism and there was hatred in Palestine between Jew and Christian, a hatred that sowed the seeds for the Christian anti-Semitism that has grown and lasted for centuries. The nascent Christian assemblages were primarily outside Palestine, mostly among non-Jews; the mission to the Jews was ended. Antioch and Rome had eclipsed Jerusalem as the center.

The Christian assemblages, often led by women in the early years of the Jesus movement, were totally male-dominated by the end of the century, departing completely from the gender equality taught by Jesus with Mary Magdalene by his side. In the space of a few decades, women were firmly relegated to what turned out to be a permanent secondary and subservient role.

Jesus himself was a Jew and quite clearly not a "male chauvinist". How, then, did his lifetime teaching of equality get lost in the burgeoning anti-Semitism and growing denigration of women?

That question and more are answered in this book. It is a chronological review of that dramatic century, a story filled with violence and prejudice, a story that as told in these pages departs from the traditional gospel accounts and laces historical fact with legend and lore.

The story enables the reader to place Jesus and his ministry and message in historical context, to better evaluate the traditional teaching about Christianity.

Dan Walker
Copyright, Escondido, California
January, 2001

CHAPTER ONE

The Birth of Jesus

Any story of the beginnings of Christianity should, almost by definition, begin with the birth of Jesus. That Jesus the man existed, taught and was crucified cannot realistically be denied, although there are some who persist in doing so. Even laying aside the writings contained in the New Testament, the historians Josephus, Tacitus, Suetonius and Pliny themselves provide as much historical support for Jesus as exists for many another ancient figure whose historical existence is accepted without cavil.

Note: The scholars prefer CE (Common Era), and BCE (Before Common Era) to be politically – or ecumenically – correct, but this book will stick with the old-fashioned BC and AD.

Christians have for well nigh two millennia honored the birth of Christ as the beginning of their calendar at the birth of the 1st century.

Many of the world's billion-plus Muslims count their calendar from AD 622; millions of Jews count their traditional time from 3761 BC.

Then there are more than a billion Chinese who take their calendar's origin back to 2637 BC.

Contrary to all those Catholic calendars, Jesus was most likely not born in the year AD 1 or even the year 1 BC to celebrate his first birthday in AD 1. Most scholars agree that Jesus joined the human race in 5 or 6 BC, just before the death of Herod the Great in 4 BC as recorded by that remarkable Jewish historian Josephus. The year-of-birth miscalculation was an understandable human mistake. It was in about 530 that a Scythian monk, abbot of a Roman monastery (Dionysius Exiguus, a noted theologian, astronomer and mathematician of his day) decided to use the birth of Jesus as the beginning of a new Christian calendar.

The monk erred by several years, possibly (no one really knows) linking Jesus' birth to Herod's death in making his intended shift from the Roman calendar (which measured from the founding of Rome) to the proposed new calendar measured from the birth of Jesus. When the mistake was discovered years later, the new calendar was firmly ensconced and it was obviously too late to make the correction.

Jesus nominal parents were Joseph and Mary but, before the birth of Jesus, the gospels do not tell us much about the relationship between these two people. Matthew and Luke both refer to Mary and Joseph as being "engaged" or "betrothed" (depending on which version of the New Testament is consulted) "before they lived together". (Mt 1,18; Lk 2.5; New Revised Standard Version uses "engaged", Revised English Bible chooses "betrothed") Thus, "engagement" or "betrothal" is the only description the gospels have of the relationship between Jesus' nominal parents.

Actually, a betrothed couple living together and practicing sexual intercourse for a period of time before the formal marriage and before the bride moved into the husband's home was not unusual at that time.

Legends of Mary and Joseph

The legends have a very colorful description of the way in which Mary and Joseph got together; this version is from Joseph Gaer's *The Lore of the New Testament*:

Ever since the temple was built by Solomon, there have been virgins in its courts. And when they came of age, they returned to their homes and were given in marriage. But there is one in the temple who refuses to leave and marry. We have consulted the oracle to learn in whose keeping she should be entrusted, for she can no longer remain in the temple. And we were commanded to gather the men here and have them place rods in the Holy of Holies. On the morrow, when the rods are taken out of the holy place, we shall be given a sign as to whom Mary should be given in marriage.

Joseph the Carpenter sought a wife, heard of the virgin in the temple, and owned a short rod which unbeknownst to him had been passed down in his family from Moses through King David:

Joseph did not know the rod's history, or the powers that resided in it, when he handed it in among the three thousand others to be placed in the Holy of Holies. Early the following morning the men of Judah assembled in the outer court of the temple. An incense offering was made and the high priest intoned the prayer. And as he prayed the angel Gabriel came and stood at the right of the altar on which the incense burned, and said: There is here a short rod which you brought in with the rest, but neglected to take out with the others. When you have returned it to the one to whom it belongs, the sign shall be given.

The high priest looked about him and he saw the short rod belonging to Joseph of Nazareth. He picked it up, went out into the court, and called out in a loud voice: Joseph, come and receive your rod! Joseph came forward with a trembling heart. He had thought that the rod had been discarded, because of his age, and he would not himself ask for its return. Now he came forward to receive it. And as his hand stretched out to take the rod, a dove, whiter than snow, its wings tipped with gold, appeared from the heavens and alighted on Joseph's head. Then the dove flew up to the pinnacle of the temple and disappeared. And as the rod passed from the high priest's hand to Joseph, its head burst into clusters of almond blossoms. This is our sign, said the high priest, that God wishes you to receive the maiden Mary.

After the betrothal ceremonies, Mary was received by Joseph into his house in Nazareth. And with her came her five companions, whose names were Rebekah, the plump one; Sephora the bookish; Susanna the joyous; Abiegea the restful; and Calah the favored. Some say that the five virgins who came to Joseph's house with Mary were: Forgiveness, Rest, Perfection, Covenant and Holiness.

Gospel Nativity Stories

The gospel Luke has the new parents Joseph and Mary taking the infant Jesus from their Nazareth home to Bethlehem for an Empire-wide census ordered by Caesar Augustus. (Lk. 2.3-5; some say that Capernaum, not Nazareth, was the home, citing the mention of that town as "home" in Mark 2.1) Luke mentions that at the time of the census, Quirinius was governor of Judea and Herod was king of Palestine. However, historical facts seriously undermine all of this. The Roman records show no such census. And Herod died two years before Quirinius became the Roman legate governing Syria. Quirinius did order a census in AD 6 for the area he governed (which included Judea) but this would not have affected the Nazarenes in Galilee since it did not require people to travel to ancestral homes.

So why this Lucan contrivance? Interestingly, no such account appears in the birth description of Matthew and neither Mark nor John has any birth account. Scholars speculate that the author of Luke was preoccupied with giving legitimacy to a Jesus that was descended from the kings of Israel. Micah had prophesied that Bethlehem, the city of David, would one day produce again a ruler of Israel. (Micah 5.1) So, it was essential to the Lucan story that Joseph and Mary be in Bethlehem for the birth. How to do it? Voila, the census. Matthew's author felt no need to go to such lengths and cut to the chase by simply stating that "Jesus was born in Bethlehem." (Mt. 2.1)

Skeptical scholars find significance in the repeated efforts in the nativity accounts of Matthew and Luke to tie the birth of Jesus to stories and prophecies from what the evangelist-authors referred to as the "scriptures".

Note: There are three major traditions involving the Hebrew Bible or, as it is sometimes called, Hebrew Scriptures. The version widely used in Palestine at the time of Jesus and when the authors of the gospels were writing was in Greek and called the Septuagint (also referred to as LXX), a name derived from the supposed authorship by seventy selected wise men. Early Christian communities adopted the LXX because most members who were literate read Greek but not Hebrew; Greek was the lingua franca of much of the Roman world. The second version is the Masoretic text, the traditional Jewish text written in Hebrew. This text has been remarkably maintained over the centuries and large portions were word-by-word verified by the Dead Sea scrolls. The version that Protestants know is an English translation called the Old Testament, a name disliked by the Jews because of the implication that it is replaced by our New Testament.

The nativity accounts featuring the virgin birth of Jesus were written by the authors of Matthew and Luke late in the 1st Century. Possibly, some writers theorize (with scholarly backup) that these accounts were added to earlier versions of the gospels in an effort to convince Jews still enamored with Judaism to join the growing ranks of the Christians.

Some speculate that the authors of Luke and Matthew concocted the virginal birth of Jesus to counter the widespread stories about Jesus the bastard, stories that could very well have become prevalent late in the 1st Century when these gospels were written. A time when (as will be described in some detail in these pages) hostility between Christian and non-Christian Jews intensified at the end of the Jewish revolt.

This view is supported, some scholars say, by the language describing the incident when the twelve year old boy Jesus gets separated from Mary and Joseph in Jerusalem and they later find him discoursing with the teachers in the temple. In addressing Jesus, Mary uses normal family terminology: Your "father and mother", your "parents", "your father and I". (Lk. 2.33, 41-42-48) This, scholars suggest, indicates that the author of Luke thought of Jesus in a normal father-mother-son fashion (as, apparently, did the author of the earlier written Mark which has no virginal birth story), but then in revising his gospel later in the century, wrote in the virginal birth concept.

The scholarly skepticism extends to the traditional story about the three "kings of orient" who followed a star to the baby Jesus, finding him in a stable lying beside Mary in a manger, surrounded by farm animals. The objection, quite simply, is that the two gospel accounts of Jesus' birth do not support the story. Neither mentions kings. (Mt. 2.7-11; Lk. 2.1-12)

Matthew features some wise men or astrologers coming to visit; Luke describes a group of shepherds making the trek. Nowhere is the number three mentioned and no one knows when or how this numerical tradition started, except that since ancient times the number three has had significant, sometimes mystical, overtones in both mythology and religion.

Three kings are described in the *Travels of Marco Polo*. In Robert W. Funk's *The Acts of Jesus: What Did Jesus Really Do?*, that account is paraphrased:

The three are kings whose tombs Marco visited in Saveh, Persia. He was told by locals that the three kings brought gifts of gold, frankincense, and myrrh in order to learn whether the new child was a king, a god, or a healer. If he accepted the gold, he was an earthly king; if he accepted the frankincense, he was a god; and if he accepted the myrrh, he was destined to be a leader.

The baby Jesus accepted all three according to the legend Marco Polo learned on his travels. In return, the story continued, Jesus gave the three kings a small closed chest. They later opened the box and found that it contained a stone. Jesus had evidently made them the present of a stone to indicate that they would be firm and constant in their new faith.

Since the kings did not know this, they threw the stone into a well. As soon as the stone fell into the well, a burning fire descended from heaven and filled the well. The kings took some of the fire and carried it to their own country where they worshiped it as a god. This is how they came to be fire-worshipers, explains Marco Polo.

Matthew severely limits his description of the birth site by stating that the baby Jesus was found by the wise men in a "house". There's nothing further. The quest by Luke's shepherds does go a little further; they find the baby "lying in the manger"; this is described as an animal feeding trough in the Infancy Gospel of James (22.3-4), hidden under some hay to avoid being found by Herod's men. The meager words supplied by Matthew and Luke ("in a house", "lying in the manger") are the only ones that provide gospel support for all the endless Christmas nativity scenes, plays, children's books, pageants, carols and stories.

Matthew does have his wise men following a "star" which leads them to the newborn baby; Luke's shepherds see a startling light in the sky and somehow proceed to Bethlehem. Who knows the source of these tradition stories? Perhaps early Christians recall seeing some phenomenon in the sky early in the century and tied it after the fact to the birth of Jesus. Those desiring to believe in these accounts find solace in an astrological calculation attributed to Johannes Kepler, a German astrologer (1571-1630). He describes a conjunction of Jupiter and Saturn in the constellation Pisces taking place in 7-6 BC which arguably could have the appearance of a star.

Or perhaps it was just that the author of Matthew was enamored of the idea of associating the birth of Jesus with a heavenly star because of the widely-known Roman traditions combining the appearance of a star with both royalty and divinity. For example, Roman literature describes a miraculous star at the birth of Mithridates the Great and the flight of a comet in the sky at the commencement of the games staged by Augustus in honor of Julius Caesar. The popular reaction was that the comet was Caesar's soul ascending to heaven.

Just two years later in 44 BC, the Roman Senate decreed that Caesar was a god, inspiring Virgil's line, "Behold the star of Caesar came forth as a sign." Following this motif, Caesar Augustus coined a silver denarius with his bust on one side and on the reverse side a comet or star with the words "Divine Julius".

Folk Lore Nativity Stories

The folk lore of the 1st Century about Jesus' beginning is dramatically different from both the gospel accounts and the storied stable birth treasured by today's Christians. The legendary story begins with Joseph and pregnant Mary riding a she-ass into the crowded city of Bethlehem. Knowing that the hour of confinement was near, Joseph found a cave to shelter Mary and then set out to search for the necessary midwife. He found one named Salome and brought her to minister to Mary. The ensuing story of the birth of Jesus in the cave is beautiful; this excerpt featuring music and light in the dark cave is from *The Lore of the New Testament* (another version of Jesus' birth in a cave appears in the 2nd Century apocryphal *Infancy Gospel of James*):

In the cave where Jesus was born, deep in the recess and low on the ground, there was a little nest made of leaves and fine roots, with a cuplike hollow in the middle. And the dweller of that nest was a plain little snuff-brown bird, about half a span in length. He was a humble and shy bird, for, indeed, he had nothing to be proud of. He spent his days in the thickets, searching for insects and berries and fruit. And at night he returned to his lowly nest in the cave where it was always dark.

One night the snuff-colored bird was awakened by a light as bright as sunlight at noon. And the cave was filled with the sound of angels singing. The little bird who had never sung before joined in with the angels, singing after them the song they sang. Ever since then, this little bird called Luscuinia has not stopped singing.

The legend goes on to describe the light provided by a small beetle whose black wings were marked with yellow:

One night the insect saw a sudden light fill the cave, and in the center of the light sat a woman with an infant in her arms. And surrounding them were a host of angels, singing. He was wondering how he could go out with the good tidings when an angel took a sparkling jewel from his hair and placed it upon the tiny insect. The bright green light of the jewel lighted the insect on his way. The beetle was permitted to keep the jewel, and he has it to this day. Some call this insect a firefly; others call it a click beetle; and some call it snapping bug. In every country in the world it is known by a different name, but it is the same lightning bug that lived in a cave near Bethlehem.

The lore, the legends and Luke all agree that Mary was not married when Jesus was born. Most scholars today bypass the virginal birth issue. QED from these premises, Jesus was a bastard. If virginal birth is laid aside, who was the father? Overwhelmingly, the centuries-old teaching has been Joseph. Today, some scholars are doubters. But if it is not Joseph, how to explain the numerous brothers and sisters of Jesus?

The Virgin Birth

The virgin birth concept is not peculiar to Christianity; its roots lie deep in ancient mythology. Virginal birth is a common feature in stories of the Greco-Roman gods, a source which Matthew is fond of citing, and also crops up in the Hebrew Bible. As noted earlier, Matthew frequently ties the life of Jesus to events and prophecies of that Bible. Matthew avers (Mt. 1.23) that the nativity of Jesus was predicted about 750 years earlier in Isaiah 7.14. Translated from the Hebrew, the passage reads: "The Lord himself shall give you a sign; a young woman (*alma*) will conceive and bear a son and shall call his name Immanuel – which means 'God with us.'"

In his quotation of the passage from Isaiah, the author of Matthew, writing in Greek, translated the Hebrew word "alma" to the Greek word *parthenos* which can mean either "young woman" or "virgin". Then, in translating the Greek into English, the King James Bible translated the critical word as "virgin", thus supporting the virginal birth concept.

Modern editions of the Bible are not in agreement on which translation to use. The King James progeny heavily favored by Protestant conservatives stick with "virgin". (King James Authorized Version (KJAV) and New International Version (NIV)). Not surprisingly, so do the Catholic versions. (New American Bible (NAB) and New American Standard Bible (NASB)).

Other editions chosen by non-conservative Protestants are ambivalent. The Revised English Bible (REB) popular in Great Britain uses "young woman" in the Old Testament translation of Isaiah 7.14, but chooses "virgin" in translating Matthew's quotation from Isaiah. The reverse is true in the heavily-used Revised Standard Versions (RSV and NRSV) which carry water on both shoulders. In the NRSV, the passage in Isaiah (Isaiah 7.14) is translated "virgin", but in the Matthean quotation, the Greek word is translated as "young woman" – but with an ambiguous footnote stating "Gk the virgin", whatever that means.

In Paul, there are two passages that have been interpreted by some scholars as referring to the birth of Jesus (Gal. 4.4; Rom. 1.3). The wording of Galatians seems to refer to a normal human conception and birth; "born of a woman" is the phrase used and scholars note that this was a common idiom for "human being." Romans uses the words "descended from David according to the flesh". But this is ambivalent and could well be referring to the Jewish tradition that the messiah has to be descended from David.

This view is supported by two incidents recorded in Luke which are taken directly from earlier-written Mark – the incident where the boy Jesus is found teaching the priests and the confrontation where Jesus rejects family in favor of his mission to proclaim the Kingdom of God. Both episodes use normal family terminology (e.g., "parents", "your father and I"). (Mk. 3.20-21, Lk 1:32-35, 2.11, 17, 19, 41-51.)

Of course, it is not at all conclusive that Paul fails to explicitly mention a virgin birth in his letters -- clearly he knew more about Jesus than appears in the letters we have and he wrote more letters than those included in the New Testament.

Everyone agrees that Mary was the mother of Jesus; repeatedly, he is identified in the New Testament as "Jesus the son of Mary". Somewhat odd, scholars point out, since in those days men were usually identified with their father. But Joseph's name could have been omitted by the gospel writers in order to protect the doctrine of virgin birth. Or perhaps they just wanted to emphasize Mary.

So, if you lay aside virgin birth conception, was Joseph the father of Jesus? Probably, say most of today's scholars, although there is far from unanimity on the subject. Some scholars speculate about the possibility of rape or seduction; some cite the old Greco-Roman and Jewish traditions involving a Roman soldier named Pandira or Pantera.

Just as the two authors of the birth accounts drew on scripture prophecies and stories, the men writing Matthew and Luke gave Hebrew legitimacy to Jesus through elaborate genealogies tying Jesus to well-known figures in the history of Israel. Matthew (Mt. 1.2-16) starts with Abraham and ends with "Joseph the husband of Mary, of whom Jesus was born." Luke goes the other way (Lk. 3.23-38), starting with Jesus as "the son (as was thought) of Joseph" and goes up the genealogical ladder. However, he does not stop with Abraham and, perhaps because he was a Gentile traces the genealogy all the way to "Seth, son of Adam, son of God", perhaps to show that Jesus was truly representative of human kind.

Mysteriously, Matthew's genealogy includes four women, not all of whom were Jewish and all of whom had life stories that could well have been offensive to Jewish sensibilities even though all four were portrayed as heroines: Tamar, a widow who was picked up by her father-in-law, Judah, who makes her pregnant (Gen 38); Ruth the Moabite widow who seduced Boaz and dubiously claimed Boaz as her husband (Ruth 4); Rahab, an acknowledged prostitute of Jericho who took Israeli spies into her home (Josh 2); and the beautiful Bathsheba who was seduced by King David who then had her husband, Uriah, murdered (2 Sam 11). Perhaps, some say, the author of Matthew was trying to say, "Don't judge Mary too harshly for conceiving a son out of wedlock; look at these seemingly blemished women, each of whom was a heroine."

Scholars have noted with interest that Mark has Jesus called "Son of Mary"; "Is not this the carpenter, the son of Mary?" (Mk. 6.3) Perhaps recognizing that using this terminology instead of identifying the son with the father was highly polemical, the parallel passages in Matthew change "son of Mary" into "son of Joseph" or "son of the craftsman". After all, scholars note, this description of Jesus was used in describing an incident occurring in Jesus' home town and these townspeople calling their neighbor "son of Mary" could be viewed as an outright insult, implying that Jesus had no proper father and was a bastard.

Scholars differ widely as to when the illegitimate birth of Jesus was first raised by Jews as an attack on the legitimacy of Christianity. David Friedrich Strauss, the seminal writer on the historical Jesus, wrote that "this Jewish blasphemy merely gave Christian dogma its due", referring to the assertion of virgin birth first made late in the 1st century by the authors of Matthew and Luke. Thus, the argument: Which came first late in the century, the virgin birth concept to which Jews responded by calling Jesus a bastard or the Jewish story about Jesus' illegitimate birth to which Christians responded by introducing the virgin birth concept? No one knows the answer.

Celsus, a pagan writing about 178, cites a Jewish informant who claimed that the virgin birth was invented by Jesus himself to overcome a story that he was the son of an adulterous relationship between Mary and a Roman soldier named Panthera (curiously, this appears to be a distortion of the word *parthenos*, meaning virgin). Celsus' writing itself is not preserved; all we have are reproductions written by a contemporary Christian author, Origen.

The story of Jesus' illegitimate birth was codified over the centuries in what is called "Toledot Yeshu", a widely circulated story in Jewish communities where it provided for many uneducated Jews virtually all they ever knew about Jesus.

The story commences with Miriam, the mother of Yeshu, and his father (they were unmarried) Joseph Pandira. Pandira and Miriam's betrothed, a man named Yochanan, desert Miriam and she raises the child who becomes irreverent and misbehaves toward the rabbis. When his illegitimacy is disclosed, he is expelled from the community. He invades the temple in Jerusalem to steal the "ineffable name", which he writes on a scrap of leather inserted into an incision on his thigh. This empowers him to work miracles.

Calling himself the virgin-born Son of God and Messiah of Israel, Yeshu attracts a following in Galilee. But the leading Jews invest the "name power" into Yehuda (obviously patterned on Judas), who defeats Yeshu and takes his leather strip. Yeshu escapes but is caught by the authorities as he tries to steal the leather strip. He is stoned and hung on a cabbage stalk – no tree would bear his body. Yeshu is buried but his followers steal the body and throw it in a ditch, claiming that the empty grave establishes that Yeshu had risen from the dead.

Good Queen Helena, a believer in Yeshu, wants to punish those who killed him but the falseness of his story is proven when his body was found, tied to the tail of a horse and dragged before her. Shimeon Kepha (obviously Simon Peter) then uses the name of Yeshu to work miracles and bring a new religion into existence.

However it happened, Jesus was born into the land of Palestine. Before picking up the story of him as boy and man, a look at this land is imperative.

CHAPTER TWO

The Land of Jesus' Birth

Palestine was the land of the 12 tribes of the people of Israel for almost 4000 years going back to the time of Abraham. In 63 BC it was conquered by Pompey, ending nearly a century of Jewish independence, and Palestine then became the far eastern wing of the Roman Empire. Divided into provinces ultimately ruled by Rome, it was a narrow rectangular land, about 200 miles long and 50 miles wide at its broadest. Somewhat smaller than the state of Massachusetts.

Geography of Palestine

The areas of Galilee to the north and Judea to the south were divided by the land of Samaria. The Samaritans started out as rebellious Jews living in the mountains of Judea. They had an ancient religious history going back to the conquest of the northern kingdom of Israel by Assyria in 722 BC. They explain their name as being derived from the word

"Shomerin" (guardians) since they claimed to be the guardians of the true religion of Israel.

The Samaritans had their own version of the Hebrew Bible, limited to the five books of Moses. Defeated in war by David, they acquired a perhaps deserved reputation as trouble makers and losers and constructed their own temple on Mt. Gerazzim, viewing it, not Jerusalem, as God's holy place. It was later destroyed by the Judeans.

The book of Sirach dismisses Samaritans contemptuously as degenerates: "My whole being loathes two nations, the third is not even a people: Those who live in Seir and Philistia, and the degenerate people who live at Shechem (a town in the heart of Samaria)".

Samaria was regularly avoided by travelers going to Jerusalem and not just the people of Judea but also the Galileans thoroughly detested the Samaritans. The city of Caesarea Maritima was built on the Mediterranean Sea in northern Samaria. North of Samaria and about 75 miles north of Jerusalem is the portion of Palestine traditionally called Galilee, an area rich in resources. In the 1st Century, it was geographically at the center of both north-south and east-west trade routes, much more propitiously located in that respect than Judea. It was in part a verdant land, greener and more fertile than often-barren Judea.

Traditionally, Galilee has been divided into Lower and Upper Galilee. Lower Galilee, an agricultural area rich with grain and cereal, commences with a fertile plain which, going north, rises into a series of gentle, rolling hills not over 2000 ft. in height. The towns, including Nazareth, climbed hillsides studded with lush grape vines and fruitful olive trees. This was the area described vividly in some of Jesus' parables. There were fields divided by hedgerows and stone fences; flocks of sheep pastured on the hillsides.

About an hour's walk from Nazareth on a hillock in a valley was the town Sepphoris and twenty miles away at the eastern end of that valley was the site where the city of Tiberias was built on the shores of the Sea of Galilee in the time of Jesus.

The broad expanse of farmland in Lower Galilee was the main route between Egypt and Syria and the place where the greatest of the pharaohs, Tutmosis III, defeated Hyksos and forged a world empire. Centuries later, this plain witnessed the ferocious battles between Saul and the Philistines.

Upper (northern) Galilee has a rugged, mountainous (3000-4000 ft.) terrain which is plagued with heavy rainfall and strong winds. This was a natural bandit and rebel hideaway place and it is also, as we shall see, the area fought over by the Jewish general Josephus who was defeated by the Romans at the beginning of the Jewish revolt. The fort city Gischala was in northern Galilee and 20 miles to the northeast the city of Caesarea Philippi was built.

Caste conscious residents of Judea and the city of Jerusalem apparently "looked down" on Galilee as a land of pagans, plotters and rebels. Indeed, they seem to have disliked Galilean Jews even more than the Samaritans. The appellation pagan arose from the fact that a number of its inhabitants were of mixed blood and open to what was termed "foreign influence".

In the midst of Galilee lays the Sea of Galilee (called the Sea of Tiberias in John's gospel), a deep blue, heart-shaped lake about twelve miles long and eight miles wide, mostly framed by cliffs. At the time of Jesus, its waters supported a thriving fishing industry and on its shores were numerous harbors for the fishermen. On the northern shore was the town of Bethsaida where the gospels have Jesus recruiting Peter, Andrew and Philip to become among the first of his disciples.

Josephus and the Roman historian Pliny locate Bethsaida east of the Jordan River, which would have placed it within the domain of the tetrarch Philip, son of Herod the Great. John 12.21 chooses the west side of the river in Galilee. Archaeological probes have confirmed the former location. In later years, Philip, son of Herod, took an interest in

Bethsaida, raising it to the rank of a city and renaming it Julias after the wife of Augustus and mother of the emperor Tiberius.

Peter and Andrew moved their fishing operation out of the domain of Philip and into the territory of Herod Antipas, Philip's half-brother, settling in Capernaum on the western shore of the Sea of Galilee. Another town on the sea was known by the Greek name Taricheae and the Aramaic name Magdala, a Hellenized corruption of the Hebrew *migdal*, meaning "tower". Magdala was a fish processing center, probably used by Peter and Andrew. It was the home of Mary of Magdala, Mary Magdalene.

Also on the western shore was the town of Tiberias, what would be called today a "resort town"; nearby was a village named Emmaus which Josephus praises for its warm baths. Tiberias was favored by Roman officers and had a large Gentile population. Also, according to Josephus, Herod "admitted poor people, such as those that we collected from all parts, to dwell in it. Nay, some of them were not quite free-men, and these he was benefactor to, and made them free in great numbers; but obliged them not to forsake the city, by building them very good houses at his own expenses, and by giving them land also."

The River Jordan, fabled of story and song, runs south about 70 miles from the Sea of Galilee to the Dead Sea (Lake Asphaltitis). On the west bank of the Dead Sea lies a barren area called the Wilderness of Judea. Just a few miles west of the wilderness is Bethlehem and, north a few miles, Jerusalem, the heart of Judea and the capital of Palestine. Just west of Jerusalem is Bethany, the village of Lazarus, Mary and Martha, as featured in the gospel of John. Mark has Jesus using this town as his residence when visiting Jerusalem.

Palestine was important to Rome as a "buffer state" between the Roman Empire and Egypt, the Empire's breadbasket. Jerusalem was the "big city", the commercial and religious center of Palestine, with a population variously estimated at somewhere between 50,000 and 100,000. While Jerusalem has been described by some historians as a "Hellenized city", the best scholarly analysis calls this an exaggeration; only about one-tenth of the residents spoke Greek. Hebrew was most often used for writing and Aramaic was the spoken tongue throughout Palestine. The Latin spoken by the Romans added to the more widely used Hebrew, Aramaic and Greek made Jerusalem truly a quadrilingual city.

The Reign of Herod

Herod the Great, king of Palestine by grace of the Romans, was a ruthless tyrant who ruled with an iron hand for 33 years. Although he considered himself a Jew, his liking for Greek ways of living was not popular with the traditional Jews who also viewed him disdainfully as only semi-Jewish. The Herodian dynasty was of the race of Idumeans who had been forcibly converted to Judaism around 120 BC and traditionalists among the Jews yearned for a leader of the Davidic line. Finally, not popular among conservative Jews was the practice of polygamy and Herod reputedly had ten wives. He was widely criticized for his marriage to Herodias, the widow of his half-brother Philip, a union that was deemed illicit by the Judeans.

History records Herod as a master builder, a reputation evidenced by the massive ruins of his fortified summer palaces, various shrines he had constructed throughout Palestine and portions of cities he built, including Samaria (later Sebaste) and the harbor city of Caesarea Maritima. Herod also endeavored to mitigate his bad reputation among the Jews by rebuilding the holy temple and vigorously developing Jerusalem.

But Herod was always canny enough to keep his back door protected, carefully nurturing his relations with Rome as both "friend and confederate" of the Senate and the emperor; they must have been pleased to have this strong ruler keep control of a sometimes rebellious Palestine. His cruelty and ruthlessness did not bother the Romans who were notoriously partial to their puppet kings who kept order while constantly toadying to Rome. Their titles were tolerated but they were kept on a relatively tight rein.

Herod was both a strong leader and a high liver. Josephus records that he maintained a wine butler; in those days, beer was viewed as a barbarian beverage and whoever could afford it drank wine. Dionysus, the Greek god of wine and revelry, was honored even in Jerusalem.

Herod's wine drinking proclivities are featured by the Israel Museum in Jerusalem which has displayed a wine jug found by archaeologists in the unearthed wine cellar at Herod's winter palace in Masada. A shard found at the site contains Herod's name, written in faded brown ink. Research indicates that Herod imported the wine from Italy and must have been something of a "wine snob" since the wines available locally were highly regarded.

The museum's curator, Dayagi-Mendels, is quoted in a press account as saying that Herod was what today might be called a "party animal": "Very famous for his lavish life-style, Herod gave big parties and banquets and did lots of entertaining."

Herod maintained his power over Palestine and his reputation for cruelty right up until the time of his death in 4 BC One story has it that as he lay dying in his summer palace near Jericho, he commanded that prominent men of the town be executed upon his death to ensure that the city would be enveloped in mourning at the time of his funeral.

The Turbulent Post-Herod Years

After the death of Herod, Palestine spiraled down from dictatorial control to virtual chaos. The historian Josephus draws a harsh picture of governmental disarray, describing a land filled with riots and anarchy. Perhaps exaggerating, as was Josephus' sometimes wont, he relates that "a great and wild fury spread itself over the nation".

This is a good point to raise a warning flag regarding Josephus as historian. Shaye J.D. Cohen in his *Josephus in Galilee and Rome* concludes that he "can invent, exaggerate, overemphasize, distort, suppress, simplify, or, occasionally, tell the truth." Overall, though, today's scholars find him reliable much more than just occasionally.

Herod had many wives, many children and many grandchildren; Josephus lists them all in his *Antiquities of the Jews;* he also notes that within a hundred years, "the posterity of Herod, which were a great number, were, excepting a few, utterly destroyed." Josephus' translator inserts a footnote at this point: "Whether this sudden extinction of almost the entire lineage of Herod the Great was not in part as a punishment for the gross incests they were frequently guilty of, in marrying their own nephews and nieces, well deserves to be considered." As we shall see, this incest was not limited to nephews and nieces – it may also have intertwined brothers and sisters.

In an effort to bring the rebellious provinces under control after Herod's death, the Romans named his son, Archelaus, as ethnarch – representative of the emperor – over the most critical district which included Judea, Samaria and Idumea. However, Archelaus could not "walk the walk" of his father and erred too heavily on the side of cruelty and oppression, far exceeding even his father's heavy handed style of ruling. After a tumultuous reign, Archelaus was deposed in AD 6, recalled to Rome and shortly thereafter banished to Gaul.

Judea was then for a short time attached to the Roman province of Syria where the legate was P. Sulpicius Quirinius; he commanded the Roman legions stationed there as a peace-keeping force for the eastern provinces of the empire. Actions by Quirinius apparently arising out of a census ordered by him led to an uprising in Galilee where Judas the Galilean urged his compatriots to rise against the Romans. Taking advantage of the peasants' rebellious feelings, Judas led a band of them out of the mountains of Upper Galilee and wasted agriculture areas and towns in Judea.

Judas the Galilean was not the first trouble-maker to emerge from Galilee; his father named Hezekias whom Josephus describes as an "arch-robber who overran the country", had been executed by Herod the Great. Josephus records the death of Judas the Galilean and states that "his followers were scattered." However, his sons were not killed and lived, as we shall see, to be crucified by the Romans in later years.

Josephus' description in his *Antiquities* of *the Jews* of the rebellion of Judas the Galilean is quite grandiose: "All sorts of misfortunes also sprang from these men, and the nation was infected with this doctrine to an incredible degree; one violent war came upon us after another, and we lost our friends which used to alleviate our pains; there were also very great robberies and murders of our principal men." Josephus paints Judas the Galilean and his men as leading "a philosophic sect" which brought great troubles to Palestine – probably a reference to the Zealots.

About that time, the Romans took over direct control of Judea through an appointed prefect or procurator (there is historical confusion as to the use of the title; procurator has been the most commonly used but in 1961 an unearthed inscription identified Pontius Pilate as a "prefect of Judea.") Under this system which remained in effect for decades, the prefects were the financial and military administrators for Palestine. They dwelled in Jerusalem or at Herod's palace in Caesarea and kept order with a light armed force, but had the centurions commanded by the legate of Syria at their beck and call when needed.

Another of Herod's sons, Philip, was given as tetrarch the extreme northern area of Palestine; he ruled for 38 years. He embarked on a building program, constructing in the region of Paneas on the Jordan River a new capital named Caesarea Philippi. He also built up and then renamed Bethsaida as Julias, after the emperor's wife. Herod Antipas, his half brother, became tetrarch over an area including Galilee and Perea and he was responsible for building not too far from Nazareth a new city, Tiberias.

Although the areas over which the sons of Herod were given titular and civilian power were in some respects regarded as semi-independent kingdoms, the Romans kept stronger controls than they had when Herod the Great ruled the land. The sons carried on their father's despotic reputation for cruelty in suppressing disorder but they lacked Herod's savvy with respect to Empire politics. Neither was given the almost total ruling latitude accorded by the Roman Senate to Herod and neither was immediately given the title of king.

The well-documented stories about the marital escapades of the "Herod boys" are fascinating. Herod Antipas' second wife was Herodias. She had been previously married to another Herod and they had a daughter named Salome. And this Herod was not monogamous; he was first married to a Nabatean princess whom he left to marry Herodias. More of Herodias later in connection with the death of John the Baptist.

The division of Palestine which followed from the death of Herod created a variety of governmental problems. Taxes were increased and, since they were already high, this resulted in even more resentment among the Palestinians. What Josephus calls "the restlessness abroad in the land" escalated. An over-taxed, disaffected and impoverished public, particularly the peasants in Galilee, was deeply resentful of its Roman rulers, harboring increasing bitterness toward the ruling classes.

Life in Palestine

The people of Jerusalem apparently experienced a relatively stable life in the first part of the century after the brief rebellions were quelled, the Roman prefects ensconced, and the sons of Herod settled down. Currencies and pay levels seem to have been relatively stable. Using Roman monetary values as a reference, a day worker would make about three sesterces (four sesterces equaled about one Roman denarius, one

Greek drachma, one-fourth of a Jewish shekel). Slavery was widespread throughout the Roman empire and the freed slaves, who still owed some duties to their former master, constituted a large percentage of the populace.

Maintaining a slave was expensive, costing around 400 sesterces a year; an able bodied slave could be bought for anywhere from 500 to 1,000 sesterces. A Roman soldier earned 900 sesterces annually and a governor of a province was highly paid – up to one million sesterces annually, and that amount was about the net worth of a Roman senator. And to put it all in context, Pliny the Younger placed his wealth at about 20 million sesterces.

There was much restlessness in the rural areas of Palestine, a very cruel land for the peasant farmers. Historians have pointed out that the life of the nominally free peasants in rural Palestine was frequently far worse than that of a metropolitan slave. At least the more valued city slaves were reasonably well fed, clothed and housed. In most of Galilee among the peasant farmers, life was harsh, poverty was the rule, not the exception, and famine and displacement from their meager plots of land were not unusual. And the lives of the laborers and artisans were not much better.

Taxes in Palestine were horribly high. The onerous tithes to support the temple, obligatory for all Jews, took 20% of every farmer's production. On top of that, the Romans assessed a land tax of 1% of the value of the land plus a crop tax of 12% on production.

The right to collect taxes was sold by the Romans to Palestinian entrepreneurs and the collectors were given a quota to fulfill. They paid a fixed amount to the Roman masters for their "franchise", the right to collect the taxes, and were then allowed to add for themselves whatever they could extort from the peasants. Needless to say, the tax collectors were despised by the Palestinians.

In total, taxes captured about 35% of the value of peasants' work and produce and frequently drove peasant farmers from their land. Many, hating both the Romans and the landowners, became brigands and preyed on travelers through rural Palestine. They were ready for recruitment by the Zealots whose numbers grew apace with impoverishment in the rural areas.

John Dominic Crossan undertakes a compellingly thoughtful analysis of the Galilean peasantry in the decades following the death of Herod the Great in his recent *The Birth of Christianity*. He focuses on the rural commercialization that resulted from the rebuilding of Sepphoris and creation of Tiberias. These massive building programs, he suggests, dramatically changed broad areas from rural to urban and inevitably forced into destitution numerous peasants.

These dispossessed men and women led a marginal existence, seeking to survive, to use Crossan's terms, as "rural artisans" or "landless laborers". Many became itinerants living off the travelers and the land belonging to others. Some joined the roving bands of the Zealots. All were peculiarly susceptible to the spellbinding talk of the wandering prophets and holy men.

This Palestinian world where Jesus was born and raised was in one sense a cosmopolitan world – at least in Jerusalem – where a religiously educated Jew could be fluent in all of the languages spoken in Palestine and carry on business with the Romans and the traders who traveled through the land. In another sense, this world was controlled by a cruel invader and a strict religion with its people impoverished, victims of malnutrition and disease, and frequently driven from their homes by exorbitant taxes and the commercialization of rural areas. Particularly in the rural areas, it was a time characterized by native restlessness and constant tensions between the haves and the have-nots, the wealthy and the poor, all against the background of an ever-present nationalistic sentiment.

CHAPTER THREE

The Boyhood and Maturing of Jesus

After the birth accounts, there are again numerous parallels to the scriptures in the reported activities of Mary, Joseph and Jesus. Matthew's description of the slaughter of innocent children which allegedly drove them into exile brings to mind the Exodus story of Moses' escape from the wrath of Pharaoh. Official records provide no corroboration for this; they contain no reference to a Herodian infanticide, although there are numerous accounts of brutality by Herod.

Was Jesus' boyhood hometown really Nazareth? Mark, the earliest written, does not name it but Luke does: "When he came to Nazareth, where he had been brought up..." (Lk. 4.16) Matthew describes a lengthy visit to Capernaum during which Jesus visits Peter's home and performs a number of miracles, including the oft-repeated calming of a storm on the Sea of Galilee, after which he "crossed the sea and came to his own town", apparently Capernaum. (Mt. 8, 9) Mark describes this visit to Capernaum but does not refer to it as a residence for Jesus. Interestingly, Mark does tell of a healing of Peter's mother-in-law in Capernaum, giving rise to the belief that Peter was married when he was called to be a disciple. (Mk. 1.21-45)

The Boyhood Legends

Mentions in the four gospels of Jesus during these formative years of his life are few and far between. Perhaps because of this omission, apocryphal gospels blossomed in the 2d Century to fill in the gaps. The best known accounts appear in the Infancy Gospel of Thomas and Infancy Gospel of James. The former deals primarily with the birth of Jesus; the latter concentrates on Jesus as a boy from age 5 to 12.

Not surprisingly, the James gospel relates many stories of miracles performed by the child Jesus. Hennecke and Schneemelcher, noted writers on the apocrypha (*New Testament Apocrypha*) state that the man who drafted these bizarre stories may have been "endowed with a gift of vivid story-telling," but on the downside was "lacking in good taste, restraint, and discretion."

John P. Meier, a Catholic scholar, describes these stories colorfully as picturing a "divine brat, a malicious boy". CBQ 59 (1997) p. 522. He cites the story of Jesus throwing a childlike tantrum and having "a child who runs up against him drop dead." Meier concludes bluntly that "the portrait of this superboy belongs more in a horror movie than a gospel." John P. Meier, *A Marginal Jew, Rethinking the Historical Jesus.*

Then there are the legends, milder than the boy-brat stories, which expand at great length on Matthew's brief tale of Mary and Joseph escaping from Palestine to Egypt to avoid Herod's infanticide, returning to Palestine only after the death of Herod to establish a new home in

Nazareth, thereby fulfilling the prophecy of Hosea that "out of Egypt did I call my son". (Mt. 2.13-15)

Joseph rose before dawn, at the hour when the cock crows and the horse neighs in the stable. He placed Mary and her child on one ass, and he mounted another, and three boys and one girl followed closely behind them, as well as the old midwife Zelomi, who had attached herself to the family. They did not stop to prepare provisions for the long journey, for they carried with them to provide for their needs the gold brought to them by the Magi. Under cover of night they left Nazareth without taking leave of their kin or their neighbors, and started out in haste for the hill country and the desert leading to the borders of Egypt.

They had not gone very far when the sun came up, and they knew that Herod's men would be out upon the roads. But they did not know where to hide. At that moment they saw a laborer sowing wheat in a field along the road. The child Jesus picked up a handful of the seed and threw it by the wayside. Instantly it grew before their eyes and ripened, ready for reaping. In this tall wheat, Joseph and his family hid themselves. Soon, Herod's men came by and asked the farmer: Have you seen a woman pass here carrying a child in her arms? Yes, said the farmer. I saw her as I was sowing the wheat. The wheat is grown and ripening, said Herod's henchmen. It must have been sown many months ago. And they went away. Joseph and Mary settled in Memphis, Egypt, according to the legend, and there Jesus performed many miracles.

One day Jesus met an old shepherd and his two sons, who were very, very poor. Jesus took three staves from a tub and stuck them into the ground as his gift to these good shepherds. Straightaway the three staves grew into three fruit-bearing trees. And in the time of Cyriacus it was reported that those trees were still blooming and bearing fruit... .

And then there is the legendary trip by the boy Jesus to India:

The Prince of India went to Galilee with a retinue of men and asked directions to Marmion Way where Joseph's home and carpentry shop stood side by side. For many days the Prince of India remained in Joseph's house, talking to Jesus and his parents. And finally he asked Joseph and Mary to let Jesus return with him to India as his honored guest.

Let him come with me to my palace in Orissa, and let him enter the temple of Jagannath to study the Vedas and the Laws of Many from our wise priest, Lamaas Bramas, Ravanna pleaded. And he, in turn, can teach the wisdom of his people to Lamaas.

Joseph and Mary consented to Ravanna's request. And Jesus left with the prince, crossing the Sindh into India. The priest Lamaas loved the boy Jesus the moment he came into the temple; and Jesus liked Lamaas above all the others in Jagannath. They often walked together in the temple grounds, discoursing on many matters.

Legends about the boy Jesus were not confined to those told and retold by Palestinian followers of Jesus. Amazingly, they spread around the then-known world and even beyond the Jewish Diaspora. One boy Jesus legend has been repeated in Great Britain for centuries. This fascinating story involves Joseph of Arimathea, described in the gospels as the rich man who had been a believer in Jesus and, at the end of that cruel day, lovingly takes Jesus' body down from the cross. (Mt. 27.57) The legend is based on trips supposedly made by Joseph of Arimathea from Palestine to his tin mines in Glastonbury in Cornwall which were the source for his riches.

The legend recounts that on one of these trips, Joseph brought with him both Mary and Jesus and the boy Jesus is portrayed as walking on the green hills of England. And then, in dramatic fashion, the legend describes Joseph of Arimathea bringing the Holy Grail to Glastonbury for burial.

Strangely, this legendary visit to England by Joseph of Arimathea with the boy Jesus has also been retold over the centuries by peasants in the remote villages of Upper Galilee. (Lionel Smithett Lewis, *St. Joseph of Arimathea at Glastonbury*.)

Jesus' Education and Occupation

Turning from the legends to what can reasonably be projected from what is known, it is virtually certain that Jesus grew up among peasants in a small town in the hills of Lower Galilee. Most likely, he was educated in a synagogue setting. However, there is argument about this among the scholars. Some see Nazareth as having a population of about 1000 to 2000, which may well have supported a community religious center. Others picture Nazareth as little more than a hamlet with a population under 500. But if the gospel references are accurate, and there is little reason to doubt them in this respect, Jesus was somehow indoctrinated into the scriptures of the Hebrew Bible.

Was Jesus a carpenter? Christians have always been taught that Jesus as a youth labored as a carpenter's assistant, following in the footsteps of his father, Joseph. Mark, Matthew and the 2d Century Infancy Gospel of Thomas all use a Greek word for "woodworker" in describing Jesus' occupation. It is most unlikely that Jesus and his father were carpenters in the sense of building homes since wood was not normally used for that purpose. Probably, if they worked with wood, it was on farming instruments such as yokes and plows.

Other occupations are speculated. One author, A.N. Wilson, argues that the words *ho tekton* used by Mark (Mk. 6.3, repeated in Matt. 13.55) could have been an effort to put into Greek a Semitic or Aramaic word, *naggar*, which could mean either craftsman or scholar. (A.N. Wilson, *Jesus.*) Crossan translates *tekton* as "peasant artisan" in his *The Birth of Christianity.* There are also those who suggest that Jesus and his father were peasant farmers, pointing to the agricultural content of many of Jesus' parables.

There is fascinating speculation as to whether Jesus ever visited Sepphoris, a Palestinian town in lower Galilee excavated in the 1980's. Never mentioned in the New Testament, it is only 3.7 miles from Nazareth and its large buildings would have been clearly visible to Jesus and his family on an everyday basis. Josephus records that a wall was built around Sepphoris, making it "the metropolis of Galilee".

The original town of Sepphoris was destroyed during the earlier-described revolt in the first few years of the century. However, after being named tetrarch, Herod Antipas chose this town located on the road from Ptolemais to Tiberias as his capital and began rebuilding it in grand Hellenistic style. Then, before the reconstruction was finished, Antipas changed his mind and moved his capital in about AD 26 to the new city of Tiberias.

Jesus would have been about 20 to 25 years old when all this transpired and it is certainly not stretching to imagine that he could have plied his trade as a wood worker in Sepphoris and even perhaps picked up a smattering of Greek in this Hellenized town. Indeed, there are those among the scholars who argue strongly that Jesus spoke Greek as well as Aramaic.

Hebrew was a written language, not an oral one at that time, at least among the great mass of the population. Could Jesus read or write? Most of today's scholars are dubious, despite the recitations of scripture reported in the gospels and the ambiguous account of Jesus writing in the sand.

The Family of Jesus

Just as subject to speculation and controversy as the circumstances of Jesus' birth and upbringing is the family of Jesus. Mary is undeniably the mother of Jesus. Many writers have commented on the obvious fact that Joseph is simply not around in the ministry accounts except for being identified as the father of Jesus (e.g., Lk. 4.22: "Is not this Joseph's son?") Matthew, Mark, Luke and John picture Jesus with his mother alone, with his brothers alone, with his mother and brother together, and with his mother, his brother and his disciples – but never with Joseph. Perhaps because he died before Jesus' ministry commenced.

Mary, on the other hand, lived through her son's ministry, bore several other children, and is described by all the gospels as being present at the crucifixion. If Mary was about 14 years old when Jesus was born, as seems likely, she would have been about 50 years old at the time of Jesus' death, a relatively senior age for Palestinians of the 1st Century. And, if the books of John and Acts are to be accepted, Mary remained in Jerusalem during the early years of Christianity. Further, the legends and folk lore have her years later visiting the apostle John in his declining years at Ephesus.

Christians today know little of Jesus' immediate family beyond Mary and Joseph. Understandably, since for centuries the Catholic church effectively squelched speculation about the brother and sisters of Jesus repeatedly mentioned in the gospels. Even the Protestant churches have said little about them.

Mark 6.3 describes Jesus' family: "Is this not the woodworker, the son of Mary and brother of James and Joses and Jude and Simon? Are not his sisters with us?" Matthew 13.55 is similar: "Is not the mother called Mary and his brothers James and Joseph and Simon and Jude? And are not all his sisters with us?" Further, without using names, there are references to brothers in Matthew 12.46 and John 7.5. These brothers and sisters are further described in the apocryphal gospels of the 2d Century.

Some skeptical scholars find it just too coincidental that in the gospels, James, Jose, Simon and Jude bear the same names as patriarchs who begat the twelve sons/tribes of Israel and after three of those sons. (James equals Jacob, Joses is Joseph, Simon is Simeon, and Jude is Judah.) However, naming children after persons prominent in the history of Israel cannot have been unusual in the 1st Century.

Catholic writers have promulgated different theories to explain the gospel mentions of brothers and sisters of Jesus in the face of the doctrine of perpetual virginity for Mary. Jerome concluded that they were cousins of Jesus. Another theory (called the "Epiphanian position" argued by Richard Bauckham is that they were children of Joseph by a previous marriage. John P. Meier reviews the evidence cited to support the Epiphanian position (principally, the Protevangelium of James, a 2d Century aprocryphal gospel) and finds it wanting. Meier, a Catholic scholar, disagrees with both Jerome and Bauckham, concluding that the named brothers and unnamed sisters were "probably" siblings of Jesus (the "Helvidian Solution").

Stories describing the relatives of Jesus are many and varied. One of the principal sources is Hegesippius' five books of "Memoirs," written in about 180 and described by Eusibius.

Hegesippius maintained as did Clement of Alexandria, that James held the title of Bishop of Jerusalem. Hegesippius goes on to describe the succession of Jude and Simeon (mentioned in the New Testament as "Jesus' brothers") as bishops and the persecution of their descendants by the Roman emperors. He has Simeon serving as bishop until beyond the end of the 1st Century.

Hegesippius also identified Joseph's brother as Clopas and named Simeon as a son of Clopas to preserve Mary's virginity, rather than recognizing a prior marriage by Joseph. Simeon thus became a cousin to Jesus. This identifies the Mary of Clopas placed at the cross by John (John 19.25) – she was either the wife or daughter of Clopas. Hegesippius also has a sister of Mary, mother of Jesus; possibly the Salome named by Mark (15:40; 16:1) as also being at the cross.

It has also been suggested that Salome was Joseph's first wife and the mother of Jesus' "brothers." This could make Mary the daughter of Clopas the sister of Mary, Jesus' mother, and Clopas the father of both of the Marys. This is corroborated by gospel fragments from Upper Egypt, according to Schneemelcher. Here, confusion sets in (if it has not already). In the early infancy gospels, the father of Mary, mother of Jesus, is called Joachim. They also have Clopas as the second husband of

Anna (Mary's mother) by whom he had a daughter also named Mary (not Jesus' mother). Obviously, these identifications of Jesus' relatives go in many directions.

There is undoubted historical evidence for at least one of Jesus' siblings. James is identified as the brother of "a man called Jesus" by Josephus writing in the 1st Century about the violent death suffered by James which will be described later in these pages. He is further identified in the letters of Paul as a leader of the early post-crucifixion followers of Jesus in Jerusalem.

This discussion of Jesus' family should close with the speculation by a few scholars that Jesus may have been married for a time before he began his ministry. Pure speculation; there is no support whatsoever in the gospels or any other early writings. And then there is Paul's puzzling statement that Jesus' brothers were married. "Do we not have the right to be accompanied by a wife, as do the other apostles and the brothers of the Lord and Cephas [Paul's name for Peter]." (1 Cor. 9.5)

CHAPTER FOUR

Religion in Palestine in Jesus' Time

Our knowledge of the religious situation existing in Palestine in the first half of the 1st century is based on limited sources. We have the New Testament, the LXX (now, the Old Testament), the Masoretic (Hebrew text) of the Hebrew Bible, the writings of Josephus and the retrospective accounts of the rabbis in later centuries recorded as the Mishnah and Midrashim. Unfortunately, all of these sources leave significant gaps with respect to Judaism as it was taught and practiced in Palestine at the time of Jesus.

Judaism as the National Religion

Judaism was the national religion of Palestine. At the time of Jesus, it is described by Jewish historians as Second Temple Judaism, which lasted until rabbinical Judaism commenced in the aftermath of the Jewish revolt of AD 66. Judaism, even though it took different forms in practice, was observed by most Jews in Jerusalem; the Torah, the written law, was revered. Judaism's ceremonies and holy day celebrations, the life of the religion, revolved around the High Priest and the temple in Jerusalem, to which Jews everywhere were called for sacred holidays and to which they were required to make annual "tithes" or contributions. All Jewish males 21 and older were obligated to pay this "temple tax".

This included all Jews retaining loyalty to Judaism living in what was called the Diaspora – the Jewish communities scattered throughout the Mediterranean basin. There was a sizable group in Rome and there were significant communities in Armenia, Iraq, Iran and Arabia, as well as Egypt (Alexandria) and even as far away as Spain. In these Jewish communities, there were leaders who enforced the Jewish law. 2 Corinthians 11.24 states that these authorities were empowered to punish wrongdoers with the traditional 39 lashes (Paul records that he received this treatment).

Constant worship services, with sacrifices, were held at the temple under the direction of the priests and the Sadduccees.   But   the temple was much more than a place of worship. It was also a money center for lending and exchange, a hub for the meat industry because of the demand for sacrifices, and a seat of political power for the religious establishment.

After Herod's death, the Romans took a further step toward control over the people of Palestine by insisting on naming the Jewish High Priest. Previously, he had held office for life but that was changed to tenure at the sufferance of the Romans. The High Priest exercised his considerable power through his privy council and a governing body called the Sanhedrin.

The Sanhedrin presided over the priests of the sacred temple and maintained religious rule over the people of Palestine. The Romans were perfectly willing to permit the priests to exercise considerable civil authority so long as this helped to keep the peace. This practice of giving power to local authorities while keeping them on a relatively tight rein (and always having a body of centurions within hail) was a hallmark of the Roman Empire.

From AD 6 to 15, the High Priest was Ananus I (called "Annas" in the New Testament); he had five sons, all of whom became High Priests. He was succeeded by his son-in-law Caiaphus, who served from 18 to 36 and thus held the office at the time of Jesus' ministry and death. In all, there were 17 different High Priests between 15 and 75. Under the High Priests were the very many priests who conducted the sacrifices and otherwise supervised the practices of Judaism.

The collaboration with the Romans that characterized the High Priests extended in various forms through the priesthood. A Pharisaic group called "the Herodians" is mentioned in the gospels (Mt. 22.16; Mk. 3.6, 12.13). The priests from the privileged families in Jerusalem seem to have been notoriously pro-Roman. At the other extreme, some reacted violently to what they saw as unacceptable acts by the Romans such as the erection of a golden eagle on a gate of the temple.

Reconstruction by Herod the Great of the holy temple so dear to the Jews began in the year 19 BC and was not completed during the ministry of Jesus. The temple, in all aspects administered by the Sadducees, was surrounded by a vast courtyard so that the entire temple complex covered about thirty-five acres, an area large enough to hold over thirty football fields. The whole area was inundated with people from near and far during the three great Jewish festivals, Passover, Pentecost and Tabernacles. Jeremias, in his *Jerusalem in the Time of Jesus*, writes that pilgrims coming to Jerusalem to celebrate the Passover feast could have added between 60,000 and 125,000 people to the normal population.

The temple interior, off-limits to women and Gentiles, was about 105 feet long, 35 feet wide and 52 feet high. The temple building itself was not used for public worship; public rites took place in the surrounding courtyard which was at all times visible to the Roman legions. These veteran soldiers were kept constantly alert to the possibility of trouble and violence.

The contrast between Jerusalem's active urban commercialism with its rich religious displays and the rural poverty and simple Judaism that prevailed in much of the rest of Palestine is dramatized by Josephus' description of the splendid garments worn by the High Priest:

"A linen undergarment, and over that a blue robe. To the robe's tassels were attached alternately golden bells and pomegranates. The robe was adorned by five bands in gold, purple, scarlet, linen and blue. The cape was held by two golden brooches set with very large sardonyxes engraved with the names of the twelve tribes. The cape displayed stones in groups of three – sardius, topaz, and emerald; carbuncle, jasper and sapphire; agate, amethyst and jacinth; onyx, beryl and chrysolite. On his head, a tiara of linen wreathed with blue and circled by another crown of gold."

The Pharisees and Sadducees

The preeminent religious groups within Judaism were the Sadducees and the Pharisees. They were clearly the Palestinian religious "establishment", openly and regularly collaborating with the Romans while at the same time savoring the civil power they exercised over the daily lives and religion of the Judeans.

Scholars have for years taught that these two religious groups were also at the top of the economic heap and that, while relatively small in number, they controlled through family members a very large portion of the wealth of Palestine, reaping the benefits of a considerable amount of the agricultural production of the peasants of Palestine.

This societal power of the Pharisees, scholars speculate, did not extend into far northern Galilee. They argue that the local scribes, not the Pharisees, were most likely the vocal opponents of Jesus during his ministry. Indeed, some scholars suggest that the Pharasaic religious supremacy came only in the last quarter of the century. These scholars point out that the authors of the gospels describing vividly the conflicts between Jesus and the Pharisees wrote very late in the century and could not possibly have experienced life in Galilee during the ministry of Jesus.

Despite this perhaps doubtful doubt, the oral traditions must have been very strong that Jesus came into direct personal and hostile conflict with at least some Pharisees. By far the majority of scholars accept the existence of conflict between Jesus and the Pharisees as described in the gospels.

Jewish tradition teaches that the Pharisees were more worldly, mostly from the laity. Although their name came from the Hebrew word meaning "to separate", they were not separatists like the Essenes. As already noted, they represented a small fraction of the population even in Jerusalem and must have been even less evident in Galilee.

Josephus describes the Pharisees thusly:

They live meanly and despise delicacies in diet; and they follow the conduct of reason, and what that prescribes to them as good for them they do; and they think they ought earnestly to strive to observe reason's dictates for practice. … They also believe that souls have an immortal rigor in them, and that under the earth there will be rewards or punishments, according as they have lived virtuously or viciously in this life; and the latter are to be detained in an everlasting prison, but that the former shall have power to revive and live again.

The Pharisees emphasized the role of fate and admitted the possibility of resurrection, which the Sadducees rejected. They and their scribes ran the synagogues, the centers of community life. The scribes were particularly active in the small towns and villages; most were Pharisees. Simply speaking, they were men who could read and write, skills which separated them from the great mass of people in Palestine. In some senses in the smaller communities they were the center of religious and even judicial power.

The Pharisees accepted and followed what was called the "oral law" or "Sayings of the Fathers", hundreds of principles and interpretations generated by scribes from the 4th century BC on; it's stated purpose was to "build a fence around the Torah", the written law.

The Sadducees did not accept the oral law; they lived by the Torah and were the elite overseers of the temple. Josephus describes their "doctrine" this way:

That souls die with the bodies; nor do they regard the observation of any thing besides what the law enjoins them; for they think it an instance of virtue to dispute with those teachers of philosophy whom they frequent; but this doctrine is received but by a few, yet by those still of the greatest dignity. But they are able to do almost nothing of themselves; for when they become magistrates, as they are unwillingly and by force sometimes obliged to be, they addict themselves to the notions of the Pharisees, because the multitude would not otherwise bear them.

In Judaism, Torah meant divine teaching and the title was also used to refer to the first five books of the Hebrew Scripture known as the Pentateuch. "The law", as Paul called it pejoratively, consisted of 613 codified separate commandments and prohibitions. Virtually a code of conduct, it regulated both private and public life.

Going far beyond strictly religious matters, agriculture, trading and commerce were also covered and codified, as were choice of clothing and food and even the intimacies of sexual practices. The food requirements as codified by Leviticus were set forth in extraordinary detail. Cooking utensils had to be very thoroughly and carefully cleaned. Various animals were not only banned from eating but also from touching.

The Pharisees attempted to persuade the people to follow these regulations scrupulously, operating out of the synagogues (by AD 70, it is estimated that there were about eighty of them in Jerusalem alone). However, as the saying goes, the devil is always in the details and differences undoubtedly arose among the various sects of Judaism over the degree of strictness and detail with which these rules should be applied. And as might be expected, their actual observance in everyday life by Jews of the lower classes – and in faraway Galilee – surely must have varied even more.

There are, of course, the diatribes against the Pharisees, the "seven woes", attributed to Jesus in Matthew (and only in Matthew). Mt. 23.16-22 It is not clear, though, whether Jesus actually had that much contact with the Pharisees. Scholars speculate that, in part because of its high level of invective not characteristic for Jesus, the speech viciously attacking the Pharisees may very well reflect the intense rivalry and animosity between Christian Jews and traditional Jews that was prevalent in the last quarter of the century after the doors of the synagogues were closed to the Jews who were followers of Jesus.

So far as we know, the two most prominent religious schools of Judaism were those of Shammai and Hillel, and it was the Shammai school, more conservative than Hillel's, that was more dominant in the first half of the century. Hillel, whose reputation and following survived his death and who was, roughly, a contemporary of Jesus, epitomized what might be called the best of the Pharisees in teaching that was remarkably similar in some respects to that of Jesus. For example, both gave high priority to observance of the "Golden Rule". There is the famous story of a student asking Hillel to teach him the whole of the Torah while standing on one foot. Hillel answered tersely, saying "What you find hateful, do not do to another. This is the whole of the law."

The Qumran or "Dead Sea" scrolls have dispelled the notion that religious groupings within Judaism were limited to the Pharisees and Sadducees; the scrolls reveal a much broader variety. While religious beliefs may have in some respects differed within these groups, all shared a common religious heritage based on the Hebrew Bible.

The Essenes

One sect described in considerable detail in the Dead Sea scrolls is the Essenes who separated themselves religiously and, finally, physically from mainstream Judaism to develop their own communities where they lived in monastic-type isolation. Their beginnings may go back to 200 BC; their end came with the Roman destruction of the Qumran settlement in the summer of AD 68 during the Jewish revolt.

The Essenes were recognized historically by both Josephus and Pliny the Elder. Pliny states that their numbers were constant "for thousands of centuries", clearly an exaggeration. Josephus placed their number at "more than 4,000" and noted their presence in numerous places in Palestine. He locates a Gate of Essenes in Jerusalem, and archeologists have, indeed, found the remains of such a gate. Although the Essenes apparently had communities in other cities, the most complete information about them comes from the Qumran scrolls, found in this principal center for the sect. Its main cemetery, when unearthed, indicates a community of several hundred persons, all males.

The teaching of the Essenes was rigid, based on exceedingly strict adherence to the Law of Judaism; it advocated communal living, continence, deplored slavery and divorce and did not practice sacrifices. Emphasizing both purity and secrecy, the followers were bound to choose death over revealing their secrets. Ancient authors stress that the Essenes believed in celibacy, but this may have been limited to the leaders and the priests. The Essenes claimed that it was really they who were the "elite" of Judaism, calling themselves the "Children of Light". They believed that the end of the world was imminent and that they would find happiness either someplace on earth or in some heavenly kingdom.

Some of the writings among the Dead Sea Scrolls discuss a revered figure, stating that God "raised for them a Teacher of Righteousness", also called Unique Teacher, Teacher of the Law and Chosen One. That teacher was placed in opposition to the hated Wicked Priest, also referred to as the Liar or the Scoffer. These characters, good and bad, are never related in the scrolls to any identifiable Jewish person. And, interestingly, these figures are nowhere mentioned in any of the extensive descriptions of the Essenes by the historians Pliny and Josephus and the Jewish philosopher Philo of Alexander.

Some scholars have argued that aspects of the Essenic teachings are not dissimilar from the beliefs of the early Christians. And a distinct minority of scholars connect the above-described Essene "teacher" figures with some of the founders of Christianity. Robert Eisenman believes that the Teacher of Righteousness was James, the brother of Jesus. Barbara Thiering suggests that John the Baptist was the Teacher. She and other scholars find a close relationship between the teaching of the Essenes and that of John the Baptist – for example, the insistence on a ritual washing as a sign of repentance.

Despite the foregoing, there are very clear differences between the teaching of Jesus and the beliefs of the Essenes. Jesus' very loose interpretation of the Mosaic Law stands in stark contrast to the Essenic teaching that the Jewish law was sacrosanct; indeed, the Essenes even considered the teaching of the Pharisees to be much too lax.

The Hasidim and the Cynics

There abounded in Palestine in those years men called *hasidim* or holy men, wandering charismatic healers and miracle-workers. One of the most famous who preceded Jesus by a number of years was Honi, active at the time of Pompey. He reputedly performed miracles, claiming power over nature and the elements of wind and rain. Also reportedly active in Galilee were the Cynics. They originated with Diogenes (404-323 BC) who, according to legend, slept in a tub and once told Alexander the Great to quit blocking his sunshine.

The original Cynics were mostly wandering, ragged-appearing radicals carrying staffs, wearing dirty and ragged cloaks with the right shoulder bared, shoeless with matted hair and beard and a belted wallet (known as a "begging pouch"; actually, what we would call a knapsack). The word "cynic" comes from the Greek word for dog; the name invoked the disdain with which the cynics regarded conventional wisdom and practice. They sought happiness through total freedom.

The Cynics begged for bread and thrived on wise-sounding aphorisms. It is this practice together with Jesus similar attire which has caused some scholars to call Jesus a "Cynic sage." The only recorded female Cynic was Hipparchia who reportedly consummated her marriage to Diogenes' protégé Crates in public.

With their well-known cloaks, walking sticks and "begging pouches", the Cynics came back into public notice in the 1st Century. One place they frequented was Gadara, a Greek town east of the Jordan River. Some suggest that there was communication between these wanderers and the disciples of Jesus.

Another of the *hasidim* was Honi ben Dosa, who lived near Sepphoris close to the time of Jesus. The story goes that he survived the bite of a poisonous lizard which promptly died. Reputedly, he took the dead lizard to his home and instructed his sons, "It is not the lizard that kills, but sin." Hanina ben Dosa attracted a large following and, as this story tells and quite unlike Jesus, railed constantly against sin. There is a later Hanina ben Dosa who became a famous rabbi.

It is entirely possible, say the scholars, that Jesus listened to and learned from the wandering *hasidim* some aspects of their popular practices. Just as he listened to another charismatic wilderness wanderer, Johanan ben Zehariah, who came to be called John the Baptist.

CHAPTER FIVE

Search for Jesus the Man

However it began, centuries of Christian church preoccupation with what the scholars call Christology has too often ignored or submerged Jesus the man, the human being hidden by the clothing of divinity. In 1835, David Friedrich Strauss in his 1400 page *Life of Jesus Critically Examined* launched the effort to distinguish what he termed the "mythical" from the historical. His effort created a scholarly storm from which his personal career never recovered.

Some have said that the quest for the historical Jesus, the human Jesus, is a dead end road. So taught Albert Schweitzer at the beginning of the 20th century and his skepticism about finding the human Jesus soon became widespread among serious scholars. Albert Schweitzer, *The Quest of the Historical Jesus: A Critical Study of Its Progress from Reimarus to Wrede.* And Schweitzer's rejection of the historical Jesus was continued years later by Rudolf Bultman.

Since that time, in relatively recent years, there has been what Marcus Borg calls "a renaissance in Jesus studies" that take up the cudgel for a portrayal of Jesus the man as opposed to the divine figure. Robert Funk and Roy Hoover put it well in their book, *The Five Gospels:* "The search for the authentic words of Jesus is a search for the forgotten Jesus."

Proliferation of Jesus Books

The Jesus books have continued to proliferate. David Tracy, noted scholar, has stated that "more has been written about Jesus in the last twenty years than in the previous two thousand." And John P. Meier writes recently and tiredly that "there are enough Jesus books to last three lifetimes."

A surprisingly large number of authors, liberal and conservative, men and women, have in recent decades painted in words their individual images of Jesus the man; who he was, what he said, what he did. Daniel Harrington, Geza Vermes, John P. Meier, Karen L. King, Gerd Ludeman, A.N. Wilson, John Dominic Crossan, Harvey K. McArthur, Hal Taussig, Donald Senior, Marcus J. Borg, Norman Perrin, Gerard S. Sloyan, Martin Hengel, E.P. Sanders, Fiorenza Schussler, John Shelby Spong, W. Barnes Tatum, Gunther Bornkamm, Robert W. Funk, Steven Mitchell, Charlotte Allen, Walter Wink, Marvin Cain, Mark Allen Powell, Barbara Thiering, Luke Timothy Johnson, E.P. Sanders, Burton Mack, John Meier, Helmut Koester, John Kloppenborg, Richard Edwards, Ben Witherington III, and more.

In addition to the books, in just 1998 and 1999, the modern Jesus scholarship has been featured in all the media. His picture has appeared on the cover of countless magazines and the portrayals of Jesus the man have been dissected over and over again in newspaper articles from coast to coast, many of them generated by the controversial work of the Jesus Seminar.

The Jesus Seminar

Most Americans are unaware that one of their founding father heroes, Thomas Jefferson, wrote about his study of the gospels which was aimed at separating the real teachings of Jesus from the gospel add-ons supplied by the evangelist authors after the crucifixion. His analysis, *The Life and Morals of Jesus of Nazareth,* was first published in 1904 and is still in print.

Those, like President Jefferson, who have attempted to describe the ministry of Jesus can be divided roughly into two camps that can be called for present purposes the traditionalists and the modernists (or, to use the scholars' jargon, the postmodernists). Almost exclusively, the first group accepts if not literally at least close to face value much of what the gospels report. Three recent examples are Donald Senior's *Jesus: A Gospel Portrait*, E.P. Sanders' *The Historical Figure of Jesus*, and Luke Timothy Johnson's *The Real Jesus*.

The second approach endeavors to sift out the "real" Jesus, discarding sayings and acts that, based on careful analysis, could not realistically be traced back to the historical Jesus. With few exceptions, this description of Jesus' ministry utilizes this more selective approach. Many of these sayings and acts, while undoubtedly attributal to oral traditions with some reduced to early writings, grew out of efforts by early Christian communities to give realistic verity to the Jesus they worshipped but actually knew precious little about.

Since about 1985 when they commenced working together, a group of New Testament scholars operating under the name "Jesus Seminar" has achieved widespread notice – or notoriety, some would say. Not just a seminar in the traditional sense of a discussion group, the group should more aptly be called a consortium of scholars. These men and women (they call themselves "Fellows"), roughly 50-75 at any one gathering, assemble usually twice a year.

Most of the Fellows carry credentials as university or seminary pro-fessors; many have been or are ordained ministers. A variety of religious denominations have been represented and observers have guessed that most would term themselves Christians in belief and practice. While the membership has changed from time to time since its inception, there has been a strong permanent core.

One of the Fellows speaks for the Seminar in stating that it holds to the belief that if we can just get the 1st century straight, we might get the 21st century better.

The Seminar has most prominently devoted itself to determining the authenticity of the deeds and acts of Jesus and aspects of the life and writings of Paul. The scholars eschew matters of faith and theology, concentrating instead on historicity, utilizing the various tools of what the scholars call criticism (read, analysis) in an effort to determine as best as possible what was really said and done by two humans named Jesus and Paul.

Their discussions merit the appellation "seminar" but these scholars also make decisions – they take votes. Using a practice sometimes ridiculed by conservative scholars, they vote on answers to specifically posed questions and on authenticity of individual sayings, acts and writings with red, pink, gray and black beads dropped into a ballot box. The colors move across the spectrum of authenticity, ranging from red as believable to black as unbelievable with two shades in between (pink, probable; gray, unlikely).

A good example of the Jesus Seminar approach is its analysis of the Lord's Prayer as it appears in the gospels of Luke and Matthew. (Mt. 6.9-13, Lk. 11.2-4; see also Th. 14.1-3) The scholars voted "Our Father" red, "in the heavens" black, "your name be revered" pink. "Impose your imperial rule" black, "enact your will on earth as you have in heaven" pink. "Provide us with the bread we need for the day and forgive us our debts to the extent that we have forgiven those in debt to us", all gray.

The work of the Jesus Seminar has attracted generous publicity and created considerable controversy. Its detractors are many, ranging from those who scholarly criticize the work product to those who with vituperation attack the participants. As might be expected, the Seminar's factual rejection of two concepts, virgin birth and bodily resurrection, were particularly galling to the conservative denominations.

The critics of the Jesus Seminar are both numerous and vociferous. Among the scholars, perhaps the most challenging are Luke Timothy Johnson (*The Real Jesus*) and Ben Witherington III (*The Jesus Quest*); they have been singled out in Robert J. Miller's *The Jesus Seminar and Its Critics*.

A substantive argument advanced by the critics from the ranks of the mainstream Catholic and Protestant religions is that the Seminar's preoccupation with historical factuality can be destructive of Christian beliefs. They argue that there is danger that getting stuck with so-called "critical thinking" can lead to an arid wasteland for those who stay there too long. And in a formal religious attack, Luke Timothy Johnson argues that search for the historical Jesus simply cannot sustain any religious commitment.

These critics naturally dispute the Seminar's refusal to accept the gospels at face value while it looks to other writings that the critics denigrate, such as the Gospel of Thomas. They disagree with the notion that historical knowledge can be normative for faith and conclude that the Seminar's scholars' allegiance is to academia over Christian belief. Central to the Johnson-Witherington views is the strong belief that the Christian faith is grounded not just in the man named Jesus but more importantly in the resurrected Jesus experienced by his followers and reflected in the gospels.

Particularly singled out for attack by the critics has been the Seminar's "red is authentic" voting scheme to identify the words and deeds of Jesus most highly regarded by the Fellows. While it has been derided by vocal critics of the Jesus Seminar, it has respectable precedent. Red letter editions of the New Testament go back to those published by Louis Klopsch around the turn of the century; passages characterized by scholars as spoken by Jesus while on earth are printed in red. And this practice goes back further. In a 14th century manuscript of the gospels, the narrative text is handwritten in vermillion, the words of Jesus are in crimson and other words are in black. (Codex 16, stored in the Bibliotheque Nationale in Paris.)

Many, and most particularly those who adhere more closely to the gospel accounts of Jesus, are disturbed by the severity of the Seminar's "calls". As to the acts and deeds of Jesus reported in the New Testament, only 29 out of 176 were voted red or pink. About the same percentage (18%) of the sayings of Jesus received red or pink ballots. These figures shocked the literalists. The extremely low percentage of authenticity is, however, misleading. The sayings and deeds reviewed were not just those reported in the New Testament but also attributed to Jesus in other Christian texts from the early centuries, including the apocryphal writings such as the Gospel of Thomas. If those are eliminated, and percentage of authenticity is based only on the words and deeds reported in the New Testament, the red-pink percentage of authenticity rises considerably, much closer to 50% than 18%.

And there are other ways of looking at this result. The number of red-pink sayings, as Marvin Cain has pointed out, far exceeds the number of known sayings of any other ancient figure. And, perhaps significantly, when the sayings themselves are examined, the picture of Jesus the man changes dramatically from the traditional soothing teller of stories. In its place, says Cain, "is a Jesus who directly challenges his hearers to a new and radical understanding". And one could conclude, as Cain does, that the fact that the 91 sayings selected as authentic particularly disturbs those in established positions in the Christian denominations today is perhaps a "good validation" of the work of the Seminar.

Images of Jesus the Man

The starting point in reconstructing Jesus the man must be the rather obvious fact ignored by many Christians – that he was a Jew. By birth and by upraising; constantly reflected in his teaching. But that is not to say that Jesus could be grouped with the predominant voices of Second Temple Judaism. Actually, if Jesus were teaching today, he would be placed on the border between what we know as Christianity and Judaism. Where precisely to place him requires a careful scrutiny of the human Jesus.

All scholars agree that the oral traditions later embodied in the earliest written texts often provide the keys to finding the human Jesus. They also ruefully recognize that during the decades that elapsed between Jesus' death and the early writings, various individuals and communities worshipping Jesus collected, altered, rearranged, embellished, interpreted and even created traditions about the words, deeds and acts of Jesus.

Wandering "prophets" who visited the early home churches in Palestine and in the other areas into which the teachings of Jesus had reached, together with those who organized and attended those churches, played a role in the word of mouth development and circulation of these traditions. As we shall see, and it was to be repeated, the embodiment of these traditions in writings was an extremely slow process, still shrouded by the mists of time, which lasted through and beyond the 1st Century.

So the task undertaken by recent authors to recreate the historical Jesus is both formidable and sometimes illusory. But, while their images understandably vary, there are some discernible threads of uniformity. For example, scholars generally agree that the Jewishness of Jesus has been too long submerged. In describing the man and his message, scholars use words like radical egalitarian, itinerant sage-prophet, Cynic sage, philosopher, apocalyptic fanatic, charismatic holy man, healer, exorcist, social reformer, challenger of conventional wisdom, confrontationist. Few of these scholars see Jesus as the Messiah of Judean thought and prophecy. And, to repeat, their concern is with Jesus the man. Walter Wink has an eye-catching summary: "If Jesus had never lived, we would not have been able to invent him."

Although there are similarities in the various images of Jesus conjured up by the scholars, scholar-author John P. Meier has a perhaps realistic reaction to them all: "No one's Jesus – and no one Jesus – suits everyone."

Not just the Jesus Seminar participants but practically all of today's scholars – again excepting the literalists, the conservative evangelists and the fundamentalists – reject the centuries-old teaching that the descriptions of Jesus the man and his work as related in the gospels of the New Testament must be accepted as totally authentic because they are "the word of God". "Inspired" and "inerrant" are the technical words used by those who adhere to this approach to the gospels.

Those who write and teach about the New Testament today can be divided roughly into three groups. First are those who accept the writings totally, without cavil, without interpretation or what the scholars call "criticism"; the writings are inspired by God. These include, of course, the fundamentalists, both Catholic and Protestant, and many evangelists. The second group, agreeing that Christianity must hinge on the resurrected Jesus, places great reliance on the understanding of Jesus as derived directly from the gospels, but without taking them literally, word for word.

The third group has adopted what might be called a "show me" approach to the gospels (historical criticism, they call it), rejecting the concepts of Jesus that were implanted in the gospels by early Christians and concentrating on the human, non-divine Jesus.

Before turning directly to Jesus' ministry, some bird's-eye generalizations – while perhaps dangerous, as generalizations always are – can be drawn from the various descriptions of Jesus' activities and teaching.

They are accepted by most of today's scholars. He was all of enigmatic, down-to-earth, egalitarian, passionate, caring, charismatic, single-minded and non-ritualistic. His authoritative teaching dealt primarily with God and ordinary human beings, favoring the realities of existence with little foundation in ritual.

Jesus was constantly preoccupied with the wants, needs and concerns of ordinary people, most particularly the underdogs of Palestinian society. His primary passion was justice for the poor and powerless; he repeatedly attacked the domination system that subdued the downtrodden people of Palestine. His kingdom of God embodied a vision of a better life here and now for those who lived under religious and temporal oppression, poverty and tyranny. He was a social deviant, not a moralist.

Jesus' Ministry Begins

Jesus' ministry most likely began in about AD 25-26 when he was in his late twenties or early 30's, shortly after he was baptized by John the Baptist in the River Jordan. Mark and Matthew attest to this; Luke has The Baptist in prison at the time (Lk. 3.19-20) and John reports no actual baptism of Jesus. In any event, scholars accept as accurate the Mark-Matthew statement that Jesus started out as a disciple of The Baptist and, after John was sent to prison by Herod, went to Galilee to commence preaching "God's good news". (Mk. 1.14-15; Mt. 4.12-17)

The story of the imprisonment and death of The Baptist is well-recorded historically; Josephus describes it in some detail. Apparently, John publicly criticized the marriage of Herod Antipas to Herodias described earlier. Herod's marrying the wife of his brother, Philip, cannot have been popular with the Palestinians. Mark's story has John confronting Herod with this criticism, whereupon Herod had him arrested and executed. This was the occasion for the legend embodied in Mark's story about Salome being instigated by her mother, Herodias, to demand "the head of John the Baptizer".

While the cause of his death as related by Mark is undoubtedly mythical, the beheading of The Baptist is surely not. Josephus writes that Herod feared John's power over the masses; his "eloquence that had so great an effect on mankind might lead to some form of sedition." Herod "feared lest the great influence John had over the people might put it into his power and inclination to raise a rebellion (for they seemed ready to do any thing he should advise" and thought it best to put him to death. John was taken in chains to Herod's wilderness fortress named Machaerus located in Perea, just east of the Jordan river area where John had practiced baptism.

Then there is the theory espoused by some scholars that it was the Romans who really instigated John's execution by Herod Antipas. They argue that the story concocted by the author of Mark was intended to divert attention from Roman involvement in the execution, thereby whitewashing the Romans at a time when Christians in the 1st Century desperately desired to placate the Romans by absolving them of complicity in the death of a popular Palestinian.

For whatever reason he was killed, most scholars accept that, as noted earlier, The Baptist inspired Jesus to commence his ministry; some scholars argue that, for a time, Jesus was a follower of John (the Fourth Gospel so attests –3.22-24). In any event, it seems probable that many in Palestine viewed Jesus as a disciple and successor of The Baptist.

As noted earlier, there are some similarities between the practices of the Essenes as revealed by the Dead Sea Scrolls and the teaching attributed to The Baptist. Possibly, he may have visited the Essenes in their secluded community by the Dead Sea. There could well have been competition between John's followers and the disciples of Jesus. His cult survived, according to Acts, until the mid-50's.

The ministry of Jesus as described by Mark, Matthew and Luke appears to be shorter than the three years seemingly described in John (for example, John mentions three Passovers -- Jn. 2.13, 67.4, 11.55). The gospels also differ geographically – the first three gospels (Mark, Matthew and Luke) keep Jesus in Galilee until the fateful foray to Jerusalem. John finds Jerusalem a much more familiar haunt for Jesus, taking him there on numerous occasions. And John appears to be more accurate, scholars say, in having Jesus find his first close disciples in the Jordan Valley, The Baptist's territory, as opposed to the towns on the Sea of Galilee where Mark has Jesus collecting the disciples who became apostles.

In words, images and audiences, the ministry can best be described as a tapestry of interwoven opposites. Founded in Galilee as opposed to Judea. Helping the poor as opposed to proselytizing the rich. People oriented as opposed to institutional. Praising the laity while demeaning the priests. Teaching lessons with earthy parables as opposed to exhortation and rhetoric. Provoking thought as opposed to arousing emotions. Challenging the establishment as opposed to collaborating with authority.

Jesus frequently walked the hills, the plains, the lake shores of Galilee as a homeless wanderer, living mostly on hand-outs from earthy peasants, the am ha aretz of rural Palestine. Matthew says it aptly: "Foxes have dens, and birds of the sky have nests, but the son of man has nowhere to rest his head." His was an open-air, walk-and-talk ministry concentrated mostly in the small hillside and lakeside towns of Lower Galilee.

Jesus made brief and apparently non-consequential forays, the gospels tell us, to Sidon and Tyre on the Phoenician coast the region across the Jordan, all Gentile territory. Coupled with his outdoor meetings with disciples, Jesus undoubtedly also preached in the synagogues. But not, scholars agree, in his home town of Nazareth where he was not well received.

Jesus also taught in towns. Mark can be read to say that Jesus had a house in Capernaum and used it as a kind of school where he taught his disciples. (Mk. 2.1-2, 2.15, 3.19b-20) Scholars conclude that it is highly likely that Jesus eventually left Capernaum to avoid trouble from Herod Antipas and resumed his regular practice of countryside teaching.

The Kingdom of God

Startling though this may be to those who listen to the hard-core Baptist preachers, Jesus never taught "sin and salvation"; repentance was not essential for admission into his Kingdom of God. But a key to understanding Jesus' concept was certainly nonviolent resistance to the discrimination, exploitation, oppression and persecution that prevailed among the peasants in Palestine. Crossan suggests that Jesus himself may have been "a marginalized peasant, a dispossessed peasant trying to survive as a rural artisan or landless laborer" and striving to create a "new social situation for the Galilean peasantry".

One of the most divisive issues in Christian teaching today is under-standing of the timing of the Kingdom of God; is it here and now or merely a future or a combination of both? The famous Arnold Schweitzer concluded at the turn of the last century that the concept was futuristic because Jesus expected the imminent end of the world. Many scholars today reject that view of Jesus and his teaching.

A major contributor to the heavenly view of Jesus' Kingdom of God was the wording used in Matthew where the author called it the "Kingdom of Heaven" and the church taught for centuries that this gospel was the first and "true word" for organized Christianity. That has changed dramatically with the recognition by virtually all scholars that Mark, not Matthew, was the first written gospel and later Matthew deliberately changed the kingdom from that of God to that of Heaven.

When the teaching of the Kingdom of God is interpreted as relating to "here and now", it becomes considerably more radical and almost revolutionary. Jesus becomes not just a teller of uplifting stories about earning an existence in the hereafter but a harsh critic of the tyrannical religious and secular practices of his day. No wonder, then, that the guardians of their version of Judaism as well as civil authorities viewed him as a very real threat. Here is a man daring to flout the conventional wisdom and practices, saying to the vast majority of Palestinians who were poverty-stricken, "Blessed are you who are poor, for yours is the kingdom of God." (Lk. 6.20) And then Luke goes even further, adding a curse on the wealthy: "But woe to you who are rich. ... Woe to you who are full now, for you will be hungry. ... Woe to you who are laughing now, for you will mourn and weep." (Lk. 6.24-25)

Jesus as Teacher

Almost all commentators, Christian and non-Christian alike, are in agreement that whatever they think of him otherwise, Jesus was one of the world's greatest teachers. Was his teaching a marked departure from the conventional wisdom and teaching/preaching practices of Judaism? Certainly it was unique in methodology – there is no record of prior or contemporary sages-prophets basing their teaching on the combination of parables and aphorisms that Jesus used. His parables were often a lesson-story, mostly peasant oriented and sometimes worded to make the wisdom kernel difficult to find. Many scholars believe that his parables are the best route to Jesus' heart and mind.

In passing, Marvin Cain reminds us that the word "parable" is a translation of the Hebrew word *mashal* which can mean not only a story but a meaningful, challenging "metaphor, riddle, sharp saying". Jesus' characteristic use of parables distinguishes the gospels of Mark, Matthew and Luke from that of John, which frequently has Jesus delivering lengthy speeches. See, e.g., Jn. 5.30-47, 16.1-28. Jesus was not always story-oriented. He could also be a standup sage, tossing out deeply meaningful one-liners (aphorisms, they are called); short and provocative or challenging sayings. "Whoever has never committed a sin should go ahead and throw the first stone. ... What goes into you can't defile you; what comes out of you can. ... No prophet goes without respect, except on his home turf. ... Nobody drinks aged wine and immediately wants to drink young wine. ... Young wine is not poured into old wineskins. ... When you give to charity, do not let your left hand know what your right hand is doing. ... The one who isn't with me is against me."

After reviewing the many parables used by Jesus, Marvin Cain concludes in his *Jesus the Man* that "his revolutionary teaching ... turned the conventional wisdom of his day on its ear." This approach was certainly unique to Judaism. And the social caste of many of Jesus' followers as described in the gospels is a fair reflection of the philosophy of his ministry. Mostly peasants; poor and illiterate. Tillers of the land and fishermen of the sea. Perhaps most importantly, the dispossessed, the destitute and the outcasts and those despised by conventional society, the tax collectors, sinner and lepers. Jesus' constantly reiterated insistence that these downtrodden persons were entitled to here-and-now membership in his Kingdom of God was a teaching startlingly new to Judaism.

Table fellowship, a meal shared with others, was a hallmark of Jesus' ministry; there are constant references in the gospels to Jesus eating with his disciples.   This included sinners and "lost sheep". Voted red by the Jesus Seminar scholars was the account in Mark (Mk 2.15-17), Matthew (Mt 9.10-13, 11.18-19) and Luke (Lk 5.29-32, 15.6) of Jesus proclivity for dining with the dregs of society. Surely an affront to the Judean hardliners; in no way could they relate to his practice of constantly consorting with "toll collectors and sinners." Toll collectors were the much-despised tax-collecting agents of the Romans. Pharisees' followers exclaimed, "Why does he eat with tax collectors and sinners?"

Meals in the days of Jesus could be on occasion rather formal when eaten in the home with guests present. Reclining on couches was the fashion; resting on one elbow while eating. Feet were washed before the meal, usually by a servant or slave, and hand washing was also a Judean prerequisite to a meal. Traditionally, there were two courses – one for eating and one for drinking; each began with a benediction and a libation.

The "after dinner" portion of the meal, called the symposium, usually involved conversation on a variety of subjects; the law was a frequent Judean subject. It is entirely consistent with this practice to picture Jesus as teaching at meal symposium time. Women were ordinarily not included at meals, particularly during symposium time – and it was little short of shocking to have any of what were termed disreputable persons participating in the meal.

John the Baptist was an ascetic, eating no bread and drinking no wine. Indeed, for this reason alone he was viewed by some as being demented. Jesus was definitely not of this school; he did not practice fasting and enjoyed wine right along with everyone else. Indeed, some of his critics accused him of being "a glutton and a drunk". (Lk 7.33-35)

Jesus constantly advocated a strong trust ethic. He surely said, against the violent and war-filled pages of the Jewish Bible: "When someone slaps you on the right cheek, turn the other as well. When someone wants to sue you for your shirt, let that person have your coat along with it. Further, when anyone conscripts you for one mile, go an extra mile. Give to the one who begs from you."

A righteous Pharisee would hardly teach, as Jesus did in what must have been one of his most radical adjurations, driving home in startling words that his ministry was one of total and all-inclusive kinship: "Love your enemies....God causes the sun to rise on both the bad and the good, and sends rain on both the just and the unjust. If you love those who love you, what merit is there in that? After all, even sinners love those who love them."

Was Jesus, like Paul, strongly defiant of the Torah, the Jewish Law? Very doubtful, modern scholars say. But even the sayings deemed most likely authentic certainly reveal a relaxed attitude toward the Law – quite unlike that advocated by the Pharisees. His concern was with qualitative fulfillment of the law as against formal adherence to ritualistic commandments. An example well known to all is his statement that "The Sabbath day was created for Adam and Eve, not Adam and Eve for the Sabbath day." The ethical and moral aspects of the law were clearly more important to Jesus – indeed, controlling – than literal observance of the law.

Jesus frequently taught on his own authority as opposed to the commandments of Judaism. Although some scholars say that the words were most likely placed on Jesus' lips by the early Christian community, their content could well have been realistic to Jesus the teacher: "Our ancestors were told...but I tell you."

His thoughts on purity ("What goes into you can't defile; what comes out of you can." Mk 7.15) as well as his everyday practices with his disciples (eating with "defiled" or "unclean" hands as described in Mark 7.2) departed so significantly from the teaching of the Pharisees that it could well be deemed radical for the time. To Palestine's religious establishment, the elite of Judaism, purity was a deadly serious matter.

It was not just a matter of washing hands (although one of the longest controversies reported in Mark (7.1-13) involved just that). Purity was coupled with holiness (all who approach God must be clean) to distinguish it from pollution and defilement. It marked a separation between Judeans and pagans and permeated many aspects of both society generally and day-to-day living.

The detailed rules for "cleanliness and purity" which the Pharisees wanted the Judeans to follow as spelled out in Leviticus and elaborated on by the Pharisees and their scribes were anathema to Jesus.

The washing of hands was a cardinal requirement before eating, and not just for reasons of hygiene. Josephus writes that the Pharisees refused to eat following a visit to the marketplace until they had washed their hands in a ritualistic way. And the rules governing table fellowship not only required observance of the detailed Kosher requirements with respect to food, they also had an inviolate principle that Judeans could not eat with those considered unclean – Gentiles, for example.

Jesus also breached the purity regulations when he touched a menstruating woman. Leviticus taught that women were unclean during menstruation and anyone who touched such a woman became unclean and was charged with washing hands and clothes and keeping pure for the remainder of the day. (Leviticus 15.19) This uncleanliness extended to anything on which the unclean woman sat or reclined.

Jesus had no patience with many of the purity regulations, including not just washing hands before meals but also more important ones governing dining with non-believers and imposing detailed rules specifying what to eat and not eat. So Jesus cannot have made the establishment Pharisees happy, to say the least, when he upset the Kosher rules of Palestine by saying that "It is not what goes into the mouth that defiles a person, but it is what comes out of the mouth that defiles."

Jesus and the Gentiles

Gentiles were early defined as "foreigners, strangers or non-Jews" and were anathema to those who interpreted the Torah strictly . The practices of Jesus in consorting with them, thereby flaunting the religious proscriptions, has been cited by some scholars as bespeaking an outreach by Jesus the man beyond Judaism to the Gentiles. However, many scholars do not find in the gospels' accounts of the living Jesus any direction or command to carry his message beyond the followers of Judaism. In other words, did the living Jesus intend, foresee, and command a mission to the Gentile s led by his disciples? Or did he seek only the acceptance of a "new Israel" by the Jews of Palestine? The latter is chosen by many scholars.

This inquiry encounters first the command of Jesus to the apostles as written in Matthew. The mission is only to the Jews; it could not be more clearly stated:

"Go nowhere among the Gentiles and enter no town of the Samaritans, but go rather to the lost sheep of the house of Israel." (Mt. 20.5-6)

Then, Jesus describing his own mission from God: "I was sent only to the lost sheep of the house of Israel." (Mt. 15.24)

Except for one statement in Mark that scholars agree was inserted after the gospel was written, those are the only lifetime comments by Jesus on this subject. The most often quoted missionary statements are attributed to Jesus only after the resurrection:

"Go into all the world and preach the gospel to the whole creation." (Mk. 16.15) "Go therefore and make disciples of all nations, baptizing them in the name of the Father and of the Son and of the Holy Spirit, leading them to observe all that I have commanded you." (Mt. 28.18-19) "You shall be my witnesses in Jerusalem and in all Judea and Samaria and to the end of the earth." (Acts 1.8)

These ringing words have resounded from pulpits for two thousand years, sending missionaries to literally all corners of the world and, frequently (like the legendary lives of the apostles) to their death, often by violence.

But how do we reconcile the post-crucifixion worldwide mission charge with the narrow command of the living Jesus which sent the apostles "only to the lost sheep of the house of Israel"? Particularly when there is added the language of the living Jesus which repeatedly denigrates the Gentiles. In response to a plea by a Gentile Greek woman who begged Jesus to cast the demon out of her daughter, Mark has Jesus replying:

"Let the children first be fed, for it is not right to take the children's bread and throw it to the dogs." (Mk. 7.27)

The context makes it unmistakable that Jesus is referring to the Gentiles as "dogs". And the scene is repeated in Matthew (Mt 15:26). Then there is the well-known passage from Matthew to which many scholars give an anti-Gentile interpretation: "Do not give dogs what is holy; and do not throw your pearls before swine, lest they trample them under foot and turn to attack you." (Mt 7.6)

Some scholars pay even more attention to this quotation since it is used by the evangelist author many years after the crucifixion when the mission to the Gentiles was thoroughly underway. It has the ring of verity since the remark by Jesus must have been too firmly embodied in the oral traditions to ignore or it never would have been repeated by an evangelist writing the gospel for an audience which most certainly included Gentiles.

In any event it is the "only to the lost sheep of Israel" command recorded by Mark, the fact that the broader commands are put on the lips of the resurrected Jesus, and the denigration of Gentiles in both Mark and Matthew that has caused Cwiekowski, a noted scholar, to join others in concluding that "We find no evidence that Jesus, during his ministry, provided for Gentile participation through a distinctive mission directed to them." The Catholic New Jerome Commentary reaches the same conclusion, "There is no reference to a mission outside Israel."

But, say some, what about the command to the apostles attributed to Jesus in Mark, the earliest of the gospels: "Go into all the world." That verse, scholars explain, is in what is called the "longer ending of Mark". This ending (Mk 16.9-20) is challenged by virtually all scholars; it does not even appear in the two most highly respected Greek manuscripts, Vaticanus and Sinaiticus. A plain reading finds it totally out of context with the verses it follows, supporting the scholarly conclusion that it was added to original Mark – precisely when and by whom no one knows. Most scholars agree, however, that it was added at some time in the 2d Century. Even the conservative Wycliff Biblical Commentary (p.

1025) concludes that "almost all textual scholars" reject the longer ending.

This leads to the conclusion of many scholars that the language charging a mission to the Gentiles was deliberately put into the resurrectional appearances by the evangelist authors (and added to the original manuscript of the book of Mark) to give the authority of Jesus to what clearly had already happened and to explain away the limitation by Jesus (too firmly embedded in the traditions to omit from the gospels) limiting his mission to "the lost sheep of Israel." The words placed on Jesus lips by the evangelists writing long after his death justified ex post facto, as the lawyers say, the 1st Century switch in conversion-concentration from Jews to Gentiles which clearly had already happened.

Divorce and Family

Then there is the teaching of Jesus regarding divorce; it is one of the few teachings of Jesus recorded in the letters of Paul. Mark has Jesus absolutely forbidding divorce. Matthew's version allows divorce for infidelity. Mark seems to have Jesus saying that women might initiate a divorce (Mk 10.12) as did Roman law, but Matthew omits this.

There was considerable Judean controversy over the grounds for divorce. The strict Shammai school insisted that only adultery justified divorce. On the other hand, Hillel apparently held a considerably more liberal view, recognizing as grounds for divorce such seemingly trivial matters as bad cooking or even ugliness. Paul recognized Jesus' strict rule but added one spousal difference that justified divorce – conflict over adherence to Christianity.

The Jesus Seminar scholars found totally authentic the gospel accounts that Jesus rejected his family when they evidenced disbelief in his teaching and concluded that he was deranged. All of the gospels repeat in varying form the notion that Jesus was "mad". What was meant, undoubtedly, was not insanity as we know it today, but what was called at that time "being possessed". Persons who had the seeming ability of divination were thought to be possessed; this included prophets and the erratic "wise men" of the time. John the Baptist was one of those.

The dramatic confrontation with Jesus by his family must have been a strong tradition to have survived during the decades when Christians were seizing every opportunity to glorify Jesus. Even today, the sensitivity of Christian laity to the passages characterizing Jesus' mental infirmity as proclaimed by his family is shown by the variances in choices of words in interpreting from the Greek that characterize different New Testament versions.

The King James Authorized Version (KJAV), favored by the Christian right and Christian conservatives generally, rejects a literal translation that his "family" found Jesus to be "mad", choosing instead a softening description that "friends" found Jesus "beside himself". The New Revised Standard Version (NRSV) strengthened the earlier RSV version's "beside himself" to "out of his mind". The New International Version (NIV), New American Bible (NAB)and Revised English Bible (REB) follow suit.

However, some versions stick with the plain word "mad". For example, the Scholars Version of the Jesus Seminar uses that word based on the "red" vote of the Seminar's scholars. As noted earlier, the "mad" concept, as opposed to the milder "beside himself", could have been based on the reasoning that at that time, persons seeming to have the spirit of divination were deemed to be "possessed".

The various New Testament versions in usage today also disagree as to the reaction of those observing Jesus at the time of this occurrence. The King James versions have them "laying hold" on Jesus. RSV used the word "seized" but that was softened to "restrained" in the NRSV.

Healer, Exorcist and Miracle Maker

Even the skeptical scholars have no difficulty accepting the concept that Jesus built a deserved reputation as a healer. For example, there is the healing of leprosy in Mark 2.1-4 which all of these scholars accept as authentic. But what was called leprosy in those days most likely included milder disorders involving dermatitis such as eczema, psoriasis and various rashes. These, like lameness, partial blindness and other ailments "healed" by Jesus could well have been what the experts term psychosomatic maladies or disorders, subject to charismatic healing.

And the same is true for exorcising or driving out demons, another "miracle healing" repeatedly attributed to Jesus (and, it should be added, to many *hasidim*, the wandering "holy men" of the time). Jesus most likely did endeavor to "drive out" what were thought in those times to be demons.

The method followed by another exorcist, Eleazar, is described colorfully by Josephus after stating that "exorcism is an exceptionally powerful cure among our own people":

He (Eleazar) would hold a ring to the nose of the possessed victim – a ring that had one of those roots prescribed by Solomon under its seal – and then as the victim got a whiff of the root, he would draw the demon out through the victim's nostrils. The victim would collapse on the spot.

Indeed, exorcism of "demons" or "the devil", as well as healing, has been a feature of charismatic God-invoking preachers down through the centuries. The movie "Exorcist" demonstrates the reality that the public can attach to the concept of "possessed by demons."

God-invoking preachers down through the centuries have repeatedly claimed to have healing powers. Well-known today is the picture of the enraptured church goer throwing away his crutches as the preacher echoes to the enraptured congregation the words of Jesus, "Your faith has made you well". (Mk. 5.34, 10.52) Even outside of church, many have seen or heard of miraculous recoveries associated with the power of positive suggestion working on a receptive mind.

One of Jesus' cures of a paralytic takes place in a home in Capernaum, a fishing village on the Sea of Galilee which was the base for a number of Jesus' forays into the nearby towns of Chorazin, Magdala and Bethesda where he taught and cured. The Capernaum cure story relates that after Jesus' vocal intercession, a prostrate paralytic immediately arose and walked away. Archaeologists have recently excavated a house in Capernaum which dates to the 1st Century. Some claim that this is the house of Simon Peter where the paralytic was cured.

The so-called "miracle stories" which the Gospel of John calls "signs" include not just the cures and banishing of demons but also what are called the "natural miracles", notably the Cana wedding, the feeding of five thousand, walking on water and the raising of Lazarus. The doubting scholars place these stories in the context of the beliefs of ancient people that viewed miracles by their holy man heroes as just to be expected. In that context, there is no way that the gospel writers could hold their audiences without finding miracles for Jesus to perform. These scholars emphasize this as they conclude that the stories should be regarded as exaggerated metaphors meant to emphasize Jesus' passionate concern for people.

Jesus and Women

Against the background of a male-dominated, patriarchal, caste-oriented society, the repeated friendly association and friendly discourse by Jesus with lower class women was surely remarkable. These women were not only involved in personal discussions with Jesus, but, married and single, also became his traveling companions. The stories of Martha, Mary and the Samaritan woman at the well, even if some are apocryphal, are entirely consistent with what we know of the teaching of Jesus and openly defiant of the chauvinistic societal and religious rules of the day.

The gospels have numerous mentions of Mary Magdalene (or Mary of Magdala, her home town on the Sea of Galilee just north of Tiberias). Her time with Jesus and her portrayal by the Christian church make a fascinating story. Unquestionably, this Mary was an important disciple of Jesus; this is shown by her prominent treatment in the gospels and the favorable portrayal she received in the traditions that continued strong in the 1st Century and on into the next century as demonstrated by the apocryphal writings of the 2d Century.

According to all the gospels, this Mary accompanied Jesus during his ministry along with Joanna, wife of Chuza who was finance minister for Herod Antipas (Lk. 8.3). She was treated as equal to Peter and Joanna and was present at the crucifixion and the finding of the empty tomb. Only this Mary is mentioned as viewing the crucifixion in all four gospels.

Scholars regard as authentic the description of Mary Magdalene as a leader in the Jesus movement after the crucifixion, along with Peter and Paul. She is featured as such in the 2d Century apocrypha (Dialogue of the Savior, Gospel of Mary, Sophia of Jesus Christ). The Gospel of Mary (written probably early in the 2d Century) has her taking over active leadership of the Jesus movement after the crucifixion. The Dialogue of the Savior describes her as "a woman who understands completely."

There are also apocryphal accounts which have Mary repeatedly opposed by Peter who is quoted as stating that Mary could not have been favored by Jesus over the male disciples. Mary, on the other hand, charges that Peter hates all women. And then there is the strange statement attributed to Jesus in the Gospel of Thomas:

Simon Peter said to them, 'Let Mary leave us, for women are not worthy of life.' Jesus said, 'I myself shall lead her in order to make her male, so that she too may become a living spirit resembling you males. For every woman who will make herself male will enter the Kingdom of Heaven.' (114)

The version of Mary Magdalene as prominent among the disciples of Jesus has survived through the centuries in the Eastern Christian churches. In the Roman church, however, Mary Magdalene's reputation was undone beginning in the 4th century by church teachers who conflated Mary of Magdala with Mary the sinner pictured in Luke 7.36-50 (some versions describe her as a prostitute) and also Mary of Bethany, the woman strikingly commended by Jesus after she generously anointed his head (Lk. 14.3-9, Matt. 26.6-13; Jn. 12.1-8)

Pope Gregory the Great in the 6th Century gave a sermon which formalized for Roman Catholic believers his reconstruction slandering Mary Magdalene as a prostitute ("The repentant prostitute who was privileged to see the risen Christ"). His wrongful teaching was not undone for centuries until scholars began insisting that Mary of Magdalene was a person quite different from Mary the sinner described in Luke.

Another Mary, Mary of Bethany, has perhaps not received her just due. This Mary intruded on a male symposium (after-dinner discourse) anointing Jesus' head dramatically and prophetically as though preparing him for a funeral. This must have been an often-repeated story; it has several versions – Mark (Mk. 14:3-9) which is copied in Matthew (Matt. 26.6-13); Luke 7.36-50 using a different locale; and John (Jn. 12.1-8) where the woman is finally identified as Mary of Bethany. In all versions, Jesus commends this Mary in remarkable words that have seldom been commented upon: "Truly, I tell you, wherever the good news is proclaimed in the whole world, what she has done will be told in remembrance of her." Some say that she was the first Christian.

Could the human Jesus have been sexually aroused by a woman like Mary Magdalene with whom he had frequent contact? The 1988 Movie "Jesus", as well as many scholars, have recognized Mary Magdalene as a leading figure in the adult life of Jesus. Father McBrien, former head of the Theology Department at the University of Notre Dame, sees nothing shocking about recognizing a possible sexuality in the make-up of Jesus the man. Richard P. McBrien, *Catholicism*. Agreeing with McBrien, a majority of the Fellows of the Jesus Seminar doubted that Jesus was celibate and thought it "probable" that he had a "special relationship" with at least Mary Magdalene.

After all, says Father McBrien, the gospel portrayals of Jesus reflect a wide gamut of emotions including tenderness, sympathy, sadness, enjoyment of nature as well as beauty, hunger, thirst, anger, temptation. Why not, he concludes, add appreciation of female attractiveness?

Jesus and Judaism

There were two concepts of the "messiah" in second temple Judaism; one was a figure that, in the image of David, would be a political savior. The other "messiah" was a prophetic or wisdom figure like Moses and Elijah. The Davidic image was not highlighted by formal Judaism; as shown by the Dead Sea Scrolls, even the Essenes who passionately expected the end of the world to be nigh have little reference to a messiah and the emphasis is on a priestly, not a royal figure. Reading the gospels closely, it is intellectually difficult to accept that Jesus conceived of himself as the Davidic "messiah" of Palestinian lore; his Kingdom of God was not a nationalistic concept. That descendant of David as most popularly pictured in the lore should have been engaged in a revolutionary battle to rid Palestine of the Romans, a task which neither scholar nor preacher can argue was ever conceived or undertaken by Jesus. Scholars find nowhere in his teaching any aspiration to become a king in the image of David.

However, Jesus most certainly viewed himself as a prophet in the wisdom tradition, in the sense of one who sought to reform or transform Judaism. Bernard Lee, in his comprehensive scholarly review, *Galilean*

Jewishness of Jesus, develops the thesis that Jesus certainly did not wish to destroy or replace Judaism; rather, his mission as he perceived it was to lead the people of Palestine into a renewal of Judaism. In this sense, as a leader in the image of Moses and Elijah, the title "messiah" could well have seemed appropriate both to Jesus and to the early disciples of Jesus.

Some like to believe that Jesus desired to terminate Judaism, citing particularly the passages in John about "killing all the Jews." Ferdinand Baur, writing in the nineteenth century, argued that early Christian history reflected a contest between the Jewish wing led by James and, for a time, by Peter as against a Gentile wing led by Paul.

A contemporary, Albrecht Kitschl, carried Baur a step further; he argued that Jesus actually condemned Judaism and Kitschl led the way in teaching that Christianity should "purify" itself by eliminating its Jewish elements. This is quite a stretch, but German scholars in the pre-World War II period did to some degree follow the theme started by Kitschl. Leading, some say, to religious justifications given to German Christians for Hitler's anti-Jewish policies.

As will be developed more fully later in these pages, there are those who cite Jesus' vicious attack on the Pharisees as a beginning of anti-Semitism, citing the famous seven woes diatribe recorded in Matthew 23.15-22. Many scholars (including the Jesus Seminar) look askance at this confrontation, arguing that Jesus most likely had little contact with the Pharisees who were predominantly located in Judea, far to the south of Galilee. These scholars find the Matthean diatribe more plausible in the context of the last quarter of the 1st century after the Jewish Christians were evicted from the synagogues by the Pharisees who were then the dominant religious force in Palestine and intense rivalry and conflict resulted.

There is the same scholarly doubt about the accuracy of the description in Luke (Lk. 11.43) of Jesus repeated "Damn you, Pharisees!" charges. Rather than condemning the Pharisees, it is suggested that

Jesus may have been railing against petty local officials who did not like him and vocally opposed his activities.

Jesus as Founder of a New Religion

There are many Christians today who persist in the belief that, even if Jesus did not condemn Judaism, he still deliberately commenced and built a movement designed to break away from Judaism and become a separate religious belief. When pressed for New Testament support, they invariably point to Matthew 16.13-19 where Peter, in response to Jesus' question, "Who do you say that I am?", responds "You are the Christ". Whereupon, Jesus charges Peter to build his church: "And I tell you, you are Peter, and on this rock I will build my church...."

This charge to Peter which to many believers lies at the foundation of Catholicism is unique to Matthew; it is not in John and it does not appear in either of the other synoptic gospels, Mark and Luke, although significantly, both have the rest of the above-quoted passage. It is hard to avoid the conclusion that the "charge" is a deliberate insertion by the author of Matthew.

This is the reasoning of many scholars – except, of course, for those who insist on adhering to the doctrines of inspiration and inerrancy. Certainly not one to stray without good reason from core Catholic church doctrine (his scholarly books all have the official Catholic imprimatur), Raymond Brown, a Catholic priest, has this to say about the famous charge to Peter in his book *The Critical Meaning of the Bible*:

"Today, the majority of scholars would recognize that Mark is older than Matthew and that the sentence about building the Church upon Peter is a Matthean addition to an account which originally lacked it, as we see in Mark and Luke." (p. 75)

In other words, putting it more bluntly, the unknown author of Matthew made it up.

Conzelman and Lindeman, noted Protestant scholars, conclude in their *Introduction to the New Testament* that Matthew's words "clearly mirror the ecclesiology of the church and not the teaching of Jesus. ... He did not hand his disciples an organization with regulations and norms." Frederick C. Grant puts it more colorfully in his *Introduction to New Testament Thought*: "The church did not sail with sealed orders, to be opened at Lat. x, Long. y."

Perhaps more accurate nautically, he did not conceive of, design, or launch the ship.

What, then, did Jesus teach in this respect? Quite clearly, say the scholars, his message centered not on the founding of a separate religion but on a renewal of Israel. This is the conclusion of the 1990 edition of the highly respected New Jerome Biblical Commentary which carries the Nihil Obstat and the Imprimatur of the Vicar General for the Archdiocese of Washington. Even Catholic scholars are today rejecting the concept that Jesus had any interest in establishing a separate community or religious structure of any kind. The patent thrust of his teaching was a proclamation message, not an organizational drive.

Traditionally, the Catholic Church has ignored the scholars' doubt about the authenticity of Jesus' famous charge to Peter. But perhaps defensively, they cite the language in the gospel of Luke which describes Jesus as commanding Peter to "feed my sheep" (Lk. 22.31-32). But not just the Jesus Seminar scholars but many who do not follow their lead conclude that these passages also represent post-crucifixion construction by the followers of Jesus.

Why, then, did the author of Matthew include in his gospel this dramatic charge about creating a church? The logic is that the community for which the author of Matthew wrote near the end of the 1st Century needed, to maintain cohesiveness, the image of a "founder", a strong figure with a background of leadership and primacy in the traditions of the Jesus movement. Peter filled the bill, as we shall see, in his role as a mediator and leader during the factional fights that divided the Jesus movement in the early decades after the death of Jesus.

Jesus as Founder of the Sacraments

The next issue is the extent to which the New Testament provides for the establishment of the sacraments during the ministry of Jesus. The Tridentine dogma has taught Roman Catholics that all seven sacraments were instituted by Jesus.

First, the Eucharist. Scholars have analyzed the various accounts of the Last Supper and the Eucharistic words that appear in the New Testament; they vary somewhat, but common to all are the references to wine-blood and bread-body. I Cor. 11.23-26; Mark 14.22-25; Mt. 26.26-29; Lk. 22.15-20. This "multiple attestation" gives strong support to the credibility of these ingredients of the Eucharist. It also points to a close relationship of the ceremony to that of a 1st Century Jewish Passover meal.

As to the details of the bread and wine acts and words and the adjuration by Jesus that this be an eternal remembrance ceremony there is considerable scholarly controversy. Scholars agree that a comparison of wine to blood and bread to body could logically have been utilized by Jesus; it was not unusual in Greco-Roman times.

The words ritually spoken at the celebration of the bread and wine, "Do this in remembrance of me", appear in the Synoptic gospels only in Luke (Lk 22.19) and even there are not found in some of the ancient manuscripts. They do, however, appear in Paul's letter to the Corinthians. Shockingly to many Catholics (and lots of Protestants), the New Jerome Biblical Commentary discussion of this subject, written by the Catholic priest and scholar Raymond Brown notes the absence of these words in all the gospels save Luke, and concludes that they "probably represent post-resurrectional understandings specifying Jesus' intention."

Put bluntly, Jesus probably did not say those words; or, to put the conclusion in more scholarly language, these words were not spoken by Jesus but arose from the "liturgical creativity" of the early communities."

John, interestingly, has a last supper of Jesus with his disciples but no accompanying Eucharist – only the washing of the feet of his disciples and the admonishment, today followed by some Baptist sects, that "you shall do as I have done for you" (Jn. 13.15). John does, however, have the bread and wine, body and blood essentials in a different setting. (Jn. 6)

The descriptions of the Eucharist are quite similar in Matthew-Mark and Luke-Acts. Mark was written in about AD 70 and Corinthians in about 55; both have similar accounts. Significantly, each was apparently written independently of the other. This similarity causes some scholars to speculate that they could have had a common Hebrew or Aramaic source. However, there is a considerable body of scholarly thought that all gospel versions are most likely based on the form known to Paul which in practice came from the community churches, although some argue that it was given to him by Peter. Paul himself attributed the rite to a revelation

To put it somewhat differently, as some scholars do, the original narrative of the Last Supper is undoubtedly earlier than both the Synoptic and Pauline descriptions and was adapted to meet the needs of various communities. It became a combination of an historical recognition of the passion event as embodied in the traditions and a rite of common meal fellowship ("agape" or "love" meal) among the followers of Jesus who looked for ways to bond their community together. The emphasis is on the words "common meal", that is, a sharing of wine and bread which were served as a part of the meal.

This may well be what Paul derived from the Christian communities that he visited. In Paul's view, the sharing of wine and bread was not an event per se celebrating a remembrance of the Last Supper and finding the "body of Christ"; it was an integral part of the meal itself, of table fellowship where bread was broken and "the cup" was taken. And it is significant, some say, that this "breaking of the bread" by the early Christians was in addition to and not in place of the sacrifices and other elements of the traditional Jewish worship.

Some scholars take particular note that Didache (subtitled, *The Teachings of the Twelve Apostles*), hailed as one of the earliest writings on Christian ritual, written probably at the end of the 1st Century (although some argue for a much earlier date), fails to link the Eucharist to the Last Supper or even the death of Jesus. And many scholars point to a sequence of breaking bread and pouring wine as being traditional in Judaism and symbolic, too, of a Greco-Roman formal meal. The Dead Sea Scrolls include a description of a ritual involving bread and wine and state that "the Messiah of Israel shall extend his hand over the bread."

The fact remains that the Eucharist founded in the acts of Jesus at the Last Supper is a solidly imbedded tradition going back well into the 1st century. However, many scholars argue persuasively that it cannot fairly be concluded that Jesus "intended" in any sense to institute a ceremony or rite done in remembrance of him and certainly not a formal rite to be administered by a priesthood akin to the Jewish priesthood of the temple.

Baptism was widely practiced in the very early church. It was a rite of admission signifying both washing away of sins and reception of the divine spirit. Traced back to the baptism of Jesus by John the Baptist, it was from the beginning a water bath. John was apparently the first to use the "one-time" baptism by total immersion and couple it with repentance; this theme for The Baptist was not echoed in the teaching of Jesus who nowhere emphasizes repentance per se. The background and meaning of baptism is also stressed in the gospel of John. Paul's letters refer to taking off the "old human" and putting on Christ (virtue replacing sin) and also to anointing as a part of the ritual (2 Cor. 1.22) The theological understanding of baptism came later.

As to Jesus performing the act, the only reference anywhere in the gospels is the statement in John 3.22: "Jesus and his disciples went into the land of Judea; there he remained with them and baptized." This is offset by the affirmation in John 4.2 that Jesus did not baptize: "It was not Jesus himself but his disciples who baptized." When Jesus began his ministry, his activities related to teaching. Acts reports Jesus as saying that while "John baptized with water, you will be baptized with the Holy Spirit". (Acts 1.5) There is, of course, the post-resurrectional instruction (Mt. 28.19) "Go, therefore, make disciples of all nations, baptize them in the name of the Father, and of the Son and of the Holy Spirit." But this appears only as a charge given by the resurrected, not the living Jesus.

Thus, we do have two present-day sacraments with real connections to the living Jesus – the Eucharist and baptism, with more of the former than the latter. Were they "commanded", "instituted", or "intended" by the living Jesus? While there is little or no evidence that they were instituted by him, they do have their "origins" in the life of Jesus. Baptism by his being baptized by The Baptist, and the Eucharist by the accepted practice in the very early Jesus movement of remembering Jesus while breaking bread.

As the decades passed in the 1st Century, rites did become important to the Christian churches as they gradually felt their way into a new religion. But some find in Paul's letters written during those tumultuous years strains of the pagan Hellenistic culture and the so-called "mystery religions." Paul Tillich, in his intensive review of the history of religion in the Middle East, describes relationships between the practices of the early Pauline churches and those imported by Hellenistic converts from their own pre-Christian cults. Particularly singled out is the passion observance, which Tillich compares to the rites of Hellenistic mystery gods where participants went into the throes of deep sorrow over the death of their gods and then shifted to an ecstatic experience involving the god resurrected.

Going beyond the Eucharist and baptism, there remain the other sacraments which have become binding in Catholicism by tradition and were enunciated at separate, formal councils (Lyon, 1274; Florence, 1439; Trent, 1547). They are forgiveness of sins, confirmation, extreme unction, investiture of holy orders, and matrimony. The formal Catholic teaching is that these sacraments were instituted by Christ.

Forgiveness of original sin has, of course, been directly attributable to the death of Jesus on the cross. However, scholars argue that the texts cited for proof that the other sacraments just mentioned originated with the living Jesus are not very convincing. For confirmation, Acts 8.14ff, 19.1ff; for extreme unction, James 5:14ff, for holy orders, 1 Tim. 4.14, 5.12, 2 Tim. 1.6, 2.2; and matrimony, Eph. 5.21-33, Mt. 19.3-9. Even if one tries very hard, many scholars say, it is most difficult to find either direct or interpretative support in these texts for a conclusion that the rites were specifically instituted by Jesus.

Nothing can be found in the New Testament that ties Jesus to a marriage rite or ceremony, unless attendance at a marriage and opposition to divorce are counted. The citation often given in Catholicism is Ephesians 5.21-33 which contains Paul's direction to husband and wife: "Submit to one another out of reverence for Christ," followed by more detailed instructions on how men and women should live in marriage (e.g., "wives should submit to their husbands in everything," comparing the husband as head of the family to Christ as head of the church). Then there is the conclusion (vs. 32-33): "This is a profound mystery – but I am talking about Christ and the church. However, each man must love his wife as he loves himself, and the wife must respect her husband." Note, though, that Ephesians was most likely written very late in the century.

This is not at all to deny the religious significance associated with matrimony generally or the Judean customs of marriage; both Jesus and

Paul attest to that. Rather, the point is that there is no explicit evidence
that Jesus during his ministry authorized or participated in any rite,
ceremony, or procedure involving matrimony.

Nor is there any evidence, these scholars say, of any participation by
Jesus himself in a rite or ceremony involving investiture of holy orders,
anointing the sick (sporadically attested to in post-crucifixion years as a
church custom), or confirmation (nowhere mentioned). The critical
sacramental significance attached to all of these events is clearly post-
Jesus and Church-originated during later centuries. Again, the purpose
here is not to denigrate in the slightest the importance of these rites;
rather, it is only to point out that they have little historical origin in the
life of Jesus.

The gospels have Jesus using the Aramaic word "abba" for God,
although it is a familiar word for "father" not likely to be used as a syn-
onym for God. There are scholars who suggest that Jesus may have been
subjected to a taunting cry, "You don't have a daddy", so defensively
Jesus found his "daddy" in God. The problem with this reasoning is that
"abba" in Aramaic usage was much closer to "pater" than to "daddy".
Another thought on this subject is that Jesus wanted his followers to
think of themselves as "children of God" and so encouraged use of the
familiar "abba".

This leads to the Lord's Prayer; did it originate with the living Jesus?
Certainly not in its present form, say a growing number of scholars.
That form comes from Matthew (Mt. 6.9-13, with the normal
Protestant addition, "For yours is the kingdom and the power and the
glory forever", which comes from Didache.

These scholars start off with skepticism about any formal, memorized prayer being suggested by Jesus to his disciples. This would have
been unlike him, they say, since his teaching through parables and
aphorisms was in form and substance intended to get his followers to
think, not to engage in ritualistic verbal exchanges.

But if there is one that started with Jesus, the favorite form opted for by many scholars today appears in Luke (Lk 11.2-4):
Father, Hallowed be your name.
Your kingdom come.
Give us each day our daily bread.
And forgive us our sins, for we ourselves
forgive everyone indebted to us.
And do not bring us to the time of trial.
This short form, as every Christian knows, has been ignored by all the established churches in favor of the Matthean version.

Prophecy, Divinity and Apocalyptic Teaching

Those who emphasize Jesus as a mystical prophet most often cite his prediction of the destruction of the temple and the events surrounding his death. The latter will be discussed later in these pages. As to the former, the demise of the temple, today's scholars are virtually unanimous in concluding that this prediction in both Mark and Luke (Mk. 13.2, Lk. 19.41) was written after the Romans razed it to the ground in about AD 70.

Going beyond "short-term prophecy", did Jesus' teaching include not just speculation but prophecy or prediction about the "end of the world"? Apocalyptic teaching, the scholars call it. The scholars are divided on this question. The fundamentalists steadfastly argue that Jesus foresaw the end of the world. But did he believe it to be imminent? Witherington says "maybe"; other scholars are more certain and a large number persist in the belief that Jesus' Kingdom of God dealt totally with "the here and now".

The Baptist clearly taught an apocalyptic message; so did Paul. But nowhere in the gospels, say those who argue against that message, is there any direct apocalyptic teaching by Jesus. Indeed, they say, his humor, his liking for celebrations, his refusal to fast all point in the opposite direction. More importantly, as noted earlier, apocalyptic teaching could be inconsistent with Jesus' emphasis on the "kingdom of God" if it is interpreted as a here-and-now concept as opposed to the establishment of God's authority over the world at some time in the future.

Then, there is another view of apocalyptic thinking – that it relates not to the destruction of the earth but to replacement of today's society with one where justice and peace will prevail on the earth. Replacement of today's "mess" with a new way of living. In this sense, perhaps, Jesus with his emphasis on the kingdom of God was an apocalyptic teacher; a teacher of social apocalypse as opposed to material or earthly apocalypse.

What about the concept of Jesus as totally divine? Today, many, perhaps most Christians accept unthinkingly an almost docetic view of Jesus as God in a human skin. Of course, the fundamental Protestants as well as many conservative Catholics reject the image of an all-too-human Jesus; what they see is a human figure with a halo around his head.

But, say some, to emphasize the divinity of Jesus is to underrate him and detract from the fact that he was an utterly remarkable human. Surely there are many high-sounding, beautiful sayings in the gospels that make Jesus sound like a divine figure. For example, "Come to me, for my yoke is comfortable and my lordship is gentle, and you will find rest for yourselves." But for what it is worth, many of today's scholars find those sayings not likely to be authentic.

Turning to the more ritualistic Christians, persuasive to even them should be the reasoning of Raymond Brown that total divinity would make Jesus the man only "a play actor on the stage of time". Or, posed in the words of the fundamentalists, if Jesus was truly the son of God, why would that God want his son on earth to be merely a divine dummy rather than a human being who could think, feel, and suffer like all humans in order to be an attainable model for them to follow?

The Twelve Apostles

The gospels tell us what the apostles did day-by-day with Jesus and the end role he foresaw for them. They will "sit on twelve thrones, judging the twelve tribes of Israel" (Mt. 19.28; Lk. 22.28). However, during their time with Jesus as reported in Mark, they are not always pictured in a favorable light. They do not understand Jesus' mission, they argue about whom is the greatest, Thomas has his doubts, Peter deserts and disavows Jesus, and the self-serving sons of Zebedee seek special positions.

Interestingly, Matthew, who must have been aware of this problem when he composed his gospel, changed Mark's version dramatically to picture the apostles as followers who fully understood Jesus' teaching.

There are among the scholars, like Thomas toward Jesus, the doubters as to even the existence of a body of twelve apostles. Significantly, some say, they are not mentioned in the Gospel of Thomas, the letter of Clement written late in the 1st century, the letters of Ignatius, or in the body of the church-oriented Didache (its title, *The Teachings of the Twelve Apostles*, is a later add-on to Didache). The gospel of John nowhere uses the word "apostle". Strange, some New Testament observers have said, since the author was an apostle himself.

Some scholars (probably a minority) are skeptical that there really was a fixed group of twelve; other suggest that there may have been simply a group of close disciples meriting the Hebrew description of "sheluhim" as messengers of Jesus in the Judean tradition. These scholars argue that Jesus is not accurately quoted as using the word "apostle", pointing out that the best Greek manuscripts omit the words "whom he also named apostles" from Mark 3.14.

J.D*   83

The doubters of the 12 apostle lore also like to point out that the concept of there being 12 apostles ties just too conveniently with the 12 sons of Jacob, the 12 patriarchs foretold in Jewish lore for Judgment Day, and the 12 tribes of Israel – perhaps in order to give Judean legitimacy to Jesus. Twelve, these skeptics point out, is (like seven) associated in the scriptures with perfection.

Accepting the existence of a group of "twelve" who were particularly close to Jesus, the first question must be, "Who were they?" The New Testament has four lists (Mark 3.16, Matthew 10.2, Luke 6.14, Acts 1.13); eleven names are common to all. Thaddaeus is included only by Mark and Matthew; Judas, the son of James, appears only in Luke and Acts.

John has no list; he only twice uses the term "the twelve" and mentions Nathanael who appears nowhere in the other gospels. (John 6.67, 20.24) John fails to mention the disciples close to Jesus being sent out or otherwise sharing in Jesus' ministry. Paul defines the apostles as including persons beyond the twelve – principally himself. Luke differs; the author of Luke, also writing Acts, obviously has a very high opinion of Paul but his description of "those chosen" would clearly exclude Paul.

John, alone among the gospels, starts the selection in Judea, near Jerusalem, and as noted above has no complete list and does not even use the word. John gives a good "play" to Thomas (the name means "twin"), but as a companion to Jesus he is largely ignored in the other gospels. John has Andrew as one of the two first chosen, in Judea near Jerusalem; the second is never named by John and is speculated by some scholars to be the "beloved disciple" who rests on Jesus' bosom at the Last Supper.

Peter, John, and James are the first-named in the gospels of Matthew, Mark, and Luke, who have all twelve apostles selected in Galilee. Peter and John are well known to all and easily singled out. Confusion surrounds the men named James; Jerome's Biblical Commentary sorts them out this way:

(1) James, the brother of Jesus, called James the Just as well as James the Lesser or Younger.

(2) The apostle James, son of Zebedee called James the Greater. Active in the Christian community in Jerusalem after Easter.

(3) The apostle James, son of Alphaeus. Rarely mentioned in the New Testament, we know practically nothing about him.

Jerome in the 3d Century equated James, the brother of Jesus, with the apostle James, son of Alphaeus. But that cannot be since both Mark and John make it clear that Jesus did not have a brother among the twelve. (Mk. 3.21, 3.31, Jn. 7.5)

Nothing is known about Bartholomew. John mentions Nathaniel of Cana, brought into the twelve by Philip (thought by some scholars to be the same individual identified by others as Bartholomew). Judas (Jude) may be the man referred to as a brother of Jesus ("James, Joseph, Simon, and Jude; see Mk. 6:3, Mt. 13.55). However, this seems unlikely; many argue that the statements in John and Mark (Jn 7.5, Mk. 3.21,31) that his brothers did not believe in his divinity makes apostleship unlikely for the Jude named as Jesus' brother. More likely, some say, Jude is simply confused with Thaddeus; the latter, not the former, is identified in the two earliest gospels, Mark and Matthew.

If there was, indeed, a group of twelve close disciples called apostles, then confusion over the names should not be surprising in view of the years of transmission of the oral traditions before names could be reduced to writing.

CHAPTER SIX

The Death of Jesus

Central to any version of the events leading up to the death of Jesus is the Roman prefect, Pontius Pilate. Describing him, Josephus perhaps evenhandedly tells several stories, one praising Pilate and another painting him as a cruel despot.

The first story relates that Pilate brought an army into Palestine "in order to abolish the Jewish laws" and, during the night, "introduced Caesar's effigies, which were upon the ensigns, and brought them into the city; whereas our law forbids us the very making of images".

Sitting on his "judgment seat" with his armed personal guard hidden nearby, Pilate allowed the protesting Jews to present a petition for removal of the offensive images. When they commenced and the centurions charged into their midst, the Jews "threw themselves upon the ground and laid their necks bare", saying they would rather die than accept the religious affront. Whereupon, "Pilate was deeply affected with their firm resolution to keep their laws inviolable, and presently commanded the images to be carried back from Jerusalem to Caesarea."

The second story may have some echoes in the Gospel of Luke.

Pilate undertook to bring a current of water to Jerusalem and did it with the sacred money, and derived the origin of the stream from the distance of two hundred furlongs. However, the Jews were not pleased... and many ten thousands of the people got together, and made a clamor against him... So he habited a great number of his soldiers in their habit, who carried daggers under their garments, and sent them to a place where they might surround them.

Then, the story ends with a statement that Pilate did not spare the Jews in the least, and since the people were unarmed, and were caught by men prepared for that they were about, there were a great number of them slain by this means, and others of them ran away wounded. And thus an end was put to this sedition.

A footnote by the translator states: "These Jews, as they are here called, whose blood Pilate shed on this occasion, may very well be those very Galilean Jews, 'whose blood Pilate had mingled with their sacrifices', quoting Lk 13.1-2. The footnote goes on to suggest that this killing may have involved Galilean Jews "being commonly much more busy in such tumults than those of Judea or Jerusalem", that this may have been an intermeddling in the powers of the tetrarch, Herod Antipas, and that to correct this error, Pilate bent over backwards when Jesus was brought to him by the minions of the high priest and sent him on to Herod for disposition.

Before discussing the confrontation between Pilate and Jesus, there is the question whether Jesus really did foresee his death as the gospels repeatedly relate. Here again, many scholars part company with those who read their bible more literally. They point to the gospel of Mark, the earliest-written of the four, which seems to disclaim complete foreknowledge by Jesus. Contrary to John, written much later in the 1st Century, which teaches that Jesus knows everything and is never taken by surprise. Those scholars who stress the human Jesus and treat the predictions of death as arising out of beliefs of the early Jesus movement that developed after the crucifixion. But, laying this aside, surely all scholars would agree that the man Jesus must have been aware that he was headed for a confrontation with the religious and civil authorities.

Jesus as Troublemaker

As we have seen, it is a vast understatement to say that Jesus the man was controversial. He was a peasant-loving, rule-breaking flouter of conventional wisdom who constantly not only practiced but openly taught deviations from the strictures of Judaism. His teaching was in part at least a strong "hit" on the power structure. He seemed to delight in pulling no punches in his treatment of the established traditions and conventional wisdom of his day.

But there was much more. Jesus' emphasis on a Kingdom (or domain) of God could be termed, to use today's slang expression, "In your face, Caesar!" Even if it be argued, as some do, that Jesus would not naturally use a word meaning, precisely, "kingdom", he certainly stressed a concept that a new world order was abroad: "It will not come by watching for it. Rather, it is spread out upon the earth".

This kind of talk about a here-and-now domain under the power of another could easily be perceived as a challenge to the Emperor's domain, the Roman Empire. Particularly when it was repeated over and over again not just in Galilee but also, finally, in Jerusalem.

The Roman authorities may very well have been quite unaware of the now-famous adjuration of Jesus, "Give unto Caesar that which is Caesar's", when he was asked about the coin due to the tax collector. By the way, there was such a coin. It was the denarius of Emperor Tiberius, who was ordained a God by the Roman Senate on his death in 14 AD and was in widespread usage in Palestine and throughout the Roman

Empire during the life of Jesus. A number of them have been unearthed in archaeological expeditions in the area that was then Palestine.

Jesus also flaunted Herod Antipas, then a Palestinian monarch solidly backed by Rome. The Gospel of Luke records that when Jesus was traveling to Jerusalem, some Pharisees approached with a warning cry, "Get out of here; Herod wants to kill you." (Lk. 13.1) That is when Jesus used the word "fox" to describe Herod.

This was the same Herod who had executed John the Baptist. Even if Jesus' response is an invention of the gospel author writing many decades later, there may well be veracity in the warning; the traditions must have been strong that Jesus was aware of Antipas' hostility. Mark reports that the Pharisees and Herodians conspired to destroy Jesus (Mk. 3.6) and Luke describes a synagogue attempt to kill Jesus because he healed non-Jews. (Luke 4.28-29)

The religious and, consequently, the civil authorities in Palestine could not have been comfortable, to say the least, with the reverberations of the unprecedented, anti-establishment, "kingdom of God" teaching of Jesus through the towns and cities of Galilee. And then he visited Jerusalem during the Passover festivities and confronted and demeaned the religious authority in plain view of the multitudes of Palestinians attending the Passover festivities, many of them undoubtedly still yearning for a Davidic king.

Significantly, although the Roman prefect normally stayed in Caesarea on the Mediterranean coast, during the Passover celebration Pontius Pilate came to Jerusalem, aware that the huge multitudes of pilgrims added to the regular population could quickly erupt in disorder and violence.

Overall, Jesus surely should have been aware that his teaching had crossed the line of the tolerance accorded to the ordinary wandering, charismatic holy men of his day and the presence in Jerusalem of his teaching and huge following must have been viewed as troublesome by the authorities.

After all, the hills and mountains of Galilee had often bred revolt before Jesus' time. Not just a nuisance, he could well have been perceived as something more dangerous than a distant threat on the horizon. Remembering the fate of The Baptist, a human Jesus could logically surmise that sustained preaching of his brand of subversion might invite brutal retaliation from the authorities, both the Romans and their client king.

All persons holding posts of authority have a low tolerance for speech and acts, even those far short of rebellion, which flout their scheme of orderliness. And one of those acts by Jesus which may have been the straw breaking the proverbial camel's back was his visit to the holy temple during the Passover celebration.

We do not know, say the scholars, whether the "cleansing the temple" as reported in the gospels involved overturning the tables of the money changers by Jesus and a few of his disciples or by a larger group of violent demonstrators, possibly including the men who were crucified with Jesus.

Whatever the details of Jesus' disturbing visit to the temple, there is virtual certainty among the scholars that the incident deeply offended the temple authorities. First, picture the temple; it was not just an isolated, stand-alone building. Including the spacious grounds outside the temple building, the entire complex covered more than 30 acres, ample space for the many thousands of people visiting during the holy holidays. The crowds celebrating the Passover feast included not only Jerusalem Jews and local "looky-loos"; there were also hordes of pilgrims, not only from rural Judea and Galilee (including many who had heard the teaching of Jesus) but from throughout the Jewish Diaspora.

Whenever and wherever large crowds congregate in both ancient and modern times, they attract the hucksters; people with products to sell. We have no first-hand account, but it is eminently logical that there would have been on the temple grounds numerous stalls and wandering peddlers hawking food and other items desired by the pilgrims.

Many of these pilgrims wanted to buy pigeons or animals to give to the high priests of the temple as offerings for the daily sacrifices. Money changers to handle the variety of currencies used in Jerusalem and the Diaspora were a necessity. And pilgrims had to exchange Roman money for the temple money required to pay the priests and the Sadducees, the masters of the temple, for the daily sacrifices.

The Jesus who had a long track record of regularly flouting contemporaneous conventions could well have become angry at the marketplace hucksterism prevailing on the temple grounds and upset some of the tables or otherwise created an uproar by vocally criticizing the way the temple grounds were being utilized and the failure of the authorities and the priestly cult to preserve a higher degree of temple decorum.

Further, as reported by Mark, Jesus may well have talked in a way that sounded like prophecy about the eventual destruction of the temple and some in the vast Jerusalem crowds may well have hailed him as a Messiah. If so, it would surely have intensified the concern about him by the authorities and provided further warning that he could be a real trouble-maker. Not just for the religious leaders but also for their Roman masters who knew full well from years of empire experience that religious trouble was often a prelude to civil disorder. These rebellion-wise Romans were ever alert in the empire's trouble spots far removed from Rome and knew through bitter experience that sparks struck in large congregations of people could quickly lead to a rebellious conflagration.

It was not as though the temple episode was an isolated event of hostility to the Judean authorities who took their religion very seriously. Jesus open flouting of authority came on the heels of numerous bones of contention between him and the religious leaders over fasting, sabbath observance, divorce, purity regulations and table fellowship with disreputable persons. And to Pharisees and Sadducees who took their religion seriously, these were not minor matters.

The Last Supper and the Passion Story

Recognizing the possibility or even probability of official Judean or Roman reaction to his confrontational words and activities in Jerusalem in the midst of a major Jewish holiday with huge attending crowds, it is entirely plausible that Jesus would have met over a meal with a group of close disciples to assess the situation in the light of the troubling events of the day. Such a meal is totally consistent with Jesus' penchant for table fellowship with his disciples and this meal could have become the Last Supper.

When did the meal take place? Conventional wisdom has it as the Seder, the traditional Passover meal; that is the teaching of Matthew, Mark and Luke. They have Jesus tried and crucified on the following day, the Passover day. John differs, setting the meal one day earlier on the day of preparation for the sabbath. Both cannot be correct.

The Fellows of the Jesus Seminar go with John, noting that neither Paul nor Didache represent the meal eaten on the night Jesus was betrayed as a Passover meal. And it is possible even probable that at such a meal, Jesus could have performed some symbolic acts involving the quite common taking of bread and wine on such an occasion.

That brings us to the passion story, the varying account of Jesus' arrest, trial and death which appears in the four gospels. Historically, there can be no realistic doubt about the crucifixion of a man named Jesus. Respected ancient historians record that there was a person named Jesus who was executed by a Roman authority named Pontius Pilate. While the details differ considerably, the broad sequence of the events leading up to his death is very parallel in all four gospels.

At one time, it was agreed by many scholars that despite the differences in the passion accounts, there was enough similarity to warrant a conclusion that an early written and self-contained document describing these events was circulated in Christian communities and became the basis for the gospel accounts. Some scholars, Koester for one, argued that this document was written under the authority of Peter. Accordingly, underlying accuracy was attested and those reaching that conclusion also used the argument that the basic story line was much the same in a variety of different traditions that culminated in the separate gospels.

In recent years, Koester and other scholars have shifted away from reliance on a writing to emphasize oral traditions like those embodied in Mark, John and the apocryphal Gospel of Peter. Today, the scholars are divided. While conservatives still adhere to the classical gospel version, others flatly disbelieve much of the story and others have varying degrees of doubt.

The basics of the passion story are accepted in the extensive, two-volume study by Raymond Brown, the Catholic scholar, although even Brown was troubled by the large number of parallels between the passion story and events recorded in Hebrew scripture. Brown finds it inconceivable that, as the gospels relate, the apostles left the scene after the arrest. He believes that they must have known the details about the crucifixion – and finds it strange that what is preserved in the gospel narrative consists largely of echoes of Hebrew scripture.

For example, just taking Mark's story, there are these parallels: offering wine to Jesus (Ps 69), dividing up Jesus' garments (Ps 22), two robbers also being crucified (Is 53), the mockers activities (Ps 22, Is 2), the darkness (Am 8), the final prayer offered by Jesus (Ps 22), proffering vinegar to Jesus (Ps 69), Jesus' crying out (Ps 31), the torn temple veil (Ex 26).

Is this, as Donald Senior suggests in his *Jesus, a Gospel Portrait*, "presenting history in the perspective of faith", or is it, as the skeptics argue, simply constructing a story out of whole Judaistic cloth? Or, to put it differently, were the passion events as chronicled in the gospels interpreted by or created from the Hebrew bible?

Those who choose the former view cite the fact that not every aspect of the story can be traced to the Hebrew Bible. Examples in Mark are the fire in the courtyard (14.54), the sword fight at the arrest (14.47), and the singing following the Last Supper (14.26). None of these have scriptural precedents.

Some of today's scholars take the second alternative, urging that the passion story is in large part a created account. Notable among these scholars are John Dominic Crossan, and W. H. Kelber. Kalber writes that the account was concocted by the author of Mark; Crossan has a much more complicated explanation.

Crossan proposes that portions of the apocryphal Gospel of Peter (which most scholars have placed squarely in the 2d century) was actually written much earlier during the 1st century, probably even earlier than Mark, and these portions describe the crucifixion. Then, Crossan hypothesizes that there was behind the Gospel of Peter a writing that he calls a "Cross Gospel" which was used by the authors of all the canonical gospels to create their passion accounts. Crossan is joined by some other scholars who conclude that only a small part of the narrative comes from the memory of persons present when Jesus was crucified.

It is doubtful that the contentions of the passion story skeptics are accepted by anything approaching a majority of today's scholars. Certainly they are vehemently repudiated by particularly the conservatives of both Catholicism and Protestanism. Most scholars agree that the earliest story is that in Mark, largely copied by Matthew and Luke, John's account, many say, is derived from an independent tradition. Others argue that it was obtained from Mark.

As to the events leading up to Jesus' awful death, perhaps a good guide could be Occam's Razor which teaches that the simplest, most obvious explanation for confusing events is most likely the accurate version. Occam's Razor would teach that the truth lies in just a few, the most simple and straight-forward of the gospel-recorded events: the temple incident, the arrest, the confrontation with the high priest, the hand-off of Jesus to the Romans, the flogging and, finally, the execution on the cross. Scholars examining critically the many details depicted in the gospel recitations would add as realistic a few such as the placard being hung around Jesus' neck which was a common practice at Roman executions.

After Jesus was arrested by men from either the high priest or the Sanhedrin, it is quite logical that he would have been taken to the religious authority, the high priest. Who, as we have already seen, was a minion of the Roman authorities. In view of his subversive preaching, his disdain for the holy temple, his moralistic flouting of the Torah, a personal inquiry by the high priest is also logical. Many scholars doubt that there was any "trial" of Jesus before the Sanhedrin; too coincidentally like the trial described in Psalms, they say.

The religious authorities almost certainly and rather quickly turned Jesus over to the ultimate civil authority, the Romans. Obviously implicit in this yielding of authority was a belief that something was happening here which required civil intervention. Once Jesus got into the hands of the Romans, the religious charges found fertile civil ground. Pontius Pilate, alert for trouble, had good reason to be concerned about Jesus' unconventional and, as he would surely have put it, rabble rousing preaching presence in Jerusalem. As we have seen, he could be a brutal, simplistic ruler. He had an earned reputation for incredible ruthlessness in dealing with what he perceived to be sedition.

The story of Barabbas being spared at the instigation of the Jewish crowd in accordance with custom (Mark 15.6) is just that, a story, conclude many scholars. Even the name Barabbas, which means "son of Abba" suggests a fictional character. Perhaps in an attempt to make Mark's story more logical, Matthew creates the name Jesus Barabbas, giving to Pilate the choice of executing two men named Jesus. (Matt. 27.15-23) There is no known custom for the Roman prefect releasing any prisoner during Passover and Pilate's record for cruelty makes him an unlikely candidate to start such a precedent.

Scholars find it hard to challenge the logical conclusion that it was the Romans, not the Jews, who decreed the crucifixion result; as one author puts it, Herod may have laughed at Jesus but Pilate had him killed. Caiaphas, the high priest, may well have perceived Jesus as some kind of threat to the religious status quo, but he had no powers of execution. The Romans could not have cared about the religious implications of Jesus' differences with traditional Judaism but they could ill afford to ignore the provocative activities of Jesus before huge crowds in Jerusalem and, particularly, the political implications of his claimed Kingdom of God. This kingdom talk together with his championing of peasants suffering from Roman rule could well have been viewed as politically subversive sedition warranting the death penalty.

As earlier mentioned and as will be developed further later in these pages, the gospel accounts giving the most blame for the crucifixion to the Jewish leaders were written well after the Jewish Christians had been driven from their beloved synagogues and had every reason to hate the Jewish leadership that caused this hurtful result. Playing "gotcha", it was easy for them to reconstruct history and make that leadership responsible for the death of their beloved founder/leader.

And so it happened. Jesus became at last the victim of his own vision. Pilate had Jesus flogged and then crucified in accordance with Roman custom and Roman law. Crucifixion was reserved by the Romans for the criminals they most detested. His cross companions were perhaps rabble rousers or terrorists – such men would have been more likely crucified companions of Jesus than the robbers described in the gospel accounts. The centurions took over. As did the legends.

Pilate pronounced sentence on Jesus; and the centurion Cornelius Vrancinus took the prisoner straightaway and bound him to a marble pillar in the judgment hall. And two mighty soldiers, with scourges made of heavy leather, tipped with brass, carried out the scourging, according to the Roman custom. Some say that 828 blows were prescribed, three for each bone of the body; and others give the number as 5475 strokes, each stroke resulting in a wound.

There was a porter in Pilate's service named Cartaphilus, a knave, who tried to ingratiate himself with his master. And when Jesus came out of the judgment hall, scourged and bleeding, he struck the prisoner on the back, shouting: Go faster, Jesus! Go faster! Why do you loiter? Jesus looked at the man and said: I am going. But you shall wait until I return.

And ever since that moment the man Cartaphilus wanders from place to place. He has no home; he has no family; he has no friends. He has no one to care whether he is well or ill; whether he lives or dies. After remaining in one place long enough for a neighbor to answer his greetings, Cartaphilus moves on. At the end of each century his body assumes again the appearance of a man of thirty – the age of Cartaphilus when he struck Jesus. And thus he is doomed to live in loneliness and despair until Judgment Day.

Crucifixion was a Roman, not a Jewish form of execution, and it was reserved for political insurrection. In the tradition of the Torah, execution by Jewish authorities would be accomplished by stoning. Crucifixion was known to the Jewish people – but there was a critical difference. The criminal was first executed and then hung onto a cross as a public warning to others. See Deuteronomy 21.22-23. Joshua 10.26 describes the Amorite kings as being killed and then "hung on five trees" until the evening. The Romans accepted the hanging tradition but changed it to having the criminal die in agony on the cross after being condemned. But whether the crucifixion was after or before death, burial before nightfall was essential.

The customary place where criminals were executed on the cross was Golgotha, meaning "place of the skull." There is no reason to doubt that his close disciples, the apostles, fled in fear.

There is also no reason to doubt the multi-gospel account that the women followers remained at the cross. Mary of Magdala, Mary the mother of Jesus and James. Together with other women who had watched Jesus suffer and die after having accompanied him the 70 miles to Jerusalem from Galilee.

"E'loi, E'loi, la'ma sabach-tha'ni". My God, my God, why hast thou forsaken me? Quite likely, these were the actual words cried out by the human Jesus suffering on the cross. Some scholars use the language of today's youths to interpret these words: "What the hell is happening here?"

How many millions of humans have cried out in despair, "Why me?" And the human Jesus, who undoubtedly felt a close relationship with his God, could very well have echoed this cry of despair at the culmination of his ministry based primarily on an all-encompassing love for others.

There are four versions in the four gospels of Jesus' last words spoken from the cross and each echoes passages from Jewish scripture and this underlines again the repeated reliance of the evangelists who wrote the gospels on words and events from scripture in formulating their stories about Jesus. And the variety of the versions arguably shows how free the authors of these gospels felt they could be in finding their preferred source for Jesus' last words.

The very variety itself poses a challenge to those who like to read their bible literally. Which version does the literalist choose? The despair of Mark and Matthew, "My God, my God, why did you abandon me?" (Mk. 15.34 and Mt. 27.46); the resignation of Luke, "Father, into your hands I entrust my spirit". (Lk., 23.46); or the near-triumph of John, "[My ministry] is finished". (Jn. 19.30. Those who see a scriptural construct in the passion story note that all of these phrases are taken from the Hebrew Bible (Psalms 22.21, 31.5; Job 19.25-27.

Late in the day, the gospels state, "Jesus breathed his last." Then, there is the well-known story of the body of Jesus lovingly taken down from the cross by Joseph of Arimathea, wrapped in a robe and carefully carried to Joseph's newly-acquired tomb. (Incidentally, no geographer has ever found a place named Arimathea). At this tomb, the empty grave and resurrection events occurred (or did not occur) which have given birth to what has been for millions of people for two millenia the core beliefs of Christianity.

In stark contrast, a few scholars today are openly challenging this ending. They see the body of the dead Jesus, along with those of the criminals crucified with him, being routinely cut down from the cross by Roman centurions. And left on Golgotha hill to the carrion eaters.

As to the meaning of the cross, there is scholarly dispute. Some view it not as a symbol of sacrifice (Jesus dying to absolve mankind of original sin) but as a more positive symbol of a man willing to die for his belief in a quest for justice.

When did Jesus die? Pontius Pilate remained in authority for ten years, from 26 to 36. The scholars' best calculation has the crucifixion about midway in Pilate's tenure; that would place Jesus' death at an age of around 35 in about the year AD 30. The then-known world, principally the Roman Empire, was certainly unaware of the death on the cross of this controversial leader of a peasant movement on the fringe of the empire. And no one could have guessed how that suffering death on the cross would capture the imagination and result in the devotion of many millions of people throughout the world.

CHAPTER SEVEN

The First Twenty Years

Only twenty years after the death of Jesus, in the letters undeniably written by the human Paul, we find the human Jesus, a crucified Galilean Jew, being worshipped as the Lord Christ risen from the dead and sitting at the right hand of God. How did that momentous glorification come about?

Jesus Becomes Christ

Mark records that the recognition of Jesus first as the messiah and then "the Christ" occurred first during his lifetime when Peter recognizes him as such. Luke times the divinity of Jesus differently, taking it back to the birth of Jesus when the angel proclaims "to you is born this day in the city of David a Savior who is Christ the Lord". Then, finally, the author of John avers that Jesus, the Son of God, became Christ at the time of creation ("In the beginning was the Word…and the word became flesh (in the form of) Jesus Christ."

In the minds of most Christians, the process of Jesus becoming Christ started with the discovery of the empty tomb and the almost immediate realization that on the third day after his crucifixion, Jesus was raised from the dead and ascended into heaven. The resurrection; the Easter faith, it is often called. The Gospel of Mark embodies the early traditions of the discovery of the empty tomb and the beginning of the Easter faith but Mark as originally written (without the "longer ending") has no resurrection accounts. Paul knew of the "risen Jesus" by the time he wrote his letters in the 50's and the elaborate descriptions of resurrection in Matthew, Luke and John were written decades later in the years 85-100. This argues that the concept as finally developed took some years to build.

In other words, in the years immediately after the death of Jesus, in ways we will never certainly establish, the conclusion was reached by those telling and retelling stories that Jesus must have risen from the dead, returning by grace of God to mystify his disciples. It was only then, scholars surmise, that members of the Jesus movement began to believe in bodily resurrection and call Jesus the Christ: "How could he have been among his disciples had he not been resurrected and returned alive for his disciples to see?" Logically, this belief could have started in both Jerusalem and Galilee and then developed further in the nascent Palestinian home churches in the early decades after the death of Jesus.

The Jesus Seminar scholars voted by a wide margin to accept the proposition that belief in the resurrection began as an affirmation of faith, not the report of a supernatural miracle. These scholars rejected the "empty tomb" stories, with most arguing that these stories originated as a storyteller's inference from the affirmation that God raised Jesus from the dead. The "appearances" of the risen Jesus are viewed by them as verifications of faith, not as the basis for faith. Ancient resurrection faith was a way of affirming the possibility of social and personal transformation.

The Acts of the Apostles surely deals with the post-crucifixion growth of the Jesus movement but the canonical gospels concentrate on the birth, life and death of Jesus and provide few clues to explain the growth of Christian beliefs after his death, except (and this is emphasized by the scholars) insofar as the gospel teaching reflects attitudes and beliefs of the Christian communities in which and for which those gospels were written in the last decades of the 1st century.

What Happened to the Apostles?

Before embarking on a time-scale reconstruction of the turbulent first twenty years of Christianity, there is an initial question, "What happened to those apostles?" Conventional wisdom has it that there were originally twelve but after Judas there were eleven. Acts relates that the martyred James, son of Zebedee, was replaced with Matthias.

After the apostles who were with Jesus in Jerusalem recovered from the trauma of the crucifixion, probably in Galilee at least initially, what did they do? Quite possibly, they followed the wishes of Jesus by teaching his ministry in the area of Galilee. But did they then actually "go forth" to take the message of Jesus beyond Palestine and into the world?

Raymond Brown in *The Critical Meaning of the Bible* states the Catholic scholars' conclusion: "The image of them as carrying on missionary endeavors all over the world has no support in the New Testament or in other reliable historical sources." However, in his more recent two-volume commentary, *"The Death of the Messiah"*, Brown suggests that the prominence given to "the twelve" in Mark undoubtedly reflects the author's knowledge of and reliance on a tradition of an apostolic practice of preaching.

While Acts does mention Christianity as being practiced in thirty-two countries, fifty-four cities, and nine Mediterranean islands, it has no descriptions of specific activity by any of the apostles other than Peter, John and Philip in Samaria, Lydda, Joppa and Caesarea (Acts 8.4 to 10.30)(remember that James, the brother of Jesus, while active in the Jesus movement was not an apostle.) Not in any of the places outside Palestine where there can be no doubt about the presence of 1st Century Christian activity. Alexandria, Egypt, for one. And scholars argue persuasively that with "Acts of the Apostles" having been written late in the century, one would think that any outreach activity by the remaining apostles would have been mentioned.

To replace that silence about missionary activities by the apostles, an amazing variety of legends developed. They describe in colorful and sometimes gory detail the travels and deaths of various of the apostles, often in very far corners of the world. Some of those legends are embodied in the writings the scholars call "the apocryphal Acts." The best known of these are the Acts of John, Paul, Andrew, and Thomas. All are described at length by Heennecke and Schneemelcher and are mentioned by the early Christian writers such as Eusibius, Origen and Clement of Alexander, and also by Tertullian in the 3d Century. These writings recount in detail the journeys, deeds, and martyrdom of some of the adventuresome apostles.

They are involved in resurrections, miracles, apparitions, talking animals, and stories with all types of sexual overtones to the extreme extent of necrophilia. Continence is constantly preached for both men and women – no one knows why. For example, there is the story of Peter's daughter, a virgin, which teaches that it is better to be dead than to engage in sexual intercourse.

A story theme which repeats itself in the legends of the lives of certain of the apostles has the apostle converting married women to Christianity and teaching them to be continent. This naturally arouses the ire of their husbands who force the apostle to leave town, or, worse, subject him to violent persecution – as in Andrew's case, by crucifixion and then being eaten alive by dogs.

Encounters with serpents and animals through persecution frequent the legends; one story has Peter thrown in an amphitheater to a ferocious lion, only to realize that it was one he had baptized, whereupon the lion, to the amazement of the audience, rolls over and licks Peter's feet.

"Gadla Hawaryat," or "Contendings of the Apostles," translated from Ethiopian manuscripts and "being the histories of the lives of martyrdoms and deaths of the twelve apostles," written at the turn of the 20th Century, describes the legends. The oldest text of this writing goes back to the 14th Century, and some of the legends have been traced back to the 2d Century. At the beginning of the book, the author writes his colorful version of the meanings of the names of the twelve:

Simon, that is, "God hath heard me"; Peter, that is, "Rock"; Andrew, that is, "Mighty one" or "Conqueror"; James, that is "Grasper of the sole of the foot" or "Supplanter"; John, that is, "Joy" or "Compassion"; Philip, that is, "Lover of what is beautiful"; Bartholomew, that is, "Wine"; Thomas, that is, "Sun"; Matthew", that is "Chosen one of Lebedyos the weaver; Simon Kananawi, that is, "Simon of Kana" or "Simon Zelotes"; Judas Askorotawi (Askorot is the name of his city), the betrayer, that is, "He who hath in him wiles or excuses.

Most of the legends about Thomas have him preaching the Gospel to Parthians and Persians and then traveling to India to found the Mar Thoma Church. Today, there are in India over one million Christians who call themselves "Christians of St. Thomas." Most are Catholic, some Protestant. Of uncertain origin, their ancestors go back into antiquity. Some forms and language (Syriac) used in their religion are apparently derived from Mesopotamia and Persia. Their legend is that Thomas established a series of churches in India before was finally martyred near Madras in 72.

There are medieval references to a tomb of St. Thomas in Mylapore, India, and in 1522 the Portuguese claimed to have found it. Regrettably, the Portuguese destroyed all early records, considering the Christian Church they found to be heretical. Most of the Christians were quickly converted to Catholicism, but many refused and developed what is known as the Protestant Syrian Church in India.

Tertullian says that John, son of Zebedee, was with Peter in Rome and that after a miraculous delivery from death by boiling oil, he went to Ephesus. Perhaps a more likely story is that in the second book of Papias, which has John suffering martyrdom with James at the hands of Herod in about 62.

The Catholic tradition going back to the early centuries was that John departed Judea after the Council in about 50 and went to Ephesus. While Domitian was emperor, he was exiled to the island of Patmos and was visited there by Mary. There, also, he wrote the book of Revelations. When the exile ended under Emperor Nerva, John returned to Ephesus and in the last years of his life wrote the Gospel of John and the Epistles of John.

Jerome in the 3d Century recounts the legend of John's declining years near the end of the first century, the only apostle still alive. John was invited to preach on First Day (as Sunday was then called), and a large multitude assembled when he was carried in feeble condition into the church. The service was long and John was finally called upon to speak. When the crowd quieted, he said simply, "Little children, love one another, love one another, love one another" – and sat down, having repeated the heart of the Gospel of John.

The legendary fame of James still lives in Spain. There are a variety of stories as to how his body or bones arrived in Spain, and all are as colorful as they are incredible.

The legends begin with James visiting Spain after the Pentecost. Arriving at Saragossa, where he erected a chapel to the Virgin Mary, together with a column of Jasper in her honor. This is the legendary origin of "La Gloriosa Colonna" at the Church of St. Mary of the Pillar, one of the most venerated shrines in Spain. From there, the stories have James travelling throughout Spain, starting religious orders, building churches, and converting thousands to Christianity. He then returned, say the stories, to his martyrdom in Jerusalem where the legends have an angel in a variety of ways transporting his "body" back to Spain. Miraculously appearing at Iria Flavia on July 25, 813, it was "discovered" in a variety of ways and finally installed at a shrine in Compostela.

As years went by, the legend of James captured the hearts and devotions of people throughout Spain. Thousands of them contributed to the construction of the shrine which came to be called Saint Iago or St. James de Compestela. St. James became a symbol for the Spanish soldiers and the Christian crusaders who came to Spain and raised his banner during the centuries-long wars against the Moors. Those wars ended in 1492 when Ferdinand and Isabella celebrated the total victory with a tribute to Compostela. The Spaniards soon made a tradition out of pilgrimages to the shrine of St. James, and it attracted Christians from all over Europe. The number of pilgrims visiting Spain rivaled those trekking to Rome and Jerusalem.

James has become a dominant legendary figure in the Spanish traditions – both as a national hero and a saint. The people of Spain still credit him with their freedom from the Moors and the consequent brief tenure of Spain as one of the leading countries in the Christian world. No other apostle has achieved the role of national hero-saint that is occupied by James.

Eusibius records the legend that Philip preached in Phrygia and later died at Nierapolis in the Mid-East. Polycrates, bishop of Ephesus in the second century, refers to two daughters of Philip the apostle who lived in Hierapolis. This story may stem from confusion with a Philip the Deacon identified in the Acts of the Apostles (Acts 21.8) who was also alleged to have daughters in this area and, according to the writer Papias, were prophets and associated with miracle stories. The tradition later developed that the apostle Philip was crucified head downwards at Hierapolis during Emperor Domitian's persecutions of the Christians.

One version of the events before Philip's death deals with his conversion of the wife of the Roman proconsul. In revenge for the loss of his wife as a bed partner, the proconsul had Marianne, Philip's sister dragged naked through the streets, but her body was protected from view by a heavenly cloud. The legends also have Bartholomew being crucified with Philip but released before he was dead because of Philip's prayers. Philip's remains are said to have been brought to Rome in the 6th Century, where they lie in the Basilica of Apostles.

Continuing with the legend of Bartholomew after he survived the double crucifixion with Philip, he went to India, where he allegedly brought with him and preached from the Gospel of Matthew. He left India to preach in Armenia, where he met his death after being flayed alive by King Astyages of Albanapolis in Armenia.

Jude, also called Thaddeus, is barely mentioned in the gospels (John 14.22-23) but is the traditional author of the book carrying his name in the New Testament.

The legends join Thaddeus with Simon, the Cananean, Simon Zelotes (both Cananean and Zelotes mean zealous), who acquired his name, the stories say, because of his zeal for the Mosaic law before he joined Jesus—not because he was a member of the group of rebellious Judaists known as Zealots. The Eastern tradition has Simon dying in peace at Edessa. The Roman Catholic tradition has him preaching in Egypt, joining with Jude on a missionary trip to Persia and then to Mesopotamia, where both were martyred.

There is an apocryphal Acts of Andrew and it describes Matthias as being in the City of the Cannibals – a Greek fiction that was translated into Syriac, Armenian, and Coptic, and so achieved wide circulation. The traditional legends have Matthias preaching in Judea and then travelling to Cappadocia and around the Caspian Sea. He allegedly preached among savage pagans and was persecuted and finally crucified at Colchis.

The same traditional legend has Andrew deputized by the Lord right after Matthias: "Go thou unto the City of the Cannibals; and Andrew thy brother shall go unto Lydia and shall preach therein." Andrew became a bishop in Lydia, where he wrought many miracles. From there Andrew travelled with Bartholomew to Macedonia where they met with persecution and then ended up in the City of the Cannibals. More hazardous adventures followed. His untimely end came when he converted the wife of the Roman proconsul, teaching her continence. The proconsul required Andrew to lead pagans in sacrifices to pagan gods. Andrew refused and he was crucified. The converted wife, the story goes, had him buried with loving care in her tomb.

A different legend is repeated in *Andrea,* one of the oldest poems in the English language, which weaves a story of Andrew and Matthias meeting death in the legendary Land of the Cannibals. Andrew's relics are said to be interred at the Church of the Apostles in Constantinople where they were placed by Constantine the Great, but were taken by the crusaders in 1204 to Cathedral of Amalfi in Italy.

Andrew is the patron saint of fishermen, Burgundy, Hungary, and Russia; there was a tradition that he preached in Kiev. Scotland also installed him as its patron saint, and Andrew is thoroughly embedded in the traditions and symbols of Scotland. In the 8th Century, when Scotland was at war with England, priests carried a large standard decorated with St. Andrew's cross. King Achaias of Scotland saw it illuminated by the sun at dawn and took it as a sign of God. After his badly outnumbered army won, the white cross on a blue background became Scotland's national symbol.

The original tie of Andrew to Scotland according to legend was the 4th century movement of his relics (an arm bone and several fingers and toes) by an abbot named Regulus, as directed by an angel, from Patras, Italy, to File, Scotland, where he built St. Andrew's Church. A feast in his honor is observed in the archdiocese of St. Andrew on May 9 of every year.

These are but a few; there are many other legendary stories of the apostles which embody different versions of their travels and deaths, almost always by martyrdom. Other than those named in Acts, though, Christianity has no real record of their lives or deaths. That they somehow served the call of Jesus after the events of the crucifixion and Pentecost seems certainly possible but unproven. And the extreme variety and remarkably enduring nature of the legends in so many parts of the world underscore in quite another way the worldwide impact of Jesus and his lifetime disciples.

The Jesus Movement in Jerusalem

After this "legendary apostolic digression", back to Jesus movement reality in Jerusalem. Aside from the Pauline letters which provide only sketchy information, our principal source for the activities of the Jesus movement disciples in Jerusalem in the early years following the crucifixion is the book called "Acts of the Apostles".

Starting perhaps with Eusibius who wrote in the 3rd century, Acts has been traditionally heralded as a solid, credible foundation story of early Christianity. Unnumbered writers have accepted Acts as gospel for what happened historically just as the canonical gospels have been accepted religiously. But times have changed; scholars today, many of them, are arguing that Acts simply cannot be read as history. Some go so far as to label it "a work of imaginative religious literature."

First, there is the undeniable fact that it was written very late in the century, at least fifty years after the death of Jesus. The reference by the author of Acts to "the traditions" on which he relied must mean oral stories told and retold during those decades after the crucifixion. There are no known written accounts (except for the letters of Paul of which Acts seems strangely to be unaware) on which Acts could have been based. And fifty years is a long, long time to maintain accuracy in orally repeated recollections.

There is the further problem that the author of Acts quite clearly had his own "irons in the fire". Not just writing history, he had an agenda of his own. A theological agenda related to elevating the status of Paul, a figure which dominates the pages of Acts. The story of Paul is told in a manner that scholars describe as "romance" literature of the ancient world. Not unlike many of today's novels, it highlights a hero who survives shipwreck, imprisonment, starvation and physical attack to carry out a personal mission.

The historicity of some of the most dramatic events involving the Jesus movement in Jerusalem as recorded in Acts is challenged by some of today's scholar-historians. Viewed with skepticism are the Pentecostal accounts in Acts 5.1-11, Stephen's martyrdom in Acts 6-8, Peter's escape from prison in Acs 12, and Philip's evangelization of the Ethiopian eunuch in Acts 8. However, the same scholars have found authentic the story of the execution of James by Agrippa I in Acts 12.1-2.

Particularly under attack by some scholars is the insistence of Acts that Jerusalem is *the* cradle city for the Jesus movement; Luke has it constantly radiating out of Jerusalem. Many scholars today agree that the death of Jesus initially resulted in a dispersion of Jesus' followers from Jerusalem with some of them later returning to Jerusalem. Mark, written many decades earlier than Acts, focuses on Galilee, not Jerusalem. Its emphasis on the sayings of Jesus during his ministry can be argued to place the movement's origins in Galilee. John emphasizes that the apostles returned to Galilee after the crucifixion and drops the story at that point. Luke and the author of John ignore the possibility of a post-crucifixion Galilean Jesus movement.

Matthew, often hailed as the organizational gospel for the Catholic church, says nothing about any activities of Jesus' followers in Jerusalem after the crucifixion. It is only Luke (written by the same evangelist that penned Acts) that combines a resurrection appearance in Jerusalem with a description of the followers remaining in that city.

But then there is Paul who assuredly wrote first hand and with detail-relating credibility about the "pillars" of the movement in Jerusalem. Persuaded by the agreement of Paul and Acts on numerous items (although there are surely differences), many if not most of today's scholars overcome the doubts expressed above and continue to accept as basically accurate much of Acts' account of those early days of the Jesus movement.

Acts relates quite plausibly that early on there were Jesus followers in Jerusalem who, clearly in the minority, mixed with their brethren among the traditional Jews in a normal living fashion. If, as probably most scholars agree, it was the Roman authorities and not the Jewish people who must bear responsibility for the crucifixion, this would explain a lack of hostility by the Jewish population of Jerusalem and their leaders toward the followers of Jesus in the early decades after the crucifixion.

Realistic too is Luke's reports (Lk 24.46-53) that the Jesus followers maintained their homage-paying visits to the holy temple and also used the community-center synagogues. And that they shared homes and daily living events with other Jews and with the large number of Greek-speaking Hellenists who had taken up residence in Jerusalem.

Possibly significant is the tradition described in Acts of the Jesus followers' communal living practices: "They had all things in common; they would sell their possessions and goods and distribute the proceeds to all, as any had need." (Acts 2.44-45) This description is echoed in the later account of Paul collecting donations for the poor in Jerusalem from the various Christian communities that he nurtured.

In describing the religious activities of the Jesus movement, Paul refers to "churches of Judea in Christ." The Greek word translated as "churches" would more accurately be understood as "assemblies". Although Paul does not identify any such in Jerusalem, there is no good reason to question that the disciples in that city did have "assemblies". Thus, most likely did the practice arise among the Jewish followers of Jesus of participating in temple worship and synagogue activities while at the same time pursuing their own developing religious beliefs. Acts relates that Peter and John went frequently, perhaps daily, to the temple (2.46, 3.1, 5.12, 21). The "breaking of the bread" in their homes in remembrance of Jesus was in addition to observance of the sacrifice rituals at the temple.

Thus could have developed in Jerusalem the "house churches" that characterized the Jesus movement in other cities. Meetings in homes where Jesus was discussed collectively could very well have included in those early years a "table fellowship" or meal at which those present shared memories of the teaching and acts of Jesus, perhaps amplified by visitors from Galilee who had seen and heard Jesus as he wandered from town to town.

Peter does play a substantial role in the burgeoning Jerusalem Christian community, along with the apostle James, son of Zebedee, and James, the brother of Jesus. John is also mentioned in Acts and is described in the Pauline letters as a leader of the Jerusalem Christian community. Unquestionably, James, the brother of Jesus, was a leader of the more conservative Christian Jews, honoring the law and traditions of Judaism. He is also viewed by some scholars as being kind of "chairman" of missionary activities, holding perhaps a supervisory role over both Peter and Paul.

Acts tells the dramatic story of trouble starting in Jerusalem with the strait-laced, tradition-bound Jews when the followers of Jesus persisted in openly pursuing their beliefs in such matters as public healing and proselytizing others. The initial trouble makers could well have included all of Peter, John and both of the men named James. It is unknown whether these men took up residence in Jerusalem after the crucifixion or were, as some scholars argue, temporary visitors from Galilee. Some surely made Jerusalem their home; James the brother of Jesus was one.

Whether as visiting guests or resident activists, these men could easily have offended (as Jesus had before them) "the priests, the captain of the temple and the Sadducees", as Acts relates. (Acts 4.2-3) Acts focuses on James and Peter as leaders but whether these two were actually jailed and then miraculously freed as meticulously detailed in Acts (Acts 5.17-21) can be left to speculation. But delicious to read is the account of the respected Jewish leader Gamaliel giving that often-quoted advice to "leave these men alone because if this undertaking is of human origin it will fail, but if it is of God, you will not be able to overthrow them" (Acts 6.36-39).

Jumping for a moment from Jerusalem to Rome, the Jews in the latter city had severe problems at this time. Josephus relates that Fulvia, a highly placed Roman lady who had converted to Judaism, sent "purple and gold" to the temple at Jerusalem at the request of dishonest priests who planned to and did convert the valuable present to their personal use. Fulvia's husband tattled to Tiberius and the outraged emperor retaliated by banishing "all the Jews" from Rome. Josephus says 4000 Jews left Rome at this time and his account seems to be confirmed by a later Roman historian, Suetonius, in his *Tiber*, Sec. 36.

These must also have been somewhat tempestuous times elsewhere in Palestine. Josephus describes tumult in Samaria when a large group of aroused Samaritans came armed to the village of Tirathaba and were trapped on narrow mountain roads by Pilate's centurions: "Some of them they slew and others of them they put to flight. As to those fleeing, the centurions "took a great many alive, the principal of which, and also

the most potent of those that fled away, Pilate ordered to be slain."
Antiquities of the Jews, Book XVIII, Chapter 4.

In about AD 34, the tetrarch Philip died, having served with moderation for 38 years. Two years later, the Samaritans petitioned Vitellius, legate of Syria, to take action against Pilate because of his cruelty in dealing with the Samaritans. Word got to Rome and Pilate was recalled to Rome in 36, having served ten tyrannical years. A new prefect, Marcellus, was named by the Romans but he was unable to quiet the riotous inhabitants. The unrest continued, and Vitellius, the legate of Syria, was ordered by Rome to take his powerful legions to Jerusalem to restore order.

This could well have been the turbulent time in Jerusalem when there was active persecution of at least the Greek-speaking followers of Jesus as Acts relates (Acts 9.1-2). These Hellenists possibly rejected temple worship and the Jews retaliated by shutting off common funds from the Greek widows who were wholly dependent on those funds. The apostles refused to get involved in this dispute, and a compromise was reached by giving the Hellenists their own administrators. At about this time, many of the persecuted Hellenists apparently left Jerusalem and moved to other cities in Palestine and Asia Minor, forming or joining existing Christian communities in such places as Samaria, Antioch in Syria, Phoenicia and Cyprus.

Arrival of Saul of Tarsus

In the midst of this turbulence in Jerusalem, Saul of Tarsus arrived on the scene as a rabid persecutor of those who believed strongly in Jesus. The peace that had been achieved in the Jewish community between Jesus believers and non-believers was gone.

Acts describes Saul, who became Paul, as witnessing the stoning death of Stephen. (Acts 8.1: "Saul approved of their killing him".) Acts goes on to describe Paul's "ravaging the church by entering house after house; dragging off both men and women, he committed them to prison." Then, on the road to Damascus to continue his persecution there, Paul saw a vision that converted him to being a devout follower of Jesus.

Acts provides no hint of Paul's physical appearance but he was described some years after his death as "a man small of stature, with bald head and crooked legs...with eyebrows meeting and nose somewhat hooked." This vivid word-picture is in the 2d Century apocryphal "Acts of Paul and Thecla", a story of a young girl who hears Paul preaching through her open window and gives up everything to flee with Paul to a religious life.

Whatever Paul's actual appearance, it is undeniable that with his fiery temperament and wide-ranging travels on behalf of Christianity, he has provided centuries of controversy, ranging (as the conservative Expositor's Bible Commentary quotes from varying descriptions) from "prince of the apostles" to "an ugly little Jew" who placed his own perhaps unduly Hellenistic imprint on the teaching of Jesus; from the "Paul of faith" to the "archenemy of Peter and the truth".

Interesting speculation but not very credible, say scholars, are the musings of a recent author, A.N. Wilson, that Paul may have been in Jerusalem at the time of the crucifixion. The author speculates that Paul, who wrote in one of his letters that he bore on his body "the marks of the Lord Jesus" may have been the man named Malchus who was wounded at the time of Jesus' arrest.

Paul had begun life as a devout Jew and repeatedly proclaimed this throughout his missionary life: "I was of the Pharisees, a Hebrew of Hebrews." Born in Tarsus in about AD 5, he was the son of a Pharisee and traditionally raised as a Palestinian Jew. Tarsus was one of three leading university centers in the Roman Empire and Paul may well have learned some Roman law as a young man. His birth in Tarsus, a city with direct ties to Rome, gave him automatic Roman citizenship. Tarsus at that time was a cultural center and, while Aramaic was the everyday language, many of its educated citizens must have spoken Greek; as his letters demonstrate, Paul was very comfortable with that language as well as written Hebrew.

The Greek revealed by his letters was, however, the non-literary, street Greek. Scholars argue that he could not have been taught in the classic Greek educational tradition. This analysis causes some students of Paul to disbelieve that he crafted the speech replete with Stoic philosophy which Acts records his giving at the Areopagus in Athens.

Paul had absorbed a detailed knowledge of the Hebrew scripture and bragged of his learning at the feet of Gamaliel, a respected member of the ruling Sanhedrin who was known as a follower of the more liberal Hillel school of Judaism. No one knows, of course, but the disputes between the liberal views of Hillel and the strict adherence to the law advocated by the Shammai school may have sowed the seeds for Paul's later vitriolic tirades against the Jewish law.

Paul is thought by some scholars to have been married at one time. His trade was tent-making and leather-working; he used those crafting abilities during his missionary travels. Paul's physical affliction is described in his Letter to the Corinthians and some speculate that it was epilepsy. Small in stature (this much about his physical appearance we know for certain), like some other passionate leaders such as Alexander the Great and Napoleon who preceded and followed him, he made up for his size with his tremendous energy and ambition combined with extraordinary fervor, persistence, and persuasiveness.

Caligula and Herod Agrippa I

Moving the story from Palestine to Rome, Emperor Tiberius died in AD 37 and the Senate elected Caius Caligula, aged 29, to be his successor, significantly changing the life of Agrippa, the grandson of Herod the Great. Agrippa had lived in the imperial household in Rome from age five, enjoying the friendship of Drusus, the emperor Tiberius' son. However, when he achieved manhood he became impoverished and got into serious money problems. While traveling and without funds, He borrowed substantial sums from a Roman official in Puteoli and then welched on the debt by leaving town. This greatly offended Tiberius but Agrippa got back into his favor by borrowing three hundred thousand drachmae (Josephus' account) from the royal Antonia, the emperor's sister in law, to pay off the debt which had offended Tiberius.

Then, on an occasion when he was riding in a chariot with Caligula, young Agrippa foolishly remarked that it would be just fine if Tiberius, who was disliked by the Romans as a tyrant, would be succeeded by Caligula. The chariot driver overheard the conversation and tattled to Tiberius. Agrippa was thrown into irons. Antonia managed to bribe his guards to see that he was at least treated decently. When Tiberius died, the new emperor Caligula, still friendly to Agrippa, "sent for him to his house, put a diadem on his head and appointed him to be king of the tetrarch of Philip... and changed his iron chain for a golden one of equal weight."

Thus, shortly after the crucifixion of Jesus, King Herod Agrippa acquired governing power over the territory ruled by Philip plus the tetrarchy of Lysanias. Traveling to his homeland, he "demonstrated to the men that saw him the power of fortune, when they compared his former poverty with his present happy affluence."

The new King Herod Agrippa I visited Alexandria on his way home and the famous Jewish writer Philo recorded that he was met with demonstrations against him and the local Jews. The demonstrations were tolerated by the Roman prefect, Flaccus, who managed in the process to insult the newly royal Herod and there ensued a virulent per-secution of the Alexandrian Jews.

The other Herod, Herod Antipas whom Jesus called "the Fox", still reigned as tetrarch of Galilee. His wife, Herodias (she who importuned

Herod to take the life of John the Baptist in the gospel story) apparently was envious of Agrippa's newfound prominence and authority in Palestine. She and her husband importuned Caligula to make him a king and, to further their cause, made charges against Agrippa. Agrippa retaliated by telling Caligula that Herod had offered armed help to an enemy of the emperor who ruled in Parthia. When Herod confessed that this was true, Caligula ended his 43-year reign and stripped Herod Antipas of his tetrarchy. Both his territory and his treasury were given to King Agrippa I. In AD 39, Antipas was banished by Caligula to Lyons, a city of Gaul.

Hopes were raised throughout Palestine that this new ruler of all the land over which his father had held sway could lead the way to a new era for the Jews. Historians say that he was to be the last hope of averting a disastrous rebellion in Palestine.

In Rome, for the first two years of his reign, Caligula gained the goodwill of Romans but then, according to Josephus, "he went beyond the bounds of human nature in his conceit of himself." As some historians say, his madness came to the fore. He villified the Senate and the Roman nobility and subverted the powerful and traditional equestrian order. Finally, he asserted his own divinity. Orders went out from the emperor that all shrines and places of worship must display his image. Then matters got worse in AD 39 when Caligula ordered that his statue be placed in the holy temple, a move that totally outraged the Jews.

According to Josephus, Caligula ordered his legate in Syria, Petronius, to enforce the royal edict by sending his legions into Judea. But Petronius procrastinated and wintered the soldiers in Ptolemais, near Palestine, saying that he would invade Judea in the spring. Then, many Jews petitioned Ptolemais to disobey Caligula's order. Petronius was convinced that he should not proceed and advised Caligula by letter that the Jews were threatening war over the matter.

Meanwhile, Herod Agrippa I intervened with Caligula, entertaining him magnificently. When the emperor asked Agrippa what favor he desired in return, Herod pleaded the cause of the Jews in Palestine. Emotionally moved that Agrippa had not asked anything for himself, Caligula rescinded his order to Petronius: "If thou has already erected my statue, let it stand; but if thou hast not yet dedicated it, do not trouble thyself further about it, but dismiss thy army, go back and take care of those affairs which I sent thee about at first, for I have now no occasion for the erection of that statue. This I have granted as a favor to Agrippa."

But then Caligula received the letter from Petronius advising him of the threat made by the Jews. Caligula immediately wrote Petronius that if he thought the Jews' threats were of more importance than the emperor's command, he should commit suicide, "for I will make thee an example to the present and to all future ages, that they may not dare to contradict the commands of their emperor." Fortunately for Petronius, he did not receive this letter until after Caligula died in AD 41 to be succeeded by Claudius.

Emergence of Antioch as Christian Center

Sometime during these years and before AD 40, the first assemblages of Jesus movement followers in Antioch occurred. Antioch was no small town. With a population perhaps in excess of 300,000, it was the third city in the Roman Empire after Rome and Alexandria. A beautiful city located on a fertile plain in northern Syria near the Mediterranean Sea, it was known as the Queen of the Orient; its broad colonnaded streets were lit by lamps at night.

Antioch was a center for Hellenistic learning and culture in Syria and also had the largest Jewish population in that country, about 30,000. Those who converted from Judaism to Christianity, along with the Gentiles who joined them, became early known as troublemakers; they were given the name "Christians" (followers of "Chrestus") by the

Roman authorities and began to be recognized as a separate sect of Judaism having an identity distinct from that of the overall Jewish community. Because of this, some call Antioch the cradle of Christianity, giving it equal prominence with Jerusalem.

Meanwhile, Paul came to Jerusalem after a period of absence to visit Peter and James, the brother of Jesus. This would have been in about AD 38. The Christian Jews must have received him with some trepidation in view of his previous persecution activities. On this occasion, Paul later wrote, he met only Peter among the apostles, but Acts states that Barnabas "took him to the apostles." (Acts 9.27) Indeed, it is hard to see how Paul could have stayed for any time with Peter in Jerusalem without coming into contact with the other leaders of that relatively small Christian community.

Many argue that Paul simply must have learned from Peter at this time some of the basic facts of Jesus' life and teaching; Paul's fervor for his new-found faith makes any other conclusion difficult to believe. But it is passing strange that none of the events of Jesus' life, none of Jesus' memorialized sayings, are reflected in Paul's letters. In the "house churches" that he surely visited, he must have shared in the stories about Jesus. Perhaps it is a reflection of the mindset of the early followers of Jesus that Paul's letters (at least the ones we have), insofar as Jesus is concerned, are preoccupied with the crucifixion and the critical need for faith in Jesus over all else.

When the new King Agrippa returned from Rome to Palestine, Josephus reports that he hung up in the temple the golden chain which had been given to him by Caligula -— possibly as a reminder of his former impoverished state and the dramatic reversal of his fortune which occurred when Caligula became emperor. To enlist the support of his countrymen, he gave the residents of Jerusalem a measure of tax relief. Then, to assert his new powers, he installed his choice as high priest, a man named Simon Cantheras. At that time, Judea was treated by the

Romans as a part of Syria so that civil power was vested in the Syrian legate. This left Cantheras with a pretty free hand in Judea.

In 39, satisfied that all was well in Palestine, Agrippa went to Rome where he stayed for two years. After the Petronius episode and Caligula's death, Claudius took over as emperor and Agrippa returned to Palestine. Agrippa removed the high priest Cantheras, replacing him with a man named Jonathan from the traditional family of Ananus. Jonathan had close ties to Pallas, secretary to Claudius. The "power" situation in Judea then went back to the former system where the Ananus family held the religious power and the Romans both directly and through Agrippa held the civil power.

Agrippa took further steps to ally himself with the religious establishment in Jerusalem. He gave substantial tax relief to the inhabitants. Then, Claudius, acting upon the petitions of both Agrippa and the remaining Herod who had a small domain northeast of Judea, decreed that the Jews should be allowed to follow their ancient customs without interference. This brought King Agrippa even closer to the religious power structure.

According to Josephus, Agrippa had a mild temper, unlike this father, but he was also a builder, like his father. Josephus records that he lived continually at Jerusalem and carefully observed the Judean laws. "He therefore kept himself entirely pure, nor did any day pass over his head without its appointed sacrifice." Agrippa was also very rich; his revenues were given by Josephus as "twelve million drachme", the equivalent of over a million dollars. He lived quite extravagantly, gave generous gifts, and held grand exhibitions for the populace in true Roman style. As a result and despite his grand income, he had to "borrow great sums from others."

Jesus Movement Encounters Trouble

Perhaps understandably, Agrippa came down on the side of the religious establishment when trouble broke out between the followers of Jesus and the traditional Jews.

Throughout the early years after the crucifixion, they had persisted in their home worship, often postponing it until Sunday because they were at the synagogue until sundown, the end of the Jewish sabbath.

The Christians gathered in these "house churches" on a weekly basis and the practice grew of sharing a meal of bread and wine in memory of Jesus, possibly telling stories as they recalled the life and times of Jesus. Apparently, they chose in early years to avoid the Jewish sabbath. Or, it may have simply been a practical adjustment; it could have been caused by the inability of Christian Jews to move about or meet together until after sundown on Saturday, the Jewish sabbath. There is ancient Christian lore of a celebration during the night between Saturday and Sunday. Gradually, as the 1st Century progressed, the followers of Jesus came together on a decision to worship on Sunday as the day of resurrection, the day of the discovery of the open tomb, the third day counting the Friday crucifixion as the first.

The Jesus movement followers began to be viewed as "stand offish" and this was enhanced, scholars believe, by rumors about Jesus being illegitimate. Rumors spread that the followers practiced "secret rites". The Jewish religious leaders quite clearly did not look kindly on these people, having been particularly offended by the Hellenists. Agrippa was not an activist leader, but he was viewed as being pious and supported the Pharisees.

Possibly at the urging of the Sanhedrin, Agrippa embarked on a program of selective persecution aimed primarily at the activist Hellenists. This led to the Roman's putting to the sword in about 43 the apostle James, son of Zebedee. The other James, "the brother of the Lord," escaped the wrath of Agrippa and the Romans; the presumption is that he was protected by his efforts to persuade Christian Jews to continue to observe the Jewish law.

Acts relates that during this time, Peter was thrown into jail but later released; as earlier noted, some of today's scholars doubt the historicity of this story. Catholic tradition has Peter leaving Jerusalem at about this time to found the Christian community in Rome and become the first Bishop of Rome. However, Raymond Brown, a noted Catholic scholar, joins others in dismissing this view of Peter's activities with the statement that it is "almost inconceivable" that the author of Acts, who wrote considerably about Peter's role, would have failed to mention Peter's presence in Rome at that time if the tradition were accurate. Most likely, scholars say, Peter remained in Palestine, visiting Lydda, Joppa and Caesarea as Acts records.

During this time, the Christian community in Rome apparently caused trouble for the Jews in that city, possibly because of the Peter-Paul differences over observance of Judean proscriptions regarding circumcision and the diet laws. In about AD 42, the emperor Claudius moved against them. The Roman historian Tranquillus wrote in his *The Lives of the Caesars* that Claudius "expelled the Jews from Rome because, incited by Chrestus, they were constantly crating disturbances."

At this time, the Jesus movement could be roughly divided into three groups in varying degrees of distinction from the traditional Jews: the conservative group headed by James (and Peter, before he sided with Paul on circumcision), the liberals headed by Paul who wanted no circumcision and no enforcement of the food laws on the new converts, and the radicals (the Hellenists) who went even further than the liberals and saw no abiding significance in any of the Jewish traditions and feasts. When the Hellenists left Jerusalem, the conservative faction headed by James became dominant among Christian Jews in that city; the liberals and Hellenists were apparently centered in Antioch.

Turbulent Regime of Herod Agrippa II

In 44, King Agrippa I died while visiting Caesarea. He had reigned four years under Caligula and three under Claudius, ruling finally over a territory equivalent to that of his grandfather, Herod the Great. When Agrippa I died, his son, like his father before him, was being educated in Rome. He was only 17 when his father died and the emperor, Claudius, took this occasion to reorganize Palestine into a Roman province to be ruled by procurators on the basis that Herod Agrippa's son was too young to rule this important area. Fadus was made prefect and Longinus became the legate for Syria.

Herod's son first became a ruler of a small territory in Palestine when an uncle, Herod of Chbalcis, died; it was not until several years later that Claudius granted him the territory of Philip, to which Nero later added parts of Galilee and Perea. Assuming the title, Herod Agrippa II developed an incestuous relationship with his sister, Bernice, which caused a scandal in both Palestine and Rome.

When Fadus took over as prefect, he definitely did not share Agrippa I's toleration of and affinity for Jewish ways. Under his direction, the Romans made life difficult for the Jews throughout Palestine. Making no effort to understand Judaism and its various shades of belief and practice, they appeared to welcome opportunities to harass those who were openly religious. Then, in 48, a severe famine occurred in Judea and lasted for several years.

During the famine and the accompanying restlessness and dissatisfaction that was prevalent among the peasants, James and Simon, sons of the Judas of Galilee who had led the revolt in the early years of the century fomented trouble with the Romans and were slain as a result. Fadus was also confronted with the magician Theudas (not the rebel by the same name who was active much earlier).

Josephus tells the story of Theudas. Claiming to be a prophet in the Jewish tradition, he mesmerized his large following and led them to the

River Jordan, persuading them that he had the power to divide the river like Moses had parted the Red Sea. Fadus, alert to any growing power in his domain, sent centurions to the scene and, surprising the horde, slew many of them and took Theudas alive.

In AD 46, Fadus was succeeded as prefect by Alexander who was confronted by the continuing famine. He ruled briefly and then Cumanus took over in AD 48. Early in his reign, a riot occurred when multitudes of pilgrims were at the temple grounds to celebrate the Passover feast. Cumanus kept one regiment of his army stationed at the temple in Jerusalem, and these centurions walked "sentry duty" to keep an eye on the tumultuous crowds. Josephus tells the story:

On the fourth day of the feast, a certain soldier let down his breeches, and exposed his privy members to the multitude, which put those that saw him into a furious rage, and made them cry out that this impious action was not done to approach them, but God himself.

Cumanus tried unsuccessfully to calm the raging Jews. He called his legions to the nearby fortress Antonia which overlooked the temple. When the rioters saw the Roman soldiers, they attempted to disperse but were caught in the narrow passages and "a great number were pressed to death". Josephus asserts that 20,000 perished, but this could be a gross exaggeration.

In these years, troubles persisted within the populace of Palestine. Josephus tells a long story of a quarrel between Samaritans and Jews living in Jerusalem. It commenced when a group of Galileans were traveling through Samaria to participate in the Passover feast at the temple in Jerusalem. Accosted by robbers, a number of the pilgrims were killed. The remainder of the band complained to Cumanus but he declined to intervene.

The dispute continued and violence broke out again. Cumanus then took the side of the Samaritans and killed a number of the Jews. The Samaritans appealed to the legate of Syria and the dispute wound up in Rome. The Samaritans seemed certain to prevail until the emperor's wife, Agrippina, persuaded Claudius to decide in favor of the Jews; whereupon, Josephus concludes, Claudius caused the Samaritans to be slain.

Josephus ends this account of Palestinian turbulence with the conclusion that "after this time all Judea was overrun with robberies." Undoubtedly, the Zealots were leading dispossessed and impoverished peasants into forays against the more well-to-do Judeans.

The Paul-Peter-James Controversy

Meanwhile, in the late 40's, the Jesus movement was having its problems. In Antioch, Paul and his assistant, Barnabas, encountered a rising furor over the need for Christian Jews to abide by the rules of Judaism, including the dietary laws, observance of the traditional feasts, and circumcision. The last was to the Jews the "rite of acceptance" commanded by Abraham, roughly corresponding to the rite of baptism for Christians.

Circumcision became a major issue; did the newly converted Gentiles have to be circumcised to comply with Jewish law and tradition? Not just the babies, but the adult men? Perhaps understandably, adults strongly resisted this very painful operation.

It was not just the pain of the operation that caused resistance to circumcision by the adult Gentiles, although that had to have been a major factor. There was also the humility; in those times, men sometimes went naked before other men and the removal of the foreskin would be immediately apparent to all. The embarrassment caused some Jews who converted to Christianity to submit to epispasm, circumcision in reverse, so they could openly demonstrate their lack of circumcision. This procedure is criticized in 1 Corinthians by Paul when he urges that Jewish converts "not seek to remove the marks of circumcision."

While Paul argued strongly that circumcision should not be required for his Gentile converts, he apparently continued to believe that it was necessary for any uncircumcised Jews who adopted the Christian faith. The circumcision of Timothy, whose mother was Jewish, is reported in both Galatians and Acts; most scholars prefer the former version.

To Paul's Jewish critics, this was viewed as setting a double standard; not requiring circumcision of converted Gentiles but forcing a converted Jew to endure it.

There was also in those years the recurring problem of Jews dining with Gentiles. The strict dietary laws prohibited Jews from eating or even consorting with Gentiles who did not observe the law. Meals were family experiences. What if one member of the family was Christian and the others were not? Families and entire communities were disrupted over the issues that grew out of the commands of the dietary law; children were disowned and violence may well have erupted.

Scholars explain that this points up the multiple divisions that existed in the early Jesus movement communities. Some strictly observed the Jewish Mosaic law — mostly Jews but also some converted Gentiles. Place them to the right; all members of what Paul called the "circumcision party" or the "James people" (named after James, the brother of Jesus.

Then, moving left, came those opposed to circumcision but still accepting some of the Jewish feasts, rites, and dietary restrictions. The third group would be people who opposed both circumcision and the dietary laws but wanted to observe the important Jewish feasts and rites. Lastly, there were those who wanted a clean, total break with Judaism and all requirements of the Mosaic Law. On this spectrum, James was to the right, Paul was toward the left, and Peter was somewhere in the middle.

Paul's intensity in converting the Gentiles naturally led him to take the practical route that would be easier, not harder to persuade people to join him and this inevitably brought him into conflict with the circumcision or James people who remained steadfast in their adherence to Jewish law and custom. All of this came to a head in Paul's early years as a missionary when the James people in Jerusalem received critical reports about Paul's, in their view, relaxed approach to conversion. Understandably, this angered the James people.

Paul came to Jerusalem in about AD 49 with his compatriots Barnabas and Titus. When they met with James, Peter and John, the last three agreed that "Paul should go to the Gentiles and they to the circumcised." (Gal. 2.9-10) However, the difference over circumcision for converts was not resolved and the result was Christianity's first summit meeting – the famous Council of Jerusalem, held probably in 49 or 50.

According to Acts, the council consisted largely of a dramatic confrontation involving speeches by Peter, Paul and James, with Peter joining ranks with Paul against James in urging that circumcision be discarded as a requirement for Gentile conversion. Scholars today have considerable doubt as to the historicity of the speeches as quoted in Acts but most do accept that the rift existed and that the council concluded in favor of Paul and Peter.

Realistically, this was a watershed event; the first concrete mark in the separation of Christianity from Judaism. Although the after-struggle went on for decades, the die was cast when Peter joined with Paul.

It took decades for the circumcision party to completely lose its battle for adherence to the traditional strictures of Judaism. The liberal, break-with-Judaism group ultimately prevailed, but not until after years of escalating conflict and hostility. We can only speculate as to how the fall-out from this conflict tore families and communities apart. We do know that it resulted in the destruction of family units, ostracism, and even killings.

After the Council, Paul returned to Antioch to resume his missionary work. Later, as recounted by Paul in Galatians but not treated separately in Acts, Peter joined him and participated with Paul in the latter's practice of taking meals with Gentile Christians who did not observe the

Jewish dietary laws. As Paul puts it, "Peter lived in a Gentile and not in a Jewish way".

"For, before certain men came from James, he ate with the Gentiles; but when they came he drew back and separated himself, fearing the circumcision party." (Gal. 2.11-12)

In other words, Peter broke bread with Gentiles in open violation of the Jewish law. Perhaps both Peter and Paul had in mind the inclusive table fellowship practices of Jesus. However, and predictably, this offended the conservative Jews and he was attacked and derided for his "lax" position. Many Jewish Christians, partisans of the James party who had lost on the circumcision issue at the Council, drew the line on the dietary laws: Jews should not, could not eat with Gentiles; table companionship was intolerable and shameful.

This probably meant little to Christian Jews in Jerusalem who associated only with other Jews and naturally observed the dietary rules they shared in common, but it must have been devastating in Christian communities outside Jerusalem where Jewish Christians mingled and celebrated a meal honoring Jesus with converted Gentiles and cared not a whit about the niceties of the dietary laws.

This Peter-Paul difference furthered the split between the Jesus movement and Judaism.   Paul writes in Galatians that probably under pressure from the James people, Peter chose sides against Paul. Paul writes that he "rebuked Peter to his face" on this dietary law difference and, to Paul's dismay, his disciple Barnabas left him to join Peter.

At this juncture, Paul realistically had no choice. Arrayed against him were those he termed the "pillars" of Christianity – James and Peter and, although the writings are silent on the matter, possibly also John. So, Paul left Palestine and Antioch to go on a wide-ranging missionary trip to Europe – Macedonia, Athens, Corinth, and Ephesus.

The picture of Peter tailoring his actions in Antioch in response to messages delivered from James, does not square with the traditional view of Peter as the Christ-anointed leader of the Christians. It gives support to those scholars who argue that James was not only the leader of the Jerusalem community of followers of Jesus but also the realistic "Chairman" of the missionary out-reach program.

In any event, it is clear that at this time, James assumed sole leadership of the Jerusalem Christian community, working with a group of presbyters who apparently acted somewhat like the Judean presbyter elders of the Jewish synagogues. James obviously felt that co-existence with the Pharisees, who had the ears of their Roman overlords, the Romans, could only be maintained in the face of open hostility to those active in the Jesus movement by demonstrating strict adherence to the Jewish law.

James was openly a Christian Jew who apparently did believe that Jesus was the messiah. However, at the same time, he persisted in observance of the Jewish law to the fullest extent. This, of course, is the explanation for his not being singled out for persecution as were some of his compatriots. Hegesippius, writing in about 150 described James as one who "drank no wine or intoxicating liquor and ate no animal food; no razor came near his head; he did not smear himself with oil, and took no baths." James was apparently permitted to enter the temple and visit the restricted places reserved for the most zealous Jews where he prayed, "beseeching forgiveness for the people". He came to be called James the Just or James the Righteous.

The Spread of Christianity

Meanwhile, even in Antioch, the controversy over observance of the Jewish law did not end with the James-enforced compromise. At best, it was an uneasy peace but the table fellowship continued and an outright schism was avoided. Christian and non-Christian Jews alike continued to frequent the synagogues as community centers. Apparently, no strong effort was made thereafter to convert non-Christian Jews in

Jerusalem to Christianity; the conversion effort was concentrated on Gentiles in the Diaspora. And, as a result, the Gentile Christians began to far outnumber the Jewish Christians.

While the Jesus movement was feeling strong growing pains in Antioch and other communities visited by Paul, Christianity also found its way to Rome. Almost surely brought there by disciples (some speculate that it was Barnabas) from Jerusalem as early as the mid-40's and, as elsewhere, it began with the Jews. There was a thriving Jewish Christian community in Rome when Paul wrote his letter to the Romans in about 58.

Rome had been the first city in Europe to have a large Jewish presence. Relatively speaking, they were late-comers to Rome, having been firmly ensconced much earlier in other leading cities in the Diaspora such as Antioch, Alexandria, and Babylon. But as Rome's power grew in the then-known world, so did the number of Jews in the city, participating in the growth of trade and commerce that accompanied the rapid expansion of the Roman Empire. At the time of Jesus, Rome could have had a population of almost one million; the Jews may have accounted for about 40,000.

The Christians in Rome, Jews and non-Jews, soon got caught up in the conflicts that prevailed in Jerusalem and Antioch. The early converts were understandably on the conservative side, closer to the James-Peter views than to the more liberal Pauline teaching. Later, when significant numbers of Gentiles were converted, that division changed and the Gentiles moved into the majority role.

Suetonius in about AD 120 records that Claudius expelled at least some Christians, probably Jews, from Rome. This occurred in about the year 50 and most likely resulted from a Roman view that the Christians were "trouble makers". Suetonius notes the "disturbances caused by Chrestus" among the Jews in Rome. This expulsion is referred to in Acts (18.2-3) where the author mentions the move of Aquila and Prisca, later strong Pauline missionaries, from Rome to Corinth.

Meanwhile, believers in the Jesus movement were proliferating in a number of other cities. Prominent among them were Philippi, Corinth, Ephesus, Colossae and Damascus. Clearly, too, the movement reached northern Africa, moving from Alexandria west to Carthage. But the overall numbers were not great; one scholar, Rodney Stark, in his *The Rise of Christianity*, estimates that there were only about 1,500 Christians at that time.

Philippi, known as a "miniature Rome" was named for the royal father of Alexander the Great and was the site where Octavian (the future Caesar Augustus) defeated the assassins of Julius Caesar. The Christians were apparently not popular in this city that thrived on magic, astrology, and the pagan mystery religions. Lydia, a wealthy woman and Christian (a dealer in the much-valued "purple cloth") sheltered a Christian assembly in her home. Paul's fondness for the Jesus followers in Philippi is shown by his several letters to their churches.

There was also an early established Christian community in Corinth which had a population of about 100,000. A "hub" city, it was strategically located between two halves of the Roman Empire. Corinth was a walled city, about twice the size of Athens, and much more a Roman than a Greek city and it later became a center for Paul's conversion efforts, possibly because it was a geographic funnel for thousands of travelers from the Aegean Sea on the east to the Adriatic Sea on the west.

Pheme Perkins' *Reading the New Testament* has a detailed discussion of the problems that plagued this Greco-Roman city. Animal sacrifices to the many pagan gods worshipped by a mixture of Romans, Greeks, and Orientals at a wide variety of temples and shrines were sold by the priests in the open market. This apparently supplied a large portion of the meat used for household meals and obviously posed a problem for Jewish Christians. Should they buy or eat meat of animals which had been sacrificed to idols?

Also, the Christians, some Jews and some Gentiles, were literally surrounded by a much larger and more licentious pagan population. Free love was open and widespread in Corinth, which was justifiably called the "City of Aphrodite". To call a woman a "Corinthian female" was to cast aspersions on her virtue; to "act like a Corinthian" meant to practice frequent fornication. Paul's later letters indicate that even some converted Christians persisted in a belief that they could do whatever they wished with their bodies.

These societal problems exacerbated the existing differences among the Christians over circumcision and adherence to the dietary laws that arose out of the Antioch controversies. Tensions also developed over the celebration of common meals held in the larger homes of the more wealthy Christians (these might have included Joanna, wife of Chuza, the financial minister for Herod Antipas described in Lk. 8.3 or Manean, a close friend of Antipas mentioned in Acts 13.1). About fifty persons might be gathered for the meal, with the inner circle reclining in the dining area and the outsiders assembled in the courtyard. Poorer Christians were left out and understandably may have become resentful.

Ephesus was one of the largest cities in the Roman world, with a population possibly as high as a quarter of a million. With a strong tradition of scholarship and intellectual inquiry, it may well be a place where Paul acquired some of his evident knowledge of Hellenism. Ephesus had also the temple of Artemis, goddess of nature and fertility, a building that was one of the seven wonders of the world.

Although Paul does not refer to them in any of his letters (indeed, Paul never even mentions The Baptist), Acts states that Paul found a group of disciples of John the Baptist in Ephesus who were unaware of the teachings of Jesus. (Acts 19.1)

Ephesus, say many scholars, was most likely the Johanine community that gave birth to the unique theology embodied in the Gospel of John. This community almost certainly commenced quite early in the development of Christianity and considerable speculation exists that among the founders were the apostle John and the mysterious "beloved disciple" so frequently mentioned in John if, indeed, he was a person distinct from the apostle himself.

There may well have been Jesus believers in Ephesus (and other like cities) even before the crucifixion. Certainly there were Jews in Ephesus and some could have been early followers of John the Baptist, later converted to Jesus (just as the Gospel of John records the first-chosen disciples as having been converted from The Baptist). Paul recites that upon arrival in Ephesus, he found Apollos, a Christian Jew from Alexandria (apparently an active Christian community in Egypt at that time; nowhere mentioned, inexplicably, in Acts). Apollos and the Ephesus Christian community followed the baptism practices of John until Paul explained to them the different teaching of Jesus.

The gospel of John does recite the presence in Ephesus of a group of Samaritan converts and refers to conflicts between Jewish Christians and Jews who continued their loyalty to the conservative tenets of Judaism. Then, John refers to the arrival of Greeks, Hellenists who were early supporters of Jesus, perhaps some of those evicted from Jerusalem.

Irenaeus in the 2d Century records that John's gospel originated in Ephesus. Justin in the same century mentions John as being in Ephesus, as does Ignatius. These accounts (and the enticing story of Mary visiting John) are rebutted by those who point to the failure of Paul in his letters to ever refer to John (let alone Mary) being in Ephesus. In view of John's status as an apostle and his prominence in Jerusalem, it seems extremely unlikely that his presence would have been ignored. However, John could very well have come to Ephesus after Paul visited there; perhaps another reminder that the writers of early Christianity clearly did not claim to be either reporters or historians.

The Early House Churches

In all these cities, there were by the time of Paul's missionary trips a well-established practice of regular meetings of the Christians. Scholars speculate that these meetings may have involved not just "table fellow-ship" and discussions about Jesus but also some type of teaching and the teachers, sometimes called prophets, apparently traveled to visit other house churches in various communities.

Scholars suggest as a possibility that these meetings reflected quite divergent views of the teachings of Jesus, not unlike Christian churches of today. Some, for example, may have strongly opposed Jewish law and traditions; some could have been more traditionally Jewish, observing some of the rituals of Judaism. And the early Johannine house churches could well have adopted the quite different theology reflected in the Fourth Gospel.

Some scholars argue that the Roman household code was stressed by early Christians in response to Roman criticism that the Christians were disorderly and disruptive. The Christians could well have wanted to distinguish themselves from the pagan mystery religions in order to achieve a greater measure of community acceptance.

No evidence exists that anyone set out to create any specific type of organization or structure among the house churches in the two decades after the crucifixion, except possibly in Jerusalem where James and a group of "presbyters" apparently held sway. The concept of a bishop or single leader for multiple churches is clearly a much later development. Leadership was local; the leaders were the prophet-teachers who acted as "shepherds" plus elders and presbyters, positions inherited from Judaism. In those years there were no consistent patterns of organiza-tion, no rules of conduct, no codes of participation.

Was there, however, in those early days of the Jesus movement as a somewhat distinct religious sect a "center city" in the sense of some kind of loose control place? Conventional Catholic wisdom has for centuries suggested Rome, but that almost surely came later, say most scholars. In the years 30 to 50, Jerusalem is the city most often designated; it was from there that James issued orders to the Jesus followers in Antioch and to which Paul returned after the conclusion of his missionary trips. But in the interim between these two events, the Syrian city of Antioch, third in size in the Roman Empire after Rome and Alexandria, assumed considerable importance and, as earlier noted, some scholars today view Antioch as a birthplace for Christianity rivaling Jerusalem.

CHAPTER EIGHT

Oral Traditions to Early Writings

As the Jesus movement grew, the traditions developed and were spread by word of mouth, community by community. From Galilee, from Jerusalem, from Antioch, emanated the stories concentrating on both his ministry and the circumstances surrounding his death.

The Oral Tradition Period

The first twenty years after the crucifixion, AD 30 to 50, are often referred to by the scholars as the oral tradition period –- a time when recollections and stories about Jesus were told and retold in various communities by members of the Jesus movement and the repetition of those accounts gradually hardened into cherished traditions.

Several factors operated to intensify the spread of these traditions. Ranked first must be the dramatic nature of the story of the life and brutal crucifixion of this unusual man, together with a developing belief in the resurrection, the "signature" event of nascent Christianity. Once it became established and accepted among the followers of Jesus that he had risen from the dead and returned to confront his disciples and that belief was dramatically conveyed to others, the almost wildfire growth of what soon became a distinct sect called Christianity began.

At that time, historians tell us, memorization was a highly developed art, much more practiced than it is today. Since the skill of reading was restricted to a few, memorization was essential for conveying to others a story about sayings or an account of an observed deed. And this was the way in which not only sayings and deeds but also beliefs about their meaning were communicated and conveyed from person to person, from group to group, from community to community, from generation to generation.

Memorization and repetition have traditionally been the explanations offered for the close similarity of words and descriptions of events in the gospels which were separately written many years after the death of Jesus. However, some scholars have strongly disagreed, arguing that memorization could not possibly account for all of the almost word-for-word detailed accounts after the passage of so many years.

Second in explanation of the growth of Jesus stories is the actions of the disciples of Jesus who had traveled, slept and shared table fellowship with him. These men, many more than the 12 apostles, may well have become active messengers for his faith. Indeed, the gospels provided the model in Jesus' lifetime instructions to his messengers: *"Go on your way. See, I am sending you out like lambs into the midst of wolves. Carry no purse, no bag, no sandals; and greet no one on the road... . Whenever you enter a town, say to them 'The Kingdom of God has come near to you.'"* (Lk. 10.3-9)

These inspired individuals, men and women, must have been strongly motivated to spread the "good news" by telling personal stories involving the living Jesus; their first-hand recollections of what he said and did. Especially during those years when these believers accepted without doubt that they would see the return of their leader, that the way of life they had known before Jesus would soon be gone forever and that they would live to see the return of Jesus and the arrival of a total Kingdom of God embracing the world.

A third factor may well have been the development of a network of traveling teacher-prophets who visited the house churches scattered throughout the communities where Christianity was developing. These men (yes, and women too) could have honed or expanded their "pitch" based on encounters with the wandering disciples. Quite naturally, these teachers would want to give an element of drama to their participation in these gatherings. That drama could have been provided by telling stories as though the teacher had first-hand knowledge. Either as a pretended observer disciple or as one who gained knowledge directly from an eye-witness disciple.

Finally, think of family life at that time. People who had no TV, no radio, no books, no newspapers, no magazines. People lived literally not only hand-to-mouth but mouth-to-ear. Most word communication was oral; word of mouth prevailed almost everywhere. Further, men and women had to work hard to survive so the evening by the fireside was a natural time for family communication. And in telling -- yes, gossiping -- about happenings, the "did you hear about...?" factor inevitably came into play. The stories about Jesus, his life and death, were natural grist for this gossipy, story-telling mill. Particularly, again, because of this very unusual man, his controversial teachings and the dramatic nature of the events surrounding the crucifixion and resurrection.

For all these reasons, a web of oral traditions about Jesus was woven, grew and spread throughout the known world. Some undoubtedly became community oriented; that is, in a particular place, the stories became through repetition not only fixed in their content but also respected as being a realistic account of something that happened or something that was said, whether it was true or not. Anyone who has lived in a small town is well aware of this phenomenon. To put it differently, the stories developed lives of their own. They became reality, respected as if (traditional Christians will please pardon the age-old expression) they were "the gospel truth".

Understandably, these stories or versions of what happened or what was said or done by Jesus could also vary from community to community. Perhaps because the same original story-teller varied or shaped the account to meet the vagaries or demands of his/her audiences. Or, it was not the original teller but a leader in the community who adapted the story to make it more acceptable to or usable for the people of the community.

So, in many different ways in many different sections of the world to which Christianity had spread, a variety of traditions developed about the life and death of Jesus. They surely varied in content and details, but, again, the dramatic nature of that life and death coupled with the practiced art of memorization must surely have provided some skeleton of more-than-similarity among the various versions. And the stories about his life would more logically have arisen in the area of Galilee whereas those about his death would naturally be more basic to Jerusalem.

This, then, is the process that occurred during those critical two decades after the crucifixion, a process that found its ultimate product in the writings that are the foundation for Christianity.

Earliest Writings

The lack of immediate written accounts of Jesus life and death is frequently explained by the perception that none was needed; word of mouth sufficed and preservation mattered not since the end-time was near. Time and distance soon changed that. As the decades went by, as Christianity spread, the "second coming" receded in time, and the distances involved grew rapidly. Stories and lessons told by the preachers-prophets would not suffice. There developed a need for writings that could be read to assembled Christians. The gospels, the good news about Jesus resulted.

The roots of the word "gospel" are in Hellenism, not Judaism. The Greek word for "gospel" was a verb, not a noun, used in connection with the enthronement of a god. It meant, loosely, "bringing tidings of joy", or "bringing glad announcements". As used by the Palestinians, it referred to an "oral preaching" in a particular community, and the Christians used it in the context of conveying the good news about the salvation by Jesus Christ. Originally, it was used in the singular – bringing the message about Jesus.

What was recorded first and in what language? Taking the latter question first, the gospels with which we are most familiar were originally written in Greek, not in Aramaic with later translation into Greek as many Christians suppose. And the Greek used by the initial authors was not classic Greek. Called for centuries "Holy Ghost Greek" or "bad Greek" because of its non-classic peculiarities, it was only with the recent discovery of ancient scrolls that scholars learned that it was just "street Greek" (called "Koine") widely used in the 1st Century.

Why Greek instead of Aramaic or Hebrew? Perhaps because most of the early writings read to assembled Christians were composed outside Palestine, and most of those listening were not Palestinian Jews. This leads also to the interesting question whether Jesus did in fact speak Greek. Most scholars conclude that he did not, although he may have had some grasp of the language. And Greek did have widespread usage in Palestinian trade and culture, even outside Jerusalem and certainly in Sepphoris, very near to Nazareth.

How were the earliest writings recorded? Certainly the difficulty of recording the oral traditions and then using the written product limited circulation. Papyrus sheets were made from pressed plant pith. Numbers of sheets were pasted together and then rolled. Later, codices were made by stacking the sheets of papyrus and then binding them on one side much like today's books.

Paul's opening words written to converts to Christianity in Greece in AD 50 made up most likely the first sentence of Christian scripture ever to be written. (I Thessalonians 1.1) Paul's famous letters which came to define early Christianity followed throughout the 50's as he pursued his extensive missionary travels.

For many centuries, the first writings aside from the letters of Paul were conclusively presumed to be the four gospels appearing in the New Testament. The fundamentalists, both Catholic and Protestant, continue to adhere strongly to the belief that these gospels were the first and best accounts, written by contemporaries of Jesus who were inspired by God; that God, so to speak, was at the elbows of the men who composed them.

But scholars in recent years have been increasingly disputing this conventional wisdom. True, speculation about the existence of some early writings had been around for many years – for example, that there was an early written Hebrew version of the Gospel of Matthew. That theory has now been rejected by almost all scholars. However, there are other proposed early writings and the possibility of their reality has attracted a number of scholars. Far from a majority, surely, but quite a few.

To appreciate just why it is that the discussion of these early writings has more than a speculatively ephemeral base, imagine that the above-described story-telling-retelling about Jesus has been going on for years.

Then, imagine four men who began writing about Jesus, separately and entirely without knowledge of each other.

The first of these men could have lived in Galilee where stories spread by the disciples of Jesus who personally knew and heard him must have been instilled in the minds of many Galileans living in the cities and villages of that region. Commencing in the spring of 30, these men most likely told stories about the teaching of Jesus in northern Galilee; for example, in Peter's home village of Capernaum. And then there were the displaced and dispossessed among the peasants who talked about Jesus as they wandered to other towns and visited a variety of homes. To all of these people, the reality of Jesus was in the unique teaching, the pithy sayings, the colorful stories with which they were personally familiar.

Our hypothetical author gathered up a selection of these sayings and stories and joined them together. In a writing that concentrated on words of Jesus that would not just preserve the memories of those sayings and stories but also provide a bonding source for the community and its beliefs. Thus could have emerged a community and a writing originated in that community that scholars call "Q" for "quelle", a German word for source.

Another of these men may have been a resident of Rome at a time when Christianity was in disrepute with the Roman leaders. This evangelist had learned about the life of Jesus from early followers, possibly directly from Peter who, tradition tells, left Jerusalem for Rome during the 50's. To a literate and impressionable convert to Christianity, the urge to put some of what he had heard about the drama of Jesus into writing after the death of Peter and Paul could have been irresistible. This young man could have drafted in the 50's a story about segments of Jesus' life which came to be called "Secret Mark" and later embodied it in the Gospel of Mark.

The third imaginary author could be placed somewhere in Syria, perhaps Antioch, in the area where the sect called Christianity was actually born. Perhaps he was a disciple or a convert of a disciple who became totally enamored with the sayings of Jesus repeated over and over again by wandering prophet-teachers and desired desperately to record them. He may not have wanted the dramatic events of the crucifixion and the stories of the resurrection to eclipse the real man and lifelike teachings that he knew so well. So he also set about assembling a collection of the sayings of Jesus which later, after considerable editing and additions, became known as the Gospel of Thomas.

Our fourth and last imaginary author could have lived in Jerusalem. There, he became indoctrinated with the stories of the crucifixion. He became convinced that the Romans were not primarily responsible for that evil act; rather, it was a combination of Herod and the Jewish leaders. He also believed, possibly, that many more Jews would have been converted to the Jesus movement had not their leaders dictated otherwise. To preserve his convictions, this evangelist wrote an account of the arrest and crucifixion of Jesus.

One controversial author (John Dominic Crossan, and he has followers in the scholarly community) concludes that this unknown early evangelist wrote what he calls the "Cross Gospel" which appeared later as a portion of the well-known apocryphal Gospel of Peter. This description of Jesus' last days, these scholars contend, formed the basis for the passion story which appears in different forms in the Gospels of Mark, Matthew, Luke and John.

The Writing Called "Q"

The first three of the gospels (Mark, Matthew and Luke) are called the Synoptics (from the Greek, meaning "taking a common view") because they have so many similarities. The reason for this similarity, known for centuries as the Synoptic Problem, is rather obvious: A good part of each of Matthew and Luke duplicates Marcan verses. In

Matthew, 90% of Mark's 677 verses are repeated among Matthew's 1068, thus accounting for about 60% of the total; 65% of Mark's verses appear in Luke, accounting for about half of Luke's 1149 verses.

This does not mean that all verses repeated are identical. Some are, some are all-but identical, and some are just too close to have been separately composed. The comparisons compel the conclusion that one of these three gospels is the source for the other two. And, when closely analyzed, conclude most scholars, it becomes most logical that Mark came first.

For example, in some instances, study shows that each of Matthew and Luke (particularly the latter, written in better Greek) corrected Mark's Greek. Both changed some verse sequences and it seems apparent that the later authors of Matthew and Luke edited and rewrote. Compare, for example, the different treatment given by Matthew and Luke to Jesus' Gethsemane agony. (Mk. 14.33-36; Mt. 26.36-46; Lk. 22.43-44)

The widely-accepted Marcan priority was first developed by Holtzman in 1863 after centuries of speculation about the Synoptic Problem. One of the interesting supporting arguments is the vividness of detail in Mark – such as Mark 4.38 describing Jesus in the stern of the boat and asleep on the cushion. There are other more complicated analyses – for example, the extensive showing that the instances where the same words appear in two or more gospels almost always involve Mark.

A few scholars still argue that Matthew came first and guided the budding churches until the need arose for a more definitive treatment, yielding Luke. Then in an effort to resolve the disparities, John Mark published his version, drawing from both Matthew and Luke. This is called the "Griesbach hypothesis". And then some still urge that the author of Luke copied both Mark and Matthew, composing the balance himself.

But then there are 200-odd verses which appear in both Matthew and Luke but not in Mark. While they are not identical, the wording is so close as to force the conclusion reached by most scholars that they must have a common source. These are the verses called "Q" by the scholars and they consist almost entirely of sayings of Jesus. Some scholars go so far as to call this collection of sayings the *Gospel of Q.*

Scholars in the Jesus Seminar have reconstructed the entire Q text by putting together the verses common to Matthew and Luke and then eliminating those that come from Mark. This is an arduous and judgmental task – not all the "calls" are easy to make because in many instances the verses are very similar but not word-for-word identical.

Why is it thought by many scholars to be inevitable that Q was a written source rather than memorized oral traditions brought together by the authors of Matthew and Luke? A main reason is that it is simply hard to believe that even the well-trained art of memorization could have produced the identical or even so-similar verses that appear separately in the two gospels. There are critics who challenge the existence of a written Q, but it seems fair to conclude that the case for it is considerably stronger than the case against.

Some scholars, notably Helmut Koester, James Robinson and John Kloppenberg, have urged that there could have been successive layers in the development of Q, each written or rewritten by successive authors at different times. They contend that the original version was most likely contemporaneous with or even earlier than the Gospel of Mark in a community where the people concentrated solely on the life and sayings of Jesus; there are no references to either the birth of Jesus or the passion story in the Q verses.

This is one of the reasons for placing the Q community in Galilee where the disciples would naturally have concentrated on Jesus' ministry. The scholars enamored of this speculation point particularly to the Q verses which are termed Jesus' "mission speech" where he commands his disciples to wander without food, knapsacks or money, depending solely on the generosity of strangers. Just as did Jesus and his disciples in Galilee.

There are, however, scholars who view Q as distinctly non-Christian, arguing that its concentration solely on the sayings of Jesus argues that Jesus was to these people simply a roving sage with no divine or supernatural overtones. Finally on Q, there are the unbelievers –– scholars like E.P. Sanders who argues in his *The Historical Figure of Jesus* that Luke and Matthew copied Mark and Luke also copied Matthew. It is safe to say, though, that most of today's scholars accept the Q concept.

Secret Mark and the Gospel of Thomas

The last two writings that some scholars (not a majority) attribute to a time in the 1st century preceding the writing of the canonical gospels are the Secret Gospel of Mark and the Gospel of Thomas. Both are extremely controversial; Secret Mark even more than Thomas.

Some, probably most scholars, urge that Secret Mark is totally a 2d Century fabrication; scholars who have studied the writing carefully conclude that it presupposes the canonical gospels. However, some scholars persist in the belief that it was either a separate writing relied upon by the author of canonical Mark or even an earlier, censored version of the Gospel of Mark. The source of the controversy was discovered in 1958 by Morton Smith of Columbia University. It is a portion of a letter written in Greek, allegedly by Clement of Alexandria, a well-recorded Christian leader who lived between about 150 and 215.

Clement reports in his letter that while Peter was in Rome, Mark commenced writing his "Acts of the Lord", that which we know as canonical Mark. Clement believed that after Peter's death, Mark came to Alexandria and used both his and Peter's notes in working on a draft of his gospel. This became a "secret spiritual gospel" from which Clement then quotes.

Someone copied Clement's letter into a collection of Ignatius of Antioch's letters at the Greek Orthodox monastery of Mar Saba, near the Dead Sea, and the British scholar, Morton Smith, photographed it there. Incidentally, many scholars write about it without detailed quotation, perhaps because of what may be perceived to be the "scandalous" reference to possible homosexuality. This is Clement's quotation from what he calls Secret Mark:

And they came into Bethany. And a certain woman whose brother had died was there. And, coming, she prostrated herself before Jesus and says to him, `Son of David, have mercy on me.' But the disciples rebuked her.

And Jesus, being angered, went off with her into the garden where the tomb was, and straightway a great cry was heard from the tomb. And going near Jesus rolled away the stone from the door of the tomb.

And straightway, going in where the youth was, he stretched forth his hand and raised him, seizing his hand. But the youth, looking upon him, loved him and began to beseech him that he might be with him. And going out of the tomb they came into the house of the youth, for he was rich.

And after six days Jesus told him what to do and in the evening the youth comes to him, wearing a linen cloth over his naked body. And he remained with him that night, for Jesus taught him the mystery of the kingdom of God. And thence, arising, he returned to the other side of the Jordan.

The possible inferences of homosexuality are obvious. A recent (1983) author (Koester) on the apocryphal gospels traces the erotic interpretation to views of the 2d Century Carpocrations and their 1st Century counterparts who related nude baptism to homosexuality. The candidate for the "mystery indoctrination" at the baptismal rite was to arrive clothed only in a light white robe. Koester also posits the possibility of this erotic baptismal relationship being involved in the quarrels over baptism by different men that arose in Corinth as described by Paul in 1 Corinthians 1.11-17.

All of this caused Smith then and leads Crossan today to conclude that canonical Mark is a "censored" version of the earlier-written Secret Mark. Canonical Mark does contain a puzzling passage in the description of the arrest of Jesus which seems out of context with the verses preceding and following:

Now a certain young man followed him, having a linen cloth thrown around his naked body. And the young men laid hold of him. And he left the linen cloth and fled from them naked. (Mk 14.51-52)

Mark 16.5 is a part of the description of the women finding Jesus' tomb and "upon entering the tomb, they saw a young man sitting in the right side, dressed in a white robe." Reference is also made to the Lazarus story of John 11 which involves Martha's brother and a "cleaned up" version of the raising of a dead man from a tomb, together with the Nicodemus story of John involving a baptism ministry across the Jordan. (Jn. 3.22, 26)

Almost every line of Secret Mark bears a close resemblance to canonical gospel material. However, many scholars who have examined the subject reach a conclusion exactly the opposite of Koester. They place Secret Mark well into the 2d Century, arguing that the author, for cultic purposes, skillfully chose language from existing Mark and John in putting together the lines that came to be called Secret Mark. Some who disagree with Smith-Crossan-Koester attribute Secret Mark to an author who for his own reasons was intent on developing a mystical relationship between baptismal practices and homosexuality. And Secret Mark does clearly reflect the mystery and eroticism so prevalent in 2d Century gnostic writings.

Much more significant to the scholars is the Gospel of Thomas. It was referred to in the 3d Century by all of Hippolytus, Origen, Eusibius, and Jerome. For centuries, it was deemed lost and scholars speculated that it was one of what has been termed the Infancy Gospels. Early in this century, fragments of some sayings from the Gospel of Thomas were discovered at Oxyrhynchus. Then, at Nag

Hammadi in 1945, a Coptic copy of the complete gospel was found. Finally published in 1959, it consists of 114 sayings of Jesus, none of which involve either the birth or death of Jesus. There is no narrative, only the individual sayings.

Interestingly, the opening words, "These are the secret words which the Living Jesus spoke and Didymus Judas Thomas wrote", together with a few of the sayings of Jesus are precisely the same as those found years earlier on the three scraps of papyri found in a garbage heap at the site of the ancient Egyptian town of Oxyrhynchus and carbon-dated to about 200.

The Gospel of Thomas is included in *The Five Gospels* authored by Robert Funk and Roy Howard, principals in the Jesus Seminar. Scholars have fought volumes over its sources and nature; for example, they disagree vehemently as to whether or not the gospel is dependent on the canonical gospels some (like the fellows of the Jesus Seminar) argue strongly that it is based on independent traditions. Many scholars argue that it is a prime example of 2nd century writing which includes some realistic sayings of Jesus but incorporates gnostic thinking. One of their strongest arguments is based on the last of the sayings (#114) which is totally unlike accepted Jesus lore:

Simon Peter said to them, "Let Mary leave us, for women are not worthy of life." Jesus said, "I myself shall lead her in order to make her male, so that she too may become a living spirit resembling you males. For every woman who will make herself male will enter the Kingdom of Heaven."

Some scholars, distinctly a minority, argue that there was an early "first edition" of the Gospel of Thomas written perhaps even earlier than Mark. More widely accepted is the view that while Thomas may contain some material contemporaneous with the synoptic gospels, its composition should be placed in the next century. Two authors may be singled out of many for the strong view against placing this gospel in the 1st century. Howard Kee in his *A Century of Quests* states that "the whole of the Gospel of Thomas" is a "radical Gnostic reworking of the Jesus tradition." Birger Pearson in *The Gospel According to the Jesus Seminar* goes further, stating that Thomas is "*completely* dominated by a (probably Syrian) type of Christianity oriented to mysticism and informed by the myth of the descent and ascent of the soul."

*   *   *

These, then are the supposed writings of the 50's that some scholars argue preceded the development of the gospels canonized into the New Testament. Written mostly outside Palestine, all but the *Cross Gospel* concentrate on the human Jesus and are silent about the dramatic events transpiring in Jerusalem. But those events gravely affected Christianity and so we return to that story and the decade of the 60's.

CHAPTER NINE

The Turbulent 60's

By the year 60, Christianity had grown by leaps and bounds. Acts describes the wide-ranging missionary travels of Paul to various places such as Thessalonia, Antioch, Corinth, Ephesus, Philippi, Colossae, Damascus, Galatia, and finally Rome. Other cities in the near East and even Spain are mentioned, but Acts is surprisingly silent about the spread of Christianity into Alexandria and then along the coast of North Africa to Carthage.

Paul's Gentile Conversion Missions

Scores of books have been written about what have traditionally been called the "three missions" of Paul and the teachings that he imparted to the Christians in the communities he visited during his admittedly lengthy travels. While some scholars are today arguing that the precise nature of the "three mission" tradition does not stand up under close analysis, most continue to accept at face value the accounts contained in Acts of the Apostles.

Paul's "first mission" commenced in Antioch and went into central Asia Minor to cities such as Iconium, Lystra and Derbe before he returned to Antioch and attended in Jerusalem the famous conference discussed earlier which was called to discuss his conversion of the Gentiles. The traditional "second mission" took Paul through northern Asia Minor to Europe where he visited cities in Greece (Philippi, Thessalonica, Beroea, Athens, Corinth) before again returning to Antioch. The "third mission" involves travels between Asia and Greece and includes a lengthy stay in Ephesus and visits to Troas and Miletus on his way to Jerusalem where James continued to lead the Jewish followers of Jesus.

Paul's missionary travels were never easy; he encountered open hostility in many places.

In 2 Corinthians 11.24, he writes that "five times I have been given the 39 lashes by the Jews; three times I have been beaten with sticks; once I was stoned; I have been in danger from my own people."

In Paul's letters to the Corinthians and Ephesians, he discusses the problems affecting the house churches in those communities that have already been described. Paul also wrote other letters in the course of his other missionary travels to communities where he encountered many of the same problems he found in Corinth and Ephesus.

Paul finally returned to Jerusalem shortly before the year 60, bringing with him men from various Pauline mission churches to deliver funds collected in their communities for the benefit of poverty-stricken Christians in the temple city. Paul quickly encountered strong hostility in Jerusalem and not only from the conservative Jewish-Christian leaders who had long opposed his activities but also from the non-Christian Jews. This was the same coalition that had opposed him over the years. Some speculate that Paul may have thought that his emphasis on charity could bring the warring factions together; it clearly did not.

Paul's Last Days in Jerusalem

Paul openly disputed not only those he called "Judaists", the traditional Jews who did not accept Jesus, but also the Jews who adhered to some of the tenets of Judaism such as circumcision and the food laws forbidding table fellowship with Gentiles. James suggested to Paul that to overcome Jerusalem's hostility, he should demonstrate publicly his participation in a temple ceremonial rite important to the Jews. Also, James urged, Paul should pay part of the cost. That ploy did not work; Paul apparently insisted that his collection be used solely for charity.

Then, Paul was seen on the temple grounds with his companions from outside Palestine and was accused of a grave sacrilege – bringing Gentiles onto the sacred temple grounds, almost a "lynching offense" not requiring Roman approval for drastic punishment. A near-riot ensued. Paul was grabbed, beaten, and almost killed before the Roman guards took him into custody for his own protection.

Paul was then allowed to address the angry mob from the steps of the Fortress Antonio, but his words only escalated the rioting. The following day, he addressed the Sanhedrin to no avail. With assassination threatened, the Romans took him by night to Caesarea Maritima where he remained in jail for about two years before he finally demanded a trial in Rome, his right as a Roman citizen. That story comes later.

Palestinian Restlessness Becomes Violence

Meanwhile, in Rome in AD 54, Nero had succeeded Claudius; reportedly, Claudius was poisoned by his wife Agrippina who conspired to bring her son, Nero, into power. She succeeded; whereupon, the ungrateful Nero had his mother killed. And, as the years passed, Nero's reputation for cruelty caused many to conclude that, like Caligula before him, Nero had gone mad.

Serving as the Roman prefect in Judea in the early 60's was Felix, the first of the three called the "Terrible F's" — Felix, Festus and Florus. All were corrupt; all were tyrannical. While it was on Florus' watch that the great revolt began in 66, many students of the time blame all three of these men for playing a significant role in bringing the people of Palestine to the boiling point of rebellion.

During the reign of Felix, two lawless groups became part of the power structure in Palestine, the Zealots and the Sicarii. The Zealots as a faction had apparently began with Judas the Galilean early in the century. They were peasants, many of them dispossessed of their meager landholdings. Impoverished and bitter about their oppressive landlords, their specialty was robbery on the rural roads and byways of Palestine; Josephus calls them "robbers and murderers" who plundered both travelers and aristocratic Jewish estates. The Zealots practiced with a passion the religious rules laid down by the Pharisees. They also hated both the Romans and all Gentiles.

During Felix' tenure, serious trouble broke out between the high priest and the many other priests of the religious ruling group. These priests lived largely off the tithes, the portion of the harvested wheat that was their right to receive from what were called the "threshing floors". According to Josephus, the high priest (Ismael, selected by King Agrippa) sent "servants into the threshing-floors to take away those tithes that were due to the priests, insomuch that it so fell out that the poorest sort of the priests died for want."

Also during Felix' tenure, Josephus relates, a prophet from Egypt persuaded revolting Jewish peasants who were barred from entering the walled city that he could cause the walls to collapse. To restore order, Felix led a force of both cavalry and infantry that executed 400 of the prophet's followers and captured many more. This minor uprising is also described in Acts which relates that a tribune of Felix mistook Paul for the leader of the uprising: "Are you not the Egyptian, then, who recently stirred up a revolt and led the four thousand men of the Assassins out into the wilderness?" (Acts 21.38)

The "four thousand men" may have been either the Zealots or the Sicarii, both very active in Palestine at that time. Literally, the "assassins" were the Sicarii who came to the fore in Jerusalem in the 50's as urban terrorists; their trademark was murder in broad daylight, even in the holy precincts of the temple. Mingling with crowds, particularly at festival time, they carried short, curved daggers (sicae in Latin; hence, their name, the Sicarii) hidden under their robes for the moment of bloody use. Their prime targets for murder were members of the Jewish ruling class who collaborated with the Romans. They would strike quickly and then blend into the crowds. One of their earliest victims (Josephus says he was chosen at the behest of the prefect Felix) was the high priest, Jonathan. These are Josephus' words about this murderous group:

And then it was that the sicarii, as they were called, who were robbers, grew numerous. They made use of small swords, not much different in length from the Perisan acinacae, but somewhat crooked, and like the Roman sicae as they were called; and from these weapons these robbers got their denomination; and with these weapons they slew a great many; for they mingled themselves among the multitude at their festivals.

The violence precipitated by the Sicarii took several forms. They selected members of the ruling elite for assassination in Jerusalem and they foraged into countryside areas where they slayed prominent pro-Roman landlords, plundering and burning their estates. Fear of these murderous men spread through the establishment figures of Palestine: "anyone could be next". Josephus writes that this anxiety among the ruling class led to the hiring of armed guards and the public actions of these men fostered further unrest and rebellious feelings among the ordinary people of Palestine.

The multitudes that crowded Jerusalem during the feast times must have placed considerable strain on both the facilities and those detailed to keep order, including particularly the Roman soldiers who were ever alert for trouble. The pilgrims included not only the troublesome Zealots and Sicarii but all varieties of people traveling to the holy temple from throughout the Diaspora. The population of Jerusalem has been estimated at between 25,000 and 30,000; no one knows for sure since there are no records. But it is estimated that at Passover time, for example, as many as 100,000 could arrive, many of them camping outside the walls at night but thronging the streets and temple grounds during the day.

Josephus describes a riot which occurred when a huge multitude was visiting the temple and crowding into the courtyard area. Some outburst brought the Roman soldiers to the temple, where they began looking for troublemakers. "The Romans proceeded to the one remaining portico of the outer court, on which the poor women and children of the populace and a mixed multitude had taken refuge, numbering six thousand." Then, writes Josephus, the Romans callously set fire to the portico and "out of the multitude not a soul escaped."

So, the events in both Jerusalem and the rural areas of Palestine in the early years of the 60's heightened the already-existing tension between Jews and Romans. The Romans led by the prefects were careless in their cruel treatment of the Jews, fostering ill feeling, resentment and hatred. The descendants of Herod who shared civil control with the Romans were apparently either powerless or unwilling to take any positive steps to assuage the feelings of their people; both they and the religious powers, the Sanhedrin and the priests, continued to pay more attention to preserving good relations with Romans than attending to the concerns and well-being of the people of Palestine.

One of the Palestinian civil leaders, King Agrippa, had rebuilt Caesarea Philippi in honor of Nero, renaming it Neronias. At the same time, he increased his presence in Jerusalem by adorning the city with statues, which the populace did not at all appreciate. To curry favor, he released a number of prisoners who had been jailed for non-capital offenses and this added many penniless people to the ranks of the wandering and viciously anti-Roman Zealots whose numbers were increasing in the rural areas of Palestine. According to Josephus, "the countryside was filled with robbers". In Jerusalem, disorder became substantially worse when work was completed on the temple; this threw thousands of unemployed workers onto the streets.

Deaths of the Leading Apostles

The sixties were a turbulent and decisive decade for Jews, Romans and Christians alike. For the Christians, those years marked the deaths of several of the leading apostles.

The first to go was James. James the Just, he was called; the brother of Jesus who was not a believer during the lifetime of Jesus but became convinced by an appearance from the resurrected Jesus in the early days after the crucifixion. As earlier noted, James led the conservative branch of the Christian Jews in Jerusalem; some scholars refer to them as the Aramaic-speaking Christians. James had managed to survive the purges that plagued the Christians in Jerusalem in the 40's and 50's by attending the temple rites and zealously observing the Jewish code of conduct. But as events turned out, it was the very authorities who kept him out of trouble that caused his demise in AD 62.

The Sadducean high priest at that time was Ananas the Younger; Josephus describes him as both insolent and heartless. The prefect Festus had died and his successor Albinus was on his way from Alexandria to take office in Jerusalem. For unknown reasons, Ananus took advantage of the vacuum in the prefect's office, convened a meeting of the Sanhedrin and, Josephus reports, "brought before them the brother of Jesus, who was called Christ, whose name was James and some others; and when he had formed an accusation against them as breakers of the law, he delivered them to be stoned."

Eusibius, in his 4th century *Ecclesiastical History*, quotes both this version and the dramatically different story related by Hegesippius, who wrote in the 2nd century. Eusibius concluded that the Hegesippius version was accurate since it accorded with the story told by Father Clement of Alexandria. This is Hegesippius' violence-filled version of the death of James:

James was beseeched by the scribes and Pharisees who respected him as a just leader of the Christians to go to the pinnacle of the temple in order to dispose of a large crowd of hostile Christians. But James, reaching the Pinnacle preached the glory of the ascended Jesus. This offended the scribes and pharisees, and they said among themselves: "We do ill in affording him such a testimony to Jesus. Let us rather go up and cast him down that being afrighted they may not believe him." And they cried aloud, saying: "Ho, ho, even the Just One has gone astray!" And they fulfilled the scripture that is written in Isaiah: "Let us take away the just one, for he is troublesome to us. Therefore they shall eat the fruit of their doings." Going up therefore, they cast the just one down. And they said to each other: "Let us stone James the Just." And they began to stone him, for the fall did not kill him. But turning he kneeled down and said, "I beseech thee, O Lord God, Father, forgive them, for they know not what they do." And while they thus were stoning him, one of the priests of the sons of Rechab, the son of Rechabim, who had witness born to them by Jeremias the prophet, cried aloud, saying, "Cease ye; what do ye? The Just One is dying on your behalf." And one of them, a fuller, took the stick with which he beat out his clothes and brought it down on the Just One's head.

Thus was James, the brother of Jesus, martyred. His body, ends the Hegesippius version, was "sawn asunder," and thereafter the saw and the fuller's club were used as emblems to depict James.

The people of Jerusalem were upset at the killing of James and petitioned both King Agrippa and the new prefect, Albinus, for redress.

Albinus reprimanded Ananus angrily but Agrippa went further and fired Ananus for his high-handed conduct.

That takes us back to Paul, whom we left just as he had claimed the right of a Roman citizen to be tried in Rome, a privilege accorded to Paul as a birthright because he was born a Roman citizen in Tarsus. Before describing his return to Rome and martyrdom, a look at his writings which had begun in the 50's and ended in the 60's.

The Letters of Paul

Very few scholars doubt either the authenticity or time of writing of Paul's major letters. There are 13 letters which are today identified with Paul's name; Hebrews was long ago abandoned as Pauline. Many of these letters were written (or dictated) by Paul himself and provide the oldest literary evidence of the significance attached by the early Christians to the events involving the death of Jesus and his emergence as the Christ .

Traditionally, all the letters which bear his name were attributed directly to Paul as being written by him. Today, however, most scholars accept that as many as six are either probably or certainly not authored by Paul. These are 2 Thessalonians, Ephesians, Colossians, I-II Timothy and Titus. The greatest unanimity of non-Pauline authorship is with respect to Timothy and Titus. Also, many scholars argue that Philippians and 2 Corinthians (and possibly even Romans) are not single letters but combinations of several letters written by Paul at separate times.

Appearing first in the New Testament is Romans, a letter written by Paul to Christians he had not yet visited. Paul Johnson in *A History of Christianity* avers that "No one has ever fully understood Romans." Be that as it may, it is often described as "beautifully intellectual." Marcion in 144 drew up a canon which included ten of the Pauline letters; collections of Paul's letters are thought to have been circulated among Christian communities many years earlier. Colossians 4.16 refers to exchanges of the letters among churches and larger collections are described by both Clement and Ignatius at the end of the 1st Century and beginning of the 2d.

Troubled by some passages in the Pauline letters, many scholars argue that they were inserted into the text long after Paul's death. 1 Thessalonians 2.13-16, a violent anti-Jewish polemic, is perhaps the best example. This passage attacking all Jews seem more appropriate to the time when Jewish Christians were expelled from the synagogues late in the 1st century. Other passages deemed non-Pauline are those which denigrate women in a fashion that seems directly contrary to Paul's acceptance and praise of women in house church leadership roles.

Some of Paul's letters were apparently written in his own hand; some state that they were dictated. Shorthand was known in the Roman world. Scholars suggest, however, that dictation was not always word for word – it could mean to dictate the sense, leaving the final words to be formulated by a secretary. An example of this style is 1 Peter for which Silvanus is stated to be the secretary; Paul may have used the same technique.

Dating for the Pauline letters is made easier by the timing of his trial before Gallio described in Acts 18.12-17. There is a Delphic inscription which places Gallio in the "26th acclamation of Claudius", emperor, which would be in the first half of the year 52. Using this as an anchor date, an analysis of the letters themselves in the context of Paul's travels as related in Acts and his letters leads the scholars to place the "Early letters" (Thessalonians) at 50-52, the "Great letters" (Galatians, Corinthians, Romans, Philippians) at 53-58, and the "Captivity letters" (Philemon, Colossians) at 60-63.

Martyrdom of Peter and Paul

By the time of Paul's arrival in Italy in 60 or 61, he had worked closely with a number of active Christian communities, as evidenced by his letters to the Thessalonians, Philippians, Corinthians, Galatians, Philemon and Colossians.

On the way to Rome from Palestine, he had endured a long and arduous sea trip. The description in Acts of his arduous trip through storm-tossed seas culminating in a dramatic shipwreck on the island of Malta, so reminiscent of the *Odyssey* and the *Aeneid*, leads many scholars to conclude that the tale was concocted by the author of Acts. No such adventure is mentioned in the Pauline letters. These skeptics point particularly to the improbability of Paul being an active advisor to the ship's officers and leader of fellow passengers when he was a prisoner, most likely confined below deck.

Finally landing in Italy, Paul was taken overland to Rome and when he neared the city, was met by a crowd of Christians. Either then or shortly thereafter he encountered the apostle Peter who had been living and working with the Christians in Rome since sometime in the late 50's. Paul was soon placed under house arrest by the Romans but was allowed to preach for several years. Acts is silent about these years.

The "judgment of probability" by most scholars is that Peter did not take any formal leadership role among the Jesus followers in Rome in those years; certainly not as a bishop, which has been claimed by the Catholic church since the 3rd century. Most scholars agree that the single-bishop concept did not even come into existence until early in the 2nd century.

All was not calm with the Christians in Rome during the last years of Peter and Paul. Clement's letter written several decades later refers to "zeal and envy" accompanying severe disagreements in that Christian community. Since Roman tentacles reached throughout the empire, there had to be some awareness at the center of the empire of the tumults, even riots that accompanied Paul's conversion attempts during his missionary trips. In Rome, his passionate feelings regarding Judaism and the Jewish rejection of Jesus must have stirred up some strong feelings among those whom Paul called "the Judaizers"

Conflict of any kind in the streets of Rome would not have been viewed kindly by Emperor Nero. Concern by the Roman authorities about the Christians in Rome is reflected in writings of the historian Tacitus who described Christianity as a "detestable superstition" which is "horrible and shameful". Black magic and cannibalism (based on the references to the "blood of Christ") were among the charges made against the Christians.

Whether or not the story of Tacitus is accurate that the persecution of Christians was intensified in order to divert attention from the rumor that "crazy Nero" had himself started the devastating Roman fire of 64 (he had proclaimed his intent to rebuild Rome and it was rumored that the fire was a way to force the issue), the traditions are both strong and credible that Peter and Paul were caught up in a wave of violence and killing that engulfed the Christian community.

Certainly in such a troublesome time, the traditionalists in the Jewish community must have sought ways to placate the Roman leadership. This logic leads some scholars to speculate that Christian Jews opposed to Paul's radical teaching may have joined the non-Christian Jews in egging the Romans on against Paul – and perhaps Peter, too. Lending support to this theory are Clement's above-described reference to the Christians' "zeal and envy" and the mention in the Gospel of Matthew of Christians betraying fellow Christians.

Traditions and legends vary as to the manner in which the two great Christian leaders met their deaths. Most agree that they died separately, although Eusibius has them "martyred at the same time", quoting Dionysus of Corinth who wrote in about 170. The strongest of the traditions has Peter crucified by the Romans outside Rome and buried on Vatican Hill, with Paul being beheaded along the Ostian Way leading to

Rome. The dates were most likely in the mid-sixties. Archeological evidence is claimed by the Vatican for the presence and death of Peter in Rome. Results of excavations under St. Peter's Basilica are debated, but Pope Paul VI in 1968 proclaimed that the bones found there were positively identified as those of Peter.

Many wonder at the failure of the author of Luke-Acts who was obviously preoccupied with the life of Paul to even mention the deaths of either Peter or Paul. Writing late in the 1st century, he must have been aware of their martyrdom. One reason often suggested is that reporting their deaths at the hands of the Romans would have run contrary to the author's desire to placate the Romans, a theme recurrent in both Luke and Acts. Arousing hostility between Romans and Christians could have jeopardized the lives of Christians throughout the Diaspora.

Another version of Paul's last years was kept alive by Christian legends and is still urged by some conservative scholars, based in part on Eusibius' account of a second Roman imprisonment of Paul. This version relates that he was released from prison in about 62 and remained free until 67, revisiting the Christian communities he had founded, installing Timothy and Titus as heads of Pauline churches in Crete and Ephesus, and eventually travelling to Spain, a hope he had mentioned in his earlier letters. This version of Paul's last years has him recaptured, imprisoned, tried and executed in Rome and enables these scholars to go against the more prevalent view that Paul did not write the letters of Timothy and Titus. These scholars suggest that he wrote the letters of 1 Timothy and Titus while traveling, and then wrote 2 Timothy as his "last will and testament" during his final imprisonment.

Whenever and however they actually died, Peter and Paul left a fabulous legacy. Almost ironically, they were martyred at about the same time that the fatal Jewish rebellion broke out in Palestine, resulting in the razing of Jerusalem and destruction of the holy temple as Jesus had prophesied.

The presence and activity in Rome of these two storied Christians were emphasized by both Clement and Ignatius, church leaders at the turn of the century, and led Irenaeus a century later to call them the real founders of the church in Rome. Whether they had any formal positions or not, their presence alone gave Rome a primacy in the rapidly growing Christian churches. And through a process that is still not totally understood, it is apparent from the writings of the Christian fathers at the turn of the century that Peter had ascended over Paul as the most prominent founder of Christianity, although it was surely Paul whose missionary activities and writings had realistically been a stronger factor in shaping the new religion. His adamant positions against Jewish law paved the path for the Jesus movement and Christianity to proceed from being a cult of Judaism to becoming a separate religion.

Continuing to call the roll of the last of the apostles, that leaves John. Papias, writing in the 2d Century, has John martyred in Jerusalem in 62. Legend and lore, however, keep John alive until late in the 1st Century, writing the Gospel of John and the book of Revelations. So, about thirty years after the crucifixion of Jesus, and possibly excepting John, all the leaders of the Jesus movement were dead.

The phenomenal spread and growth of Christianity must have surprised and shocked the leaders of Judaism (if, of course, they were aware of it) and that vigor as well as the fervor it aroused in the followers of Jesus made Christianity's separation from Judaism inevitable well before the end of the century.

Scholars argue that Paul, openly disappointed at the failure of large numbers of Jews to join Christ's cause, undoubtedly hastened this result when he taught in his letter to the Galatians that Christians had superseded the Jews as God's chosen people, even though James and Peter seemed pretty clearly not to agree with that position. But even then the schism that changed the then-known world was not final. The gospels of Mark, Matthew, Luke, and John were yet to be written and the full impact of the traditions of Jesus' sayings, little reflected in Paul's letters as well as his Hellenistic-tainted teaching, were yet to be felt by Christianity.

CHAPTER TEN

The Great Jewish Revolt of 66

The discord, hostility, and violence that characterized the separation of Christianity from Judaism did not end with the martyrdom of Peter, Paul, James and John. While Romans oppressed and continued to slaughter both Christians and Jews, Jews continued to ostracize and occasionally murder Christian Jews. Mark has Jesus predicting aptly the conflict that beset the Jews both in Jerusalem and the Diaspora: "Brother will betray brother to death, and a father his child. Children will rebel against their parents and have them put to death. All men will hate you because of me..." (Mk. 13:12-13)

As the sixties wore on in Palestine after the death of James in 62, open fighting between Romans and Jews began. The seeds of the cataclysmic events that would ensue had been sown years before and it is of more than passing interest that traditional study of the 1st Century has tended to keep the development of these events quite separate. There is little mention in the books of the New Testament of the violence in Palestine that escalated just three decades after the crucifixion. And little attempt has been made by the historians to put the life of Jesus and the final separation of Christianity from Judaism squarely into the context of the causes of that violence.

The Prologue to Rebellion

The Jewish rebellion was not an over-night development. In his remarkable historical works, "The Wars of the Jews" and "Jewish Antiquities", written toward the end of the 1st Century (the first in the eighties, the second in the early nineties), Josephus seems to play down the plight of the Palestinian rural populace and stresses the violent and tyrannical Roman rulers. Josephus does make it clear, however, that as a representative of the upper class, he was basically opposed to the peasant elements involved in the revolt. His emphasis on the role of the Zealots as rebels does not probe the human causes which led these desperate and distressed peasants to revolt.

But before examining those events through the eyes of Josephus, he should be placed in his lifetime context. As will be developed in the following pages, he was a leading personage in Palestine, where he became a general over Jewish armed forces before he was captured and then released by the Romans. Living in Rome, he wrote the only detailed historic accounts we have of the great revolt of 66.

Jews have always viewed Josephus as a turncoat and look upon some aspects of his historical works with a jaundiced eye. Josephus showed his prejudice, Jewish scholars argue, by stating in the introduction to "The Wars of the Jews" that "It was the Jewish tyrants who drew down upon the holy temple the unwilling hands of the Romans." Jewish historians also criticize Josephus for blaming the destruction of Jerusalem on the Zealots because they rigidly opposed any negotiations for peace with the Romans. Josephus seems to apologize for his favorable treatment of the Romans in this passage: "If I have dwelt at some length on this topic, my intention was not so much to extol the Romans as to console those whom they had vanquished and to deter others who may be tempted to revolt."

Despite his critics, and there are many, Josephus' works cannot be easily dismissed as the works of a Flavian flunky or Jewish traitor. His review of the events in Palestine in the 1st Century, while containing some demonstrably gross exaggerations and distortions, is considered overall to be a good chronicle of the war and at least some of the turmoil that led up to it.

The Jews had for years become increasingly restive under Roman rule. They resented being ruled by even the Herods; they wished to have a leader of the Davidic line. While the Herods were at least part-Jewish, the Herodian dynasty was widely disliked by the Jewish people.

Then, add hatred for the Romans to dislike for the Herods. The Roman overloads were openly tough and contemptuous in their relations with Judaism and the Jewish people as they frequently were of the cultures and natives in the subjugated lands of the empire. Then there was the deep Palestinian resentment over taxes which as described earlier were devastatingly high, taking up to 35% of a peasant farmer's production, a crushing burden that finally drove many peasants from their small land holdings.

Finally, there was the urbanization involved in the city-building activities of Agrippa and Herod Antipas which displaced countless peasants from their land. All of these factors forced untold numbers of peasants from their homes and deprived them of a living. The result was a dispossessed, downtrodden, resentful and restless population. In his *The Historical Jesus*, Crossan reviews the evidence in detail and concludes that under Roman imperialism, events "pushed the Jewish peasantry of Palestine below 'normal' subsistence level and thus into relative, perceived, and decremental deprivation, resulting eventually in massive peasant rebellion."

Of course, as Josephus emphasizes with detailed, colorful accounts of their tyrannical rule, the Roman prefects played a significant role in igniting the revolt. Tacitus, a 1st Century Roman historian, also blames the malfeasance of the Roman prefects. These included Cumanus in 48-52, Felix in 52-60, Festus in 60-62, Albinus in 62-64, and Florus in 64-66 (Felix, Festus and Florus have been termed the "Terrible F's").

The violence incited by Felix and Festus has already been described. Florus, the last of the "terrible F" prefects, may have been the worst, making his predecessor prefects seem almost virtuous by comparison. According to Josephus, he "stripped whole cities, ruined entire populations, and almost went the length of proclaiming throughout the country that all were at liberty to practice brigandage, on condition that he received his share of the spoils. Certainly his avarice brought desolation upon all the cities." Even allowing for exaggeration, the picture of widespread violence throughout Palestine remains credible.

The notorious Zealots took advantage of this situation to incite the peasants against the Romans. Many left the countryside for the cities such as Caesarea and Jeruaslem. At the same time, in Caesarea, superior rights were granted by the Romans to the Hellenists and they built shops obstructing access to the synagogue. When the Jews complained, the Roman authorities refused to intervene. Then, Florus showed his arrogance by boldly appropriating 17 talents from the sacred Jewish treasury in Jerusalem. Sarcastically, the Jerusalem Jews publicly took up a collection for "poor Florus" and Florus retaliated by turning a portion of Jerusalem over to his soldiers for plunder. Resisting Jews were killed.

Josephus argues that during this time, Florus was determined to provoke open rebellion and took numerous taunting steps to achieve that goal. The Jews did not take the bait and repeatedly avoided violent reaction, seeking relief from both King Agrippa II and the high priest, asking them to intervene with Nero to get Florus under control. Josephus reports that King Agrippa, with his sister Bernice, whom the Jews liked, standing nearby, gave a long speech to the Jerusalem multitude urging that revolt against the Romans was worse than useless, pointing to the ease with which their massive legions had subjected the rebellious Gauls, Germans and Spaniards. Agrippa thus made it clear to the people of Palestine that in this time of their travail, he was on the side of the Roman authorities.

Historians have cited favorably Josephus' long disquisition in this speech on the military prowess of the Roman legions and the extent and strength of the army at that time. This Agrippa speech was undoubtedly composed by Josephus, not the king. Josephus was a great admirer of Agrippa, calling him a "wonderful and admirable man". This, by the way, is the same Agrippa who said to Paul, "Almost thou persuadest me to be a Christian." (Acts 26.28) And of whom Paul said, "He was an expert in all the customs and questions of the Jews."

But Agrippa's plea to avoid provoking the Romans was in vain. The Jewish temple leaders stopped the twice-daily sacrifices on behalf of the emperor and refused to pay the tribute owing to him, thereby outraging the Roman leadership even further. Finally, a Jewish mob did take to violence and, attempting to get needed arms, assaulted the fortress Masada, breached its walls, and slaughtered the Roman guards. The revolt then began in AD 66.

Rebellion Commences

Urban violence erupted first in Jerusalem when rebellious Palestinians took control of the lower city. Agrippa's soldiers tried to seize the temple area and fierce fighting continued for days. The rebels assaulted the Fortress Antonia, killing a number of the king's soldiers.

At this point, the Jewish leader Menahen, a son of one of the early Zealot leaders, Judas of Galilee, obtained arms from the Fortress Masada and returned to Jerusalem to organize the Jews, contesting for leadership with Eleazar. The high priest, Ananias was killed by a Jewish mob. Meanwhile, Florus was on the rampage in Caesarea, killing thousands of Jews and sending unnumbered more to slavery in the galleys. These actions ended any hope for peace and the revolt then gradually engulfed all of Palestine.

Gallus, the legate of Syria, was ordered to lead 30,000 Roman soldiers from Syria into Palestine to share the overall command with Cestius. Gallus headquartered in Caesarea, remaining there while Cestius marched toward Jerusalem. His forces suffered a temporary setback when the Jews laid aside their annual celebration of the feast of the tabernacle and charged through the gates to attack the Romans, killing hundreds before being forced to retreat back into the city.

Cestius responded by placing Jerusalem under siege and came perilously close to taking the city. Then, Josephus records, Cestius "retired from the city, without any reason in the world". The Roman retreat aroused the Jews under Eleazar and Menahen to attack and they harassed Cestius as his force fled to the north. Josephus records (we know not whether accurately) that Cestius lost 5,300 footmen and 380 horsemen in this inglorious retreat.

Florus and his soldiers retreated to Caesarea on the coast, leaving the rest of Palestine to the Jews, and peace reigned through the winter of 66-67. During this interlude, the Jews organized their army. The Sanhedrin confirmed Josephus as general in command of both Upper and Lower Galilee and the city of Gamala, the strongest city in that part of Palestine. Josephus brags that he "levied in Galilee an army of upwards of a hundred thousand men" (undoubtedly another Josephus exaggeration).

While assuming his command in Galilee, Josephus ran into opposition from a man named John of Gischala who conspired against him for leadership of the Galileans. The cities of Sepphoris, Gamala, Gischala and Tiberias all joined with John in a command rivalry with Josephus but that canny general outmaneuvered them all and, together with the leadership in Jerusalem, prepared for a resumed war with the Romans.

Vespasian's Legions Take the Offensive

When the spring of 67 came, so did the Romans. Nero, angry at the Romans' defeat in Palestine, called in the elderly Vespasian, son of Claudius, who had a remarkable military record. He had pacified Gaul, defeated the Germans and recovered Britain for the Romans. Vespasian took charge of the army in Syria and sent his son, Titus, to take take command of two powerful legions in Alexandria and bring them also to Syria, where they were joined by mercenaries collected from other nearby kingdoms. This combination of Roman legions and mercenaries joined forces with King Agrippa in Antioch and the Roman army now totaled 60,000 men (Josephus' perhaps exaggerated estimate). Taking the offensive, Vespasian led this army toward Galilee and must have been pleased when residents of Sepphoris came out to join him.

Josephus has a detailed description of the Roman army, its camps and its methods of warfare; it has often been cited by military historians. For example, he includes a dramatic description of the use of hundreds of individual shields raised over the heads of the soldiers, one by one, to make up a huge "tortoise shell" over an attacking force. He also includes a detailed account of the various deadly siege engines and powerful battering rams used by the Romans to capture walled cities.

Seeking to protect Galilee from the invading forces of Vespasian, Josephus centered his newly-recruited forces at Jotapata, near Sepphoris, where he hastily built a hilltop fortress on the edge of a precipice. Vespasian's army attacked, placing the city under siege, deploying their siege engines around the walls and using huge battering rams in an effort to break into the city.

Josephus dwells at length on the defenses mounted by the desperate Jews against the powerful Roman onslaught. However, after a seven-week siege, the walls of Jotapata were finally breached by the Romans. "So Vespasian gave order that the city should be entirely demolished, and all the fortifications burnt down. And thus was Jotapata taken."

Before the assaulting Romans arrived, Josephus had managed to hide himself with a group of his men and he writes that because his soldiers preferred death to dishonor, they agreed to a desperate suicidal plan. When defeat became inevitable, each soldier would kill one of his fellows and this would be repeated until only two soldiers remained. The last two would then commit suicide. But when that time came and Josephus was one of the last two surviving, the last step of the plan was aborted and Josephus surrendered to the Romans.

Brought in bonds before Vespasian, Josephus predicted that both Vespasian and his son, Titus, would become Roman emperors: "Thou, O Vespasian, art Caesar and emperor, thou, and thus thy son. Bind me now still faster, and keep me for thyself, for thou, O Caesar, are not only lord over me but over the land and the sea and all mankind." Vespasian remembered those prophetic words and took pains to see that Josephus remained as his personal captive.

The rebellion continued in the towns and cities of Galilee. Titus with his legions attacked the city of Taricheae and Vespasian brought Roman reinforcements to join him there. Taricheae is located on the shore of the Sea of Galilee; Josephus calls the lake Gennesareth. On that lake, there was a calamitous naval action in 67. The Jews debarked from their hastily assembled war fleet to raid a Roman camp and then retreated back into their boats. The Romans loaded their forces of archers and soldiers armed with swords and javelins into boats and an archery duel ensued between the two forces. The Romans won this duel and then boarded the opposing boats with their heavily armed soldiers. A massacre ensued.

Josephus describes the aftermath vividly:

During the days that followed, a horrible stench hung over the region and it presented an equally horrifying spectacle. The beaches were strewn with wrecks and swollen bodies, which, hot and clammy with decay, made the airs so foul that the catastrophe revolted even those who had brought it about. Such was the outcome of this naval engagement. The total dead, including those who died in defense of the town, numbered 6,700.

The slaughter did not end there. The surviving men of the city were force-marched by Vespasian to Tiberias. When they arrived, they were directed to the stadium where the young men were separated from the older men. The old men were then slain and the young men were divided; the strongest were sent to Nero as slaves for the emperor; the remainder were sold on the slave market. The English translator of Josephus' works footnotes that "this is the most cruel and barbarous action that Vespasian ever did in this whole war."

Vespasian then turned his attention to a siege of the key Galilean city of Gamala. After the Jewish defenders held out for weeks, with the last desperate families jumping to suicide into the precipice to avoid slavery, the Romans took Gamala. Titus then captured Gischala, forcing John of Gischala, Josephus' former opponent in the formation of the Jewish army, to flee to Jerusalem where he stepped into a leadership vacuum and, taking charge, urged the residents of the city to prepare for the inevitable attack by the Romans.

During this time, hundreds of Zealots fleeing from Vespasian's army in the ravaged countryside came to Jerusalem and sought to take control of the city and the public treasures. The city's defenders were hopelessly divided; the Zealots, led by Eleazer, were opposed by a number of the residents of Jerusalem led by the high priest Ananus. John of Gischala moved deviously in both camps and this division of the defending forces ultimately proved disastrous.

Meanwhile, Vespasian's army was, to use the military word, "mopping up" the remainder of Palestine before attacking Jerusalem which the Roman commander thought would be weakened by the disputes and bickering that grew among the residents. Vespasian was anxious to complete the Roman conquest of the rebelling Jews because of the revolts confronting the tyrant Nero elsewhere in the empire. The Romans embarked on what would today be called a "scorched earth" campaign aimed at every nook and cranny of Palestine. During this time, at about the year 68, the Qumran settlement of the Essenes on the Dead Sea that has yielded the fabulous horde of scrolls was destroyed by the Romans' veteran 10th legion.

Nero Dies and Vespasian Attacks Jerusalem

Before the Romans attacked Jerusalem, there is the story related by Josephus of the demented prophet Jesus of Ananias:

Jesus, son of Ananias, an ignorant peasant, came to the festival at which it is customary for everyone to erect a temporary shelter to God, and suddenly began to cry out against the temple, "A voice from the east, a voice from the west, a voice from the four winds, a voice directed against Jerusalem and the sanctuary, a voice directed against the grooms and the brides, a voice directed against all the people." He kept shouting this refrain day and night as he made his way through the narrow streets of the city. Some prominent citizens became so irritated at this oracle forecasting doom that they arrested the fellow and flogged him with many lashes. Without a word in his own defense or under this breath for those who punished him, he continued crying out as he had done earlier.

The leaders assumed that he was being driven by some demonic force, as was the case, and hauled him up before the Roman governor. Although cut to the bone with lashes, he didn't ask for mercy and he didn't shed a tear; rather, he would vary the tone of his lamentation in a most peculiar way and cry out with each lash, "Damn you, Jerusalem."

When Albinus began interrogating him – Albinus, you will recall, was governor – about who he was, and where he came from, and why he kept crying out, he didn't respond at all to these questions, but didn't stop repeating his dirge over the city. He kept this up until Albinus declared him a lunatic and released him.

... So he continued wailing for seven years and five months until he saw his forecast fulfilled in the siege of the city; then he found peace. You see, as he was making his rounds and shouting in a shrill voice from the wall (of the city), "Damn you again, dear city, and damn you, people, and damn you, temple", to which he added a final word, "and damn me too", a stone hurled by a catapult struck and killed him instantly. And so he died with such ominous predictions still on his lips.

Vespasian's march toward Jerusalem was delayed when Nero committed suicide on June 9, 68. The residents of Jerusalem, anticipating Vespasian's attack, brought in large numbers of Idumeans to help defend the city. The inhabitants of the city were torn; the Pharisees were reluctant to fight but others joined the Zealots who remained fired up by their hatred of the Romans. The Jewish Christians who had been led by James the Just refused to join in the revolt; it is not certain but generally concluded by those studying those calamitous years that at this time, the Christians left Jerusalem, crossed the Jordan River, and settled in Pella in the kingdom called Perea.

Many others fled from Jerusalem during 68, particularly the well-to-do class. Civil war broke out in the city. A man named Simon Giora who had been plundering towns untouched by the Romans arrived in Jerusalem where he confronted John of Gischala, now the undisputed leader of the Zealots. Pharisees supporting the revolt fought those who did not. By 69, Simon had obtained control of the city itself and John of Gischala withdrew to the temple with those who remained loyal to him. Eleazer took his followers to the fortress Masada; Josephus identifies them as mostly consisting of the Sicarii.

In Rome there was widespread turbulence following Nero's suicide. There ensued a rapid succession of emperors over a two-year period, from Nero to Galba to Otho to Vitellius. Vespasian, then in Alexandria where he was supported by the legions stationed there, was importuned by many of the Roman army commanders throughout the Empire to take over as emperor. But before leaving for Rome, he remembered Josephus' prophecy that he would become emperor. When Vitellius was assassinated in 69, Vespasian became emperor and immediately set Josephus free.

Vespasian's son Titus took command of the Roman legions in Palestine. In 70, he assembled his army in Caesarea to begin the renewed campaign and from there, four years after the revolt began, led his forces onto the siege of Jerusalem. Titus built a four-mile wall encircling the city and prevented access to and from the countryside. The population of the city was already swollen by the large numbers of peasants who had sought refuge from the ravages of Vespasian's army. Any Jews seeking to escape from the city were killed either by the Romans outside the wall or by Zealots inside.

In the city, bitter feelings, disputes and divisions continued to wrack the defending Jews. Hoping to take advantage of this conflict, Titus sent Josephus into the city to talk to the inhabitants and persuade them that the Romans were invincible and would certainly prevail in the end. His long speech is reconstructed in the *Wars of the Jews*. The speech raises interesting questions about the languages used in Jerusalem. Josephus reports that both Titus and Josephus exhorted the Jews to surrender and that Titus sent Josephus to speak "in the language of their forefathers"; most likely, he used Aramaic. Since Titus undoubtedly spoke Greek to the Jews, it is apparent that the Jews of Jerusalem did not in great part understand that language and needed to have the message given in a language they all understood.

Possibly because the Jews viewed the action of Titus in sending Josephus to make a plea for surrender as a sign of weakness, the Jews ignored his entreaties.

Fearful Jews in greater numbers attempted to escape the beleaguered city and the Romans decided to make a public display of the execution of those they caught. Hundreds were crucified in full view of those inside the walls. Josephus records that the number caught for execution was so great that "room was wanting for the crosses and crosses wanting for the bodies."

Inside the walls, food supplies were soon depleted and famine ensued. Desperate hunger "devoured the people by whole houses and families; the upper rooms were full of women and children that were dying by famine, and the lanes of the city were full of the dead bodies of the aged." Deserters escaping swallowed coins of gold; when they were captured by the Romans, they were quickly killed and bodily searched for the coins; Josephus records that "in one night's time about two thousand of these deserters were thus dissected".

The end neared when Titus' men fought their way through the narrow streets to the temple where they set the huge wooden gates on fire and the flames soon spread to the treasured cloisters of the temple. Josephus relates that Titus tried to stop the fire, but the centurions ignored him and their men, out of control, plundered the temple of its storehouse of gold. When the Jews still would not stop fighting, Titus finally ordered his legions to plunder the entire city.

Jerusalem thus fell to Titus and the revolt was ended. John of Gischala was captured by the Romans; Simon managed to hide himself but finally surrendered. Simon and John were both kept in chains by the Romans so that they could be taken to Rome following the Roman custom of publicly displaying to a cheering populace the hordes of captive rebels led by their leaders in chains.

Josephus reports (perhaps exaggerating again) that Titus during the siege crucified 500 Jews each day in order to force a surrender, that the captured Jews numbered 97,000, and that the "entire nation was now shut up by fate as in prison." Titus literally razed the holy temple to the ground except for the three towers which had been added by Herod the Great and a portion of the west wall which, according to Josephus, Titus left standing as a tribute to the "character and strength" of the city. The temple has never since been restored; the portion of the west wall still stands today in Jerusalem as a revered site for prayer.

The Triumph in Rome

The story is told by Roman historians that Titus, the victorious Roman general, was not totally anti-Jewish. He talked of taking to Rome his mistress Bernice (daughter of Herod the Great, sister of Agrippa I and Herod Agrippa, and widow of Herod King of Chalcis), but his plan was thwarted by the Roman Senate. Agrippa had allegedly engaged in incest with one of his three sisters; it is unclear whether this was Bernice.

Titus returned to Rome via Alexandria to participate with his father Vespasian, now emperor, in the grand Triumph at the center of the Roman Empire which the Senate authorized in celebration of a victorious campaign. From Alexandria, he sent ahead of his party "seven hundred men, whom he had selected out of the rest as being eminently tall and handsome of body", along with their leaders.

The magnificent Triumph honoring Vespasian and Titus was described in detail by Josephus:

For there was here to be seen a mighty quantity of silver and gold and ivory, contrived into all sorts of things, and did not appear as carried along in pompous show only, but, as a man may say, running along like a river.

The treasures of the Jewish holy temple including the "purple hangings of the sanctuary" described in Mark as well as the massive golden table and candlesticks from the temple were displayed, along with what today would be called parade floats depicting the various victories achieved by Vespasian and Titus on the way to the total victory over the Jews.

The victorious march featured the hundreds of captives from Palestine, led by their commanders in chains and pulled along by ropes.

At the conclusion of the parade and festivities, the Jewish leaders were publicly executed according to Roman custom and the captive Jews became slaves. The entire "parade" went under a newly constructed triumphal arch which displayed carved depictions of the battles of the war and the destruction of Jerusalem; the arch still stands in Rome today.

Tragedy of the Fortress Masada

In Palestine, one stronghold remained, the fortress Masada, and the Romans did not turn their attention to it until the year 74. Masada was built of rock on a sheer flat-top mountain on the shore of the Dead Sea. It was manned by Eleazar and hundreds of Jews who had followed him there from Jerusalem before the city was destroyed. Josephus states that these men took no part in the revolt, refusing military assistance to their brother Jews even during Jerusalem's last desperate days.

The siege and capture of Masada is described in detail by Josephus. The attacking Roman legions under Silva built a wall around the fortress to prevent any from entering or leaving, so that those inside knew that it was just a matter of time until they would be starved into submission. At the end, when resistance seemed fruitless, Eleazar spoke to the defenders and the substance of the speech was repeated later by a woman who had hidden herself with her children before the end came. Josephus reconstructs that speech in his *Wars of the Jews*:

For it is death which gives liberty to the soul and permits it to depart to its own pure abode, there to be free from all calamity; but so long as it is imprisoned in a mortal body and tainted with all its miseries, it is, in sober truth, dead ... But it is not until, freed from the weight that drags it down to earth and clings about it, the soul is restored to its proper sphere, that it enjoys a blessed energy and a power untrammeled on every side, remaining, like God Himself, invisible to human eyes.

Josephus relates that after hearing Eleazar's plea, the defenders resolved that slavery was not for them and death was better than capture. They soberly and carefully carried out their plans for the last day of their lives. The men first killed their women and children, each man killing his own, and then the remaining men killed each other; Josephus reports that the calamitous slaughter decimated 961 Jews. A popular Jewish story differs from Josephus' account; it has the defenders not killing each other but all together throwing themselves to death from the fortress walls into the precipice below.

The price paid by the Jews for their revolt was awesome. Their cities were destroyed; their land was ravaged; their leaders were slain. Famine and death spread throughout Palestine. Some Jews escaped to other lands in the Diaspora, but thousands of men, women, and children were taken prisoner by the Romans and sold as slaves throughout the Mediterranean area. Palestinian society and its religion, Judaism, were totally fractured. The populace was crushed further by the Roman heel. Vespasian imposed a Roman "temple tax" on everyone up to age 62 for the benefit of the temple of Jupiter Capitolinus in Rome which had been destroyed some years earlier.

It is impossible to overstate the long-range effects of this Jewish defeat. Norman Perrin describes it as a "major catastrophe" producing shock waves that deeply influenced not just Palestine and Judaism but for years thereafter even the relations between Judaism and Christianity.

Coincidentally, this last twenty years of Christianity as a cult of Judaism began immediately after the disastrous eruption of Mt. Vesuvius, an event that reverberated throughout the Roman Empire.

Emergence of a New Judaism

With the destruction of the temple and its guardians and priests, the few active Sadducees who survived lost all their power. The Essenes who before the revolt had gone into seclusion in their caves on the Dead Sea were wiped out by the Romans. Remaining to speak for Judaism were some of the Pharisees and scribes, who soon began to call themselves "rabbis".

The religious center of Judaism shifted from Jerusalem to the Palestinian city called Jamnia (or Jabnah, or Yavneh). A degree of religious power was assumed there by Pharisees under the leadership of Johanan ben Zakkai and Rabban Gamaliel II, both of whom were Pharisees of the school of Hillel. A rabbinical story (perhaps too reminiscent of the similar tale involving Josephus) has it that upon leaving Jerusalem, Johanan ben Zakkai had hailed Vespasian as emperor and was rewarded with special dispensation from the emperor to establish a "Sanhedrin of scholars".

This became a new center for Judaism and from about 75 there was developed a kind of "blueprint" for the future Judaism. Participating were the surviving Pharisees, their scribes and the remnants of the priesthood. Under their leadership, they developed a synagogue replacement for the former temple worship and this led to the transition from Pharisaism to rabbinic Judaism.

Survival of Jewish Christians

The Jewish War and the destruction of Jerusalem signaled the ending of Jewish Christian domination of the Christian movement. Tradition has it that the Jewish Christians who had fled to Pella were then led by Simeon, son of Clopas, perhaps the Simon, brother of Jesus, named in the gospels. This, it is suggested, was a natural succession of leadership after James was martyred in 62. Eusibius, writing in the 3d Century, has Simeon continuing as their leader until he was martyred early in the 2d Century in the persecution of Christians launched by the emperor Domitian, the younger brother of Titus.

As for Nazareth and Capernaum in Galilee in the post-revolt years, Josephus is perhaps understandably silent; these were small communities hardly deserving his attention. A Hebrew inscription found at Caesarea in 1962 dating back to the 4th Century does name Nazareth as a place where the priestly divisions were living after the Jewish revolt and this would seem to argue against Nazareth having been a strong Christian community during those years.

After the revolt, Jewish Christians undoubtedly sought to distance themselves from the defeated Jews in order to avoid the wrath of the Romans and this along with the attacks on Jewish law fostered by Paul must have posed difficulties for the remaining Pharisees. Despite their different beliefs and practices, however, the Christian Jews apparently continued to use the synagogues for family and community purposes. Scholars speculate that the Christians and particularly the Jewish Christians may have been viewed by the new leaders of Judaism in Jamnia as a menace to the resurgence of Judaism. The feelings of the Pharisees could also have been aroused against Christians by reminders of Jesus' predictions of the destruction of the temple.

Ultimately, the lines of orthodoxy began to be firmly drawn. The result, scholars conclude, was to bar Christian Jews from the synagogues. Not just an informal "do not visit", but a total suspension or ostracism from Jewish community life. While being ejected from the synagogues, Jewish Christians were forced to explain publicly their Christian views. Matthew records the scourging in the synagogues of Christian Jews by non-Christian Jews. Imagine the impact this must have had on Jewish families having members who were both Christian and non-Christian.

At some point in time (scholars debate the actual year) Christians were apparently made the object of a prayer-curse publicly recited at services. Those who refused were referred to as being "killed". The curse, inserted into the Jewish Prayer of the Eighteen Petitions, said in part, "Let there be no hope for the slanderers" and even went so far as to say that the Nazarenes (Christians) should "perish" and "be blotted out from the book of life."

The expulsion of Christian Jews from the synagogues is expressly described in John 9.22, 34 and 12.42 (e.g., "the Jews had already agreed that if any one should confess him to be the Christ, he was to be put out of the synagogue"). Christians retaliated by describing the Jews as "blind" to Jesus and this was the basis for the blindfolds so often placed over the eyes of Jews by painters in the Middle Ages.

As a result of all this (the repeated suggestion that Christians had replaced Jews as God's chosen people, the expulsion from their beloved synagogue, their total ostracism in the traditional Jewish communities, and the active persecution), Christian Jews could have stopped considering themselves as Jews or calling themselves Jews.

Meanwhile, the real center of the Christian movement had already shifted away from Palestine to other cities in Asia Minor and to Rome. Rome, particularly, grew in influence; so, apparently, did Antioch where the single bishop practice ultimately commenced. As Christianity moved physically away from Jerusalem, the more separated it became from Judaism, and this was hastened by the influences of the Greco-Roman culture which surrounded it.

CHAPTER ELEVEN

Writing of the Gospels

:

For almost two millenia, Christians everywhere have believed that the gospels –- Matthew, Mark, Luke and John –- were written by contemporaries of Jesus who recorded their first-hand memories within a few decades after the crucifixion. There are still some scholars who hold to that view, but the reaction of many ranges from doubt to outright disbelief.

First, the traditional teaching. Matthew and John were written by the apostles Matthew, the tax collector, and John, the son of Zebedee. The church considered the traditional authorship of Matthew most important to gospel credibility since it was viewed as the first and primary gospel as well as the authority on church structure. The apostle Matthew was an eyewitness to Jesus' command that Peter was the rock on which his church would be built and his background as a tax collector could be perceived in the orderly, accountant-like structure of his gospel. He alone among the gospels used the Greek word for church, teaching the importance of structure, discipline, and religious rites. As

one scholar puts it, you could put into a phone booth the people familiar with Luke's version of the Lord's Prayer, while Matthew's is on the
lips of practically every Christian in the world.

After writing his gospel, as church tradition has it, the apostle John
was exiled to the island of Patmos where he wrote the book of
Revelations. This tradition also has Mark and Luke providing important first-hand credibility to the story of Jesus. Both were claimed to be
contemporaries of Jesus. Luke was a physician and inseparable traveling
companion of Paul. The physician concept was thought to be corroborated by the language of Luke emphasizing disease and healing.
Reference is made to the woman with an issue of blood, which appears
in both Mark and Luke (Mk 5.25, Lk 8.43). Mark emphasizes the help-
lessness of the physicians; Luke diagnoses the case as incurable. Also,
Luke was described in the traditions as an artist who painted a picture
of the Virgin Mary. And he was not only a doctor but a pastor, traveling
evangelist, historian and writer, having a wide acquaintance with both
Christian leaders and important Roman officials. Students of Acts
emphasize the change from third-person to the pronoun "we" (Acts
16.6-10) in relating the travels of Paul to support the argument that this
actual companion of Paul wrote at least this portion of Acts.

The gospels were given their names by tradition, not signing. The
title "Gospel according to ..." which appears at the beginning of each of
the gospels comes from papyrus fragments dated much later; there is no
evidence that those names for the writings were used in the 1st Century.

The First of the Gospels

The scholars, most of them, dispute the traditions. They place Mark
before Matthew. At some time between 65 and 75, with about 70 being
the most-often chosen year, the gospel of Mark, the first written of the
gospels according to most of today's scholars, was drafted. Those were

turbulent years and all the momentous events of the sixties could surely fit the temper of the times as recorded in Mark and help persuade the scholars that it was Rome, not Syria, where the gospel was composed.

Papias of Hierapolis, writing in about 140 (his work, since lost, is quoted by 3rd Century Eusibius) records that the author of Mark was John Mark of Jerusalem who later became Peter's interpreter: "Mark made no mistake in thus writing down certain things as he remembered them. For he was careful not to omit or falsify anything of what he had heard." Based on this, Irenaeus (130-200) refers to Mark as "disciple and interpreter of Peter". Jerome, writing in the 4th Century, agrees.

Acts portrays John Mark as a cousin of Barnabas and active with Paul; his mother's home is described as being in Jerusalem where it was visited by the apostles. (Acts 12.12) Then, John Mark joined Barnabas when he split with Paul but rejoined Paul before the latter reached Rome. Paul mentions Barnabas' "cousin Mark", and a Mark is named in Philemon 24 as Paul's fellow worker. In 2 Timothy 4.11, Paul instructs Timothy to "get Mark and bring him with you." Finally, the author of 1 Peter sends greetings from himself and "Mark my son" (1 Peter 5.13). Thus, admitting that the name Mark was common in the Roman era, the conclusion can reasonably be drawn that there was a John Mark who was a companion of Paul and knew both Peter and Paul in their last years in Rome.

Despite this logic, the personal relationship of the author of first-written Mark with Peter and Paul has been questioned in recent years by numerous mainstream scholars, Catholic as well as Protestant; they regard the authorship traditions as untrustworthy. They trace the conclusions of Eusibius and Irenaeus about John Mark of Jerusalem solely to Papias who early in the 2d Century was the first to name Mark as the author. Papias is, however, a dead-end source since his works have all been lost; all that we have left as a basic source are Eusibius' quotations from Papias.

The skeptical scholars turn to Mark itself and find material clearly attributable to events occurring long after the deaths of Peter and Paul, tied to descriptions that served the interests of the church as later constituted. Close studies show, too, that the author of Mark was not intimately knowledgeable concerning Peter and was not familiar with Palestinian geography and practices. These portions of the gospel just do not square with a John Mark, longtime resident of Jerusalem where Peter goes to the house of John Mark's mother and is a frequent companion of both Paul and Peter.

There is much more; the evidence is marshaled in Frank Matera's "What Are They Saying About Mark?" Although some still disagree (a good example is Martin Hengel), even the noted Catholic scholar Raymond Brown has concluded that "we know nothing biographical about the author of Mark and it cannot be demonstrated that he was directly dependent on Peter."

A setting in Rome for the writing of Mark seems most convincing to many scholars, although some still hold out for Syria. In part, this conclusion is based on the demonstrable fact that the gospel fits the make-up of Rome's largely Gentile Roman Christian community. For example, Mark takes care to explain Jewish customs and the Hebrew Scripture is largely ignored. The persecution in the background of the gospel (Mk. 13.11-13) can be identified with Nero; portions of Mark appear clearly to be a message of faithfulness for those facing martyrdom (see Mk 8.34-38 and 10.28-30)

The Marcan view that the end-time is nigh fits the prevalent view of Christians which dissipated as the years rolled by in the 1st century. And this apocalyptic view inherent in Mark would have been buttressed by the cataclysmic events occurring in the decades preceding the year 80. These were the Jewish war, the famine and unrest in Rome, the devastating earthquakes of the year 68 in Italy, Nero's suicide, the bloody civil war attendant on the deaths of three emperors, the revolts in Germany and Gaul, and the serious unrest in both Britain and Africa.

Where did the author of Mark obtain his material? There is scholarly speculation that there was a proto-Mark, an earlier version or perhaps some written texts that were incorporated into the manuscript as we have it. Support for this view is found in the argument that some of the descriptions of Jesus' activities are just too vivid to be based solely on oral traditions. Perhaps, some scholars guess, the author of Mark used the mysterious Matthean Aramaic original that, if it ever existed (which most scholars doubt), has disappeared.

Oral traditions were almost surely the source for the author of Mark. This is about 40 years after the death of Jesus, which allowed ample time for many traveling between Palestine and Rome to carry the stories of Jesus. And then there was the presence and teaching in Rome of both Peter and Paul. Even if there cannot be established any first-hand relationship between the author and Peter, there is no denying the possibility, given the writing of the gospel in Rome, that some of Peter's lifetime lore about Jesus was passed on to that author.

Most scholars believe that original Mark ended with verse 8 of Chapter 16. The last two sentences of verse 8 as it appears in most modern editions are called the "shorter ending". Verses 9 to 20 are called the "longer ending"; they differ in vocabulary and style from the rest of the gospel. They are the only verses in Mark which describe the resurrection of Jesus They are absent from the best and earliest Greek manuscripts and in some where they do appear, they are noted as being doubtful. Scholars speculate that they were added because of the unnatural sounding of the verse 8 "shorter ending".

Most likely, say the scholars, the longer ending verses were written in the 2d Century based in part on passages in Luke (Lk 24) and John (Jn 20) describing Jesus' resurrectional appearances to Mary Magdalene and the apostles. These verses also contain the controversial teaching of Jesus that those who believe in him will "cast out demons", "speak in tongues", and, without any harm, "take up serpents" and "drink poisons"; teaching that many scholars find inconsistent with the lifetime lessons of Jesus.

One of the reasons for giving Mark time-priority over the other gospels is its simplicity. The story of Jesus' ministry is down-to-earth and told in straightforward fashion. Mark shows us a Jesus who is largely alone and frequently misunderstood by his disciples and by his relatives, as well as by his enemies. Suffering, misunderstanding, rejection, and death are the basic story lines. Some liken the gospel to a Greco-Roman tragedy in its composition and structure, providing evidence for composition in Rome.

One Marcan twist is what scholars term the "Messianic Secret", the claimed effort by Jesus to persuade his disciples to keep his divine attributes a secret. Many scholars believe that this was an inventive effort by the author of Mark to explain the non-recognition by Jews of Jesus as Messiah during his lifetime.

The Gospel of Matthew

As discussed earlier, most scholars today accept that most of the Gospel of Matthew is based on Mark, so that it had to be written later in the century. The same scholars reject the traditional view that the author was an apostle or even an eyewitness to Jesus. Why, they reason, would an eye-witness apostle need to copy so much about Jesus from someone like John Mark who had not even been on the scene?

Some scholars speculate that the author had been a scribe who originally taught the Hebrew Scripture. The conclusion of most is in favor of an unknown evangelist; totally rejected today is the theory that Matthew was a translation of a Semitic original.

Syria is viewed as the most likely place of composition of Matthew, although some scholars still hold for Caesarea Maritima in Palestine. The time is usually fixed at about 80, based partially on the reasoning that it had to be written after Mark and after what appears to be a murky reference in a parable to the described destruction of Jerusalem in Matthew 22.7.

This selection of a date late in the century is not without its problems. Scholars remain puzzled at the lack of a clear, explicit description of the destruction of Jerusalem. Some argue that the parable reference to that destruction and the prophecy of the destruction in Luke 21.20-24 were inserts by a later author into the original form of the gospel.

Timing for Matthew is also perceived, however, in the gospel's addition of elements to the story of the crucifixion that place considerably more blame on the Jews as opposed to the Romans. For example, Matthew puts these historically fateful words into the mouths of the Jews: "And all the people answered, `His blood be on us and on our children.'" (Mt 17.25) This would be a natural outgrowth of the Christian hostility towards the Jews which increased markedly as the years passed in the second half of the 1st Century. There is also the diatribe of Matthew 23 against the Pharisees which is consonant with the bitterness toward Pharisees that could have resulted from the barring of Christian Jews from the synagogues which most scholars agree occurred in about the year 80.

Antioch in Syria is the Christian community most consistent with both the text of Matthew and the times. The gospel's preoccupation with disputes between Judaism and Christianity and the intimate knowledge of Judaism support the conclusion that it was written for a community divided among Jews and Gentiles by an author who was Jewish Christian. There is great emphasis on fulfillment of cited Hebrew Scripture prophecies. Jewish expressions are frequently used – for example, Kingdom of Heaven rather than Kingdom of God, reflecting Jewish avoidance of the use of God's name.

Matthew and Luke both reflect clear dissatisfaction with the Marcan portrayal of both Jesus and Mary with not enough emphasis on the divine. Different from Mark are the word pictures of Jesus as a

profound, peace-bringing, healing teacher. Also added in Matthew are
the details of church organization and discipline; this is the only gospel
to use the word "church" ("ekklesia" in Greek).

John Meier, a Catholic scholar, argues that "Matthew's gospel must
be seen as a theological and pastoral response to a crisis of self-identity
and function in the Antiochean church." The craving for leadership is
symbolized, he and other scholars suggest, by the emphasis given to the
role of Peter: "You are Peter and on this rock I will build my church."
(Mt. 16.18)

Matthew reflects the need for cohesion in the community by its
emphasis on church structure, the passages which very probably led to
its being known as the "ecclesiastical gospel." This would have provided
the elements of permanence and stability which the community
undoubtedly needed, not only because of the factors mentioned earlier,
but because of the increasing awareness that the widely heralded end-
time was not arriving as predicted by some.

A fascinating aside on Matthew is the frequent inclusion of a rabbinical device of numbers. It cannot be accidental, say some scholars,
that there are in Matthew three temptations, three examples of righteousness, three prohibitions, three injunctions, three healings together,
three miracles showing Jesus' authority, three restorations, three "fear
nots", three sayings about little ones, three prophetic parables, three
prayers in Gethsemane, three denials of Peter, three questions of Pilate.
And the same pattern is used with seven, starting with the seven woes
and going on through seven brethren to seventy-times-sevenfold par-
dons.

Luke and Acts

Few scholars doubt that a single author is responsible for both the
Gospel of Luke and Acts of the Apostles. Some scholars call the latter

the "Acts of Peter and Paul" since they and not the remainder of the apostles are central to the narrative. Luke was probably first named by Irenaeus late in the 2d Century. Many if not most scholars today reject the traditional physician-companion of Paul theory of the author of Luke. However, there are notable exceptions, particularly those who point to the first-person plural ("we") used in Acts in describing some of Paul's travels. These scholars support the "companion of Paul" tradition for at least these portions of Acts.

Often cited by the opponents of the companion theory is the undeniable fact that Acts shows no knowledge whatsoever of Paul's letters; it seems incredible that a person close to Paul would not be aware of his many letters. Also, it is hard, some scholars say, to rationalize the portrayal of Paul in Acts with that drawn in those letters. There is no reference in Acts to the theology of Paul, and what close companion could have failed to remark on those intense views? There are also contradictions between the Pauline letters and Acts. For example, Paul in Acts is an outstanding orator; in his letters, Paul admits to being an unremarkable speaker. Finally, the author clearly did not know Palestine at all, judging by the geographical references in the two books. Arguably, a traveling companion of Paul would not have been that ignorant.

The consensus author of both Luke and Acts is "unknown evangelist", not an eye witness to Jesus, probably a non-Palestinian Gentile familiar with Hellenistic culture and the Greek language, working with written and oral sources and traditions. Many scholars agree that the widely-known speeches in Acts (e.g., those of Stephen in Jerusalem and Paul to the Greeks) are of Lucan composition, although some still stoutly maintain that they are historical.

The Gospel of Luke is viewed by scholars as attempting to shift the blame for the crucifixion of Jesus more squarely on the Jews. And it is also different in its new emphasis on women in special material that does not appear in either Mark or Matthew. These include the scenes involving Mary Magdalene, Mary of Bethany, Martha, and the woman at the well. (See Lk 7.36-50; 10.38-42.) Indeed, Luke's mentions of women (about 40, many more than any other gospel) causes some scholars to even speculate that one good source for the author was a woman.

Most scholars conclude that viewing the Synoptic gospels (Mark, Matthew and Luke) in terms of Christology – a measurement of the degree of divinity ascribed to Jesus – they move upward on that scale with Mark having the lowest and Luke, the last of the Synoptics, the highest.

Luke's desire to persuade the Romans that Christianity was a legitimate religion separate from Judaism is often commented on by scholars. They argue that the author of Luke and Acts appears to be writing not only in an effort to unite Christianity by smoothing over differences between diverse groups of Christians, but also defensively (apologetically, it is called by the scholars) to convince Roman authorities that Christians were not hostile to the Romans. Witness the fact that Luke is the only gospel which teaches its audience to "render unto Caesar the things that are Caesar's." Undoubtedly, the author was aware that the Romans were still reveling in their victory and hoped to dissuade them from including Christians in their retribution against the Jews. Acts uses verbatim speeches of Stephen, Peter and Paul to show the scheming of the Jews and the positiveness of Roman government officials.

The description of the destruction of Jerusalem, the effort to play down Roman complicity in the crucifixion, and other factors cause scholars to place the time of writing after the end of the Jewish revolt and after Gentiles took over from Jews the leading role in Christianity. All of this has caused most scholars to set the writing at about the year 85.

CHAPTER TWELVE

The Last Decades

No one knows how much the Christian communities outside Palestine and throughout the Diaspora were affected by the Jamni decree barring Christians from the synagogues. Antioch, the third city in the Roman empire after Rome and Alexandria, most likely was affected. Antioch was a melting pot for Jewish and Gentile influences, reflecting the history of Paul's conflicts there. Undoubtedly, the Antiochean Christian community was in a period of crisis reflecting the destruction of Jerusalem and the temple, the continued persecution by the Romans, and the lack of any leadership from Jerusalem.

Even during the time of Peter and Paul, as we have seen, the Christian community in Rome was predominantly Gentile, reflecting the earlier dispersal of numerous Jews from Rome. We have little to go on in reconstructing Roman Christianity in the decades after the martyrdom of Peter and Paul. After the dispersal of Jews described earlier, some Jewish Christians clearly remained in Rome; witness Aristobulus, a Jewish grandson of Herod the Great, named in Paul's letter to the

Romans. In those early years after the martyrdom of Peter and Paul, we have little to go on with respect to Christianity in Rome; we do have more sources as to other communities.

The Letters of Clement

The Corinthian church which so much preoccupied Paul is portrayed in I Clement, a letter from Rome to Corinth. In assessing the relevance of this letter, the first tough questions have to be its authorship and time of writing. The letter was fully accepted as authentic by early Christian historians. On its face, it is sent from "the church of God which sojourns in Rome" to the Christian church in Corinth. Identification of the source can be read to refer to just a brother church, or to some kind of seat of authority.

The author of I Clement is not named anywhere in the letter; it acquired the name years after it was supposedly written. In about 450, the bishop of Corinth describes the letter as one "earlier sent to us through Clement". Irenaeus in the 2d Century describes a Clement as the third bishop of Rome, and states that the letter was written "in the time of Clement", but his authority may not be too sound since he counted Peter as the first bishop, a conclusion rejected by most of today's scholars.

There are those, certainly a minority, who have argued for different and more colorful identity for Clement. One version has him as a Roman consul, Titus Flavius Clemens, Vespasian's nephew and Domitian's cousin, converted to Christianity and later executed for indolence and atheism – a charge frequently made by the Romans against the Christians. Flavia Domitilla was allegedly Clemens' Christian wife, and this may have caused some to identify her husband as the author of I Clement.

Another, more radical account has the author as a freed slave from the household of Clement. But neither of these stories supplies an answer to the most logical question which supports authenticity of the letter. How, if the author was not a highly placed person in the Christian church, could he have presumed to write on behalf of "the church of God which sojourns in Rome?"

Placing the letter in the 90's is supported by its reference to persecution which probably, scholars say, refers to the violent onslaught against the Christians led by Emperor Domitian late in the 1st Century. And Clement is the first written record of the martyrdom of Peter and Paul. The letter describes them as "the good apostles" who were the "most righteous pillars" of the church. Some place I Clement even before Luke-Acts and John and argue that the author was familiar with Matthew.

Corinth is obviously a troubled church at the time of I Clement. The dissension and turmoil which so upset Paul has apparently continued; outright chaos is threatened. There is a reference to "jealous zeal" and the removal of presbyters from office. The writer warns, based on his experiences in Rome, that divisiveness may lead to death for many Christians; a united front is desperately needed. Jewish heritage, obedience to civil order, and church structure are all stressed. Interestingly, precisely the same themes that are emphasized in Matthew, written most likely years earlier in Antioch.

Obviously, the Christian community in Corinth has looked to Rome for guidance; further evidence of the shift in the center of Christianity away from Jerusalem to Rome. And the licentiousness which so much troubled Paul has continued. However, the heartening development is that the church is obviously maturing; there has been a continued movement toward order and unity. Almost certainly, despite the travails and persecution, the church in Corinth remains well-established and growing.

The Gospel of John

The Gospel of John was quite clearly written very late in the century. Serious scholarly controversy continues to this day over its authorship. Many books have been written on the subject and the theories are widely divergent. Some support what most Christian churches continue to teach, that the Fourth Gospel was the "final apostolic testimony" by the Apostle John himself, who was also the "beloved disciple" whom, as John describes the event, Christ clasped to his breast at the Last Supper.

This reasoning has internal (within the gospel) logic – in the Synoptics and Acts, John is constantly portrayed as being with Peter; just as the beloved disciple is constantly associated with Peter in the Book of John. Also, a disciple as important as John would not ignore his identity in his own book; therefore, he must have been referring to himself in the name of the beloved disciple. Other scholars dispute this conclusion, citing the reference in John 21.2 to the "Sons of Zebedee", including John, whereas in the same chapter (Jn 21.7) there is a separate reference to the beloved disciple. They choose other identities; some even select Lazarus.

As to authorship by the apostle, Eusibius was an early doubter. Papias, writing in the 2d Century, has John martyred in 62. Those who join Eusibius and Papias cite Mark 10.39 which indicates martyrdom for both of the Sons of Zebedee (Jesus tells them that "the cup that I drink you will drink"), which could place John's martyrdom close to that of his brother, James, in Jerusalem; arguably much too early for him to have written the gospel which refers to events occurring considerably later in the 1st Century. Another argument against apostolic authorship is the gospel's mysticism and theology which appear to be far beyond what would be likely for a Galilean fisherman.

A theory developed after the Reformation held to a "late date" for the gospel, arguing that it was a product of 2d Century reflection. But then came the Rylands Papyrus found at Nag Hammadi in 1945. It contained a fragment of the gospel (Jn. 18.31-38). Carbon dated to the early 2d Century, this supported the conclusion based on events described in the gospel (e.g., the exclusion of Christian Jews from the synagogues) and other factors that the gospel was most likely written very late in the 1st Century. Many modern scholars ascribe the gospel to "unknown evangelists", dating its final editing to the last decade of the 1st Century.

A number of scholars (most notably Raymond Brown) have rather recently given a leading role in the development of the gospel to the beloved disciple as a person independent of John. They argue that the anonymous disciple of The Baptist chosen by Jesus to be his own disciple along with Andrew (see Jn 1.35-40) was the individual later described in the gospel as the beloved disciple. This incident took place, according to the gospel, in Judea, near Jerusalem. The theory speculates that there developed in the area near Jerusalem a group of disciples of Jesus who were quite independent of those in Galilee, and the beloved disciple was a member of this group; possibly also being the disciple in the courtyard pictured in John. Others suggest that he is the same as the young disciple described in Mark who stayed with Jesus after all the apostles left and was seized by those who arrested Jesus, but then fled naked from the scene.

Then, after the crucifixion, Raymond Brown's theory continues, the "beloved disciple" went with the apostle John to Ephesus – and there is strong tradition support for John developing a Christian community there. Irenaeus, for example, writing in the 2d Century has John in Ephesus. Paul certainly confirms the Christian community at Ephesus; his silence about any presence of John either argues against his having been a part of that community or supports a conclusion that John arrived in Ephesus later than Paul. Perhaps it was the students of John who traveled from Ephesus to Iran where some followers of John called Mendaeans still exist, claiming that he, not Jesus, was the Messiah.

Another highly respected scholar, Martin Hengel, argues that a John the Elder left Palestine during the Jewish War, having met Jesus as a young man and becoming one of his disciples. He modeled himself after the beloved disciple and founded a school in Ephesus, where the first version of the Gospel of John was developed. Hengel suggests that it was directed against the Petrine-oriented traditions of the Synoptic gospels, repeatedly reworked, and finally published near the end of John the Elder's life, with Chapter 21 being added later. Hengel goes on to argue that some of John the Elder's former pupils upset the Johannine community by attacking some of the theological reasoning in the gospel, and their secession from the community led to the three epistles of John and perhaps some of the changes in the ending of the gospel.

Substantial editing of the gospel is readily apparent from the text itself. Scholars generally agree that whoever wrote the first version and whenever it was written, the gospel underwent a complex development before it reached its final form, with redactors revising the material and adding new portions. And the reviser took pains to explain the non-arrival of the perousia, the second coming, and the death of the beloved disciple, whoever he was, in spite of predictions that he would live to see Jesus again.

Revelations should be mentioned along with the Book of John, since for centuries commencing with Justin Martyr it was assumed to be another work of the apostle John, written in the last stages of his life while exiled to the Island of Patmos. Most scholars today conclude that the author of this highly mystical book written poorly in Greek is an unknown Jewish Christian prophet, possibly a disciple of John, writing in the 90's at the end of Domitian's reign.

Revelations continues to be very controversial. Many read it as a guide to how the world will end. Preachers have likened its Beast of Revelations to Hitler, Stalin and even Saddam Hussein and relate the book's events to the atomic bomb and the origin of Israel.

Scholars are deeply divided on the issue of John's independence from the synoptic gospels; some argue strongly that it is derived from entirely separate traditions. Traditions which embody some of the same stories that appear in the Synoptics but otherwise are quite distinct in derivation.

Certainly, the differences between John and the Synoptics are remarkable. John has Jesus teaching during a much longer ministry; about three years as opposed to the Synoptic one. John has Jesus spending much more of his ministry in Judea and Jerusalem – at least four visits compared to the one described in the Synoptics. The names of Jesus' followers in John include some not mentioned in the other gospels. Jesus visits Jerusalem twice for the Passover event and also for other festivals. This ministry is quite different from that practiced in Galilee where Jesus concentrated on the poor.

John places the cleansing of the temple at the beginning, not the end of Jesus' ministry and the oft-repeated saying about prophets having no honor in their homes is spoken in Judea not Galilee. Indeed, some scholars speculate that the gospel was produced by disciples in Judea.

John does share the story of John the Baptist and the passion story with the other gospels, but as to the latter, there are some major differences. The Last Supper is not portrayed as a bread-and-wine event; John does not include the well-known "This is my body ... this is my blood" in the last-night account. Rather, the washing of Jesus' feet by the apostles is emphasized.

The story of Lazarus is unique to John and has led a few scholars to identify him as the "beloved disciple". The Synoptics have the Last Supper as a Passover meal; only John has Jesus crucified on the day before the Passover, and John places the cleansing of the temple at the beginning of Jesus' ministry rather than at the end. Remarkably, John uses the word "love" over 45 times; almost twice as often as in all the other gospels combined; incompatible, some say, with John's severe condemnation of "the Jews" as murderers. Then, there is the colorful story of the severing of the ear of the high priest's slave at the time of Jesus' arrest, an account that is absent from all of Mark, Matthew and

Luke. (As an aside, one recent author argues colorfully that this was Paul himself, long before he was converted.)

The variance of John from the Synoptic gospels was for centuries strangely muted in Christian educational materials; the differences frequently being put down as merely reflecting an effort by a knowledgeable apostle to "carry the story one step further", as though John was merely filling in aspects of Jesus' teaching that had not been sufficiently covered by the other three gospels. But today's scholars recognized that the differences are just too great to treat the Fourth Gospel as an intended supplement to the first three. Perhaps this helps explain why it took so very long for John to be accepted by the church authorities, lagging for decades behind the Synoptics.

The Epistles

The Petrine epistles, particularly 1 Peter, have been called a "storm center". Tradition has it that Peter himself wrote both 1 and 2 Peter. That tradition has increasingly come under attack by the scholars; the "weight" of opinion now is against apostolic authorship for both. Well-nigh unanimous is the rejection of 2 Peter ("universal doubt" is the scholars' expression); it is mostly placed well into the 2d Century, making it the last of the New Testament to be written.

Polycarp of Smyrna shows familiarity with 1 Peter early in the 2d Century; so do Papias and Irenaeus later in that century. Close analysis seems by many to support the argument that the epistle reflects knowledge of events that clearly happened long after the death of Peter. These scholars point, too, to the fact that the author is identified as a presbyter and there is no evidence that Peter himself ever held that position.

Finally, there is the argument as posed by one scholar that "it is style, above all, which damns the two letters of Peter"; the elegant Greek could not be the work of an "uneducated and ordinary"

Galilean fisherman, as Peter is described in Acts 4.13. True, if he had a wife on his Christian travels, as some argue, she could have spoken classical Greek. And in any event these arguments fall if, as many contend, Peter's secretary Silvanus used his own skill in putting down the thoughts of Peter as spoken to him.

The inclusion in the epistle of what is deemed to be a code-word for Rome used after the Jewish War, "greetings from a woman who dwells in Babylon", argues that the place of writing was Rome, probably quite late in the 1st Century. The epistle speaks of the entire church being threatened by violent persecution, and this would fit the terror imposed by Domitian late in the century much more than the selective persecution of Nero in the sixties. The conservative scholars who urge a more direct relationship with the apostle Peter place it earlier. Roman Catholic tradition has Peter living long enough to ordain Clement, so this tradition would be consonant with personal authorship late in the 1st Century, unlikely though most find it.

The best evidence of Christian beliefs in the late decades of the 1st Century could in I Peter which most scholars place in the range of the eighties and nineties. It insists on obedience to authority: "Accept the authority of every human institution whether of the emperor as supreme or of governors." (I Peter 2.13-14) Then, "slaves accept the authority of your masters (I Peter 2.18). Wives must "accept the authority of your husbands." (I Peter 3.1) Reference is made to the "fiery ordeal that is taking place among you and the fact that "the end of all things is near."" (I Peter 4.7, 12)

It was originally assumed that all of 1, 2, and 3 John was penned by the apostle. However, an unknown evangelist is today the verdict of most scholars. The author is referred to in the epistles as John the Presbyter, deeply disturbed about the splits in the Johannine community. This fits with known facts concerning the emergence and growth of gnosticism, and leads the scholars to place the date of writing very late in the 1st or early in the 2d Century. Already referred to is the theory of Hengel that these stemmed from quarrels in the Johanine community over the writing of the Gospel of John by disciples of John the Elder. On the other hand, there are some who ascribe 1 John to whomever wrote the gospel itself.

The Letter of James was first attributed to James, the brother of Jesus, "James the Just", who was a leader of the Jerusalem Christian church for years after Jesus' crucifixion and martyred in the year 62. The traditional date of the epistle was, of course, tied to James' later years. Scholars now taking a hard look at the traditions note that the view of this James as the author was unknown until the time of Origen in the 3d Century and even then was not universally accepted.

Most scholars today disagree with the traditions. James' seeming knowledge of the Pauline letters and theology (see 2.14-26) argues for a date after those letters were generally circulated and well-known, probably late in the 1st Century.

Christian Communities at the End of the Century

No one knows how many meaningful Christian communities there were by the end of the 1st Century. Mentioned earlier were Jerusalem, Rome, Corinth, Antioch, Ephesus, Edessa, Damascus, Thessalonica, Alexandria, Caesarea, Philippi, Galatia. Antioch, particularly, was a leading city in the growth of the church.

Then there is Ephesus where Paul's letters were probably first combined for general circulation and where, as earlier noted, there was probably a strong Johannine community. If there was this community in Ephesus, a widely held view of scholars, then it must also have felt the effect of the ostracism of Christian Jews from the synagogues. John 16.2 describes this expulsion as having led those affected to understand themselves as "being killed". (John writes, "the hour is coming when whoever kills you will think he is offering service to God.")

The Christian community in Antioch probably featured in Matthew and the site of the early Christian-Jewish conflicts produced the historic Christian martyr, Bishop Ignatius. Born in the 1st Century, he was probably a contemporary of Clement. Ignatius joins Clement in featuring the leadership of Peter with only secondary mention of Paul.

It was early 2d Century when Ignatius was sentenced by the Roman magistrate in Antioch to be thrown to the wild beasts in the arena in Rome. We do not know the crime that in the eyes of the Romans merited this punishment. Sent on a long death trip under guard of ten centurions, Ignatius wrote a series of five letters back to communities where he stopped on his journey, plus one to Polycarp. (Actually, at one time Christianity widely accepted more letters as having been written by Ignatius, but his authorship of these is rarely defended today by the scholars.)

The letters of Ignatius provide valuable information about the churches and Christian communities at the end of the century. Ignatius is the first known writer to use the phrase "the catholic church" to describe collectively the Christians in various communities which were communicating with each other. Ignatius became the symbol of the perfect way a Christian should give his life for Christ. Ignatius writes almost poetically of his desire to give his life "to be ground fine by the lion's teeth" in order to become "the purest bread for Christ."

Trying to place both Ignatius and Clement in the context of the development of Christian writings, there is great controversy over the extent to which these two men had knowledge of the gospels which were by then certainly being circulated among various Christian communities. Clement in the `90's clearly knew of the letters of Paul, probably an early collection; traces of Pauline thinking are found by scholars in Ignatius' letters; both authors refer to the leadership role of Paul. More difficult to find is evidence of the gospels of Mark, Matthew, and

Luke. Ignatius does refer to what he calls "gospel teachings" in his letter to the Ephesians, using what appears to be textual material from Matthew relating to the life of Jesus. Even more controversial is whether Ignatius relied on or was even aware of the Johannine writings.

Church Organization at Century End

The late 1st Century churches discussed by Ignatius, Clement and Timothy-Titus were not, of course, churches anything like those we know today. The community centers of religious activity undoubtedly continued to be the house churches. Too much visibility could not have been permitted in those years of continued persecution. And there is no reason to believe that there was much consistency of doctrine among the various communities. Some would have been closer to the more conservative Jewish Christian tradition; some, like the Hellenist Gentiles, would have been much more liberal, less tied to the older practices of Judaism. There must not have been any perceived need for inter-city organization and structure; again, Roman hostility could have suppressed any such efforts.

In Jerusalem even during the apostolic years, there had been the presbyters and elders, modeled after the practices of Judaism. This model was apparently followed in the Christian communities that flowed out of the synagogues in the Diaspora outside of Palestine. And the prophet-teachers who moved from community to community could well have been modeled after the scribes of Judaism who filled the roles of teachers and interpreters of the law.

Decision making at the church level in those turbulent years was apparently the province of the entire membership. And there was much separatism from the community; the practices and beliefs of Christianity were increasingly foreign to both the Jews and the pagan Gentiles among whom they lived. This must have led to the need, demonstrated by Matthew in the eighties, for more order and discipline as reflected in what is called Matthew's Sermon on Church Order and Life. But there was no single pattern of structure and leadership.

Paul exercised some degree of control through advice to the house churches with which he communicated. And there were the presbyters who apparently did honor the Eucharist or other rites but did act as teachers and, to some degree, "tenders of the flock" by coping with communal problems. Later in the century, however, this gradually changed. The letters of Timothy and Titus reflect a more structured organization and gradually the presbyters began establishing some kind of centralized control over the various house churches in a single community.

Doctrinal similarities must have increased with the advent of more communication among the communities and the circulation of first Paul's letters and later the gospels of Mark and Matthew.

A need for leadership was inevitable and, as earlier noted, it is evidenced by the writers of Timothy and Titus. Ignatius in about 110 is the first to write about a single bishop presiding over presbyters and deacons and the language used indicates that this is a very recent development. I Peter, written probably about 20 years earlier, refers not at all to bishops but speaks of the elders as being in control. Prior to Ignatius, there were single bishops in some Asia Minor cities, including certainly Antioch and Ephesus, but Ignatius' letters suggest that it was not a universally accepted structure. For example, Ignatius in writing to Rome does not address or even mention a single bishop there. Most scholars (including Catholic writers in the New Jerome Biblical Commentary) agree that the three-tier, multi-church structure with a single bishop at the top was not established in Rome until probably the middle of the 2d Century.

The mysterious writing called *Didache* and subtitled *Teaching of the Twelve Apostles,* is usually placed at about the turn of the century by scholars although there are some, as earlier noted, who bring it back several decades earlier. *Didache* contains considerable discussion of churchly order and instructions for church offices. Its recitation of the Lord's Prayer is widely used; Didache is the source for the ending, "For Thine is the Kingdom and the power and the glory forever." Scholars strongly disagree as to what Christian community *Didache* describes. Most do see a direct relationship with the traditions of the Matthean community of Antioch, and find a dependence on the Gospel of Matthew.

By the closing decades of the 1st century, leadership of the Christian churches shifted from Jewish to Gentile domination. Acts (15.23) describes Jerusalem as the center for Christians in Antioch, Syria, and Cilicia, but by the end of the century, according to some scholars' reading of I Peter 1.1 and I Clement, Rome is reaching out to Christians in North Asia Minor and Corinth. And the leaders are non-Jewish (e.g., Ignatius, Clement, Polycarp). After Paul, the effort to convert Jews in the Diaspora diminished substantially. And in the last years of the century, the polemic against Jews increases in the letters of Paul, Revelations ("the synagogue of Satan", Rev. 2.9; 3.9") and the Gospel of John ("You are from your father the devil", John 8.44).

At the same time, as exemplified by Hebrews (written, most scholars agree, c. 80-90), the doctrine taught by Paul that there was a second covenant favoring Christians replacing the first covenant favoring Jews came more into ascendancy. (Hebrews 8.1-13: "In speaking of a new covenant, he [God] had made the first one obsolete.")

However, during these years a decline in Pauline influence seems apparent. His adventuresome and confrontationist Christianity went out of style. There was no need for it as the conversion effort shifted from Jews to Gentiles. The nascent churches sought unification, not dispute. They apparently found it in the memory of Peter who had led the effort for compromise when Paul confronted the conservative Jews earlier in the century.

This is exemplified by the Gospel of Matthew. It clearly rejects Paul teaching in having Jesus stress "every jot and tittle" of the law. (Mt. 5.18) This gospel also elevates Peter as a symbol for the struggling Christian community for which the author wrote. Acts (written late in the 1st Century makes it clear that Peter stood somewhere between Paul and James and was criticized by both (see Gal 2.11-14) and the Petrine trajectory in the 2nd Century carried on the image of Peter as one who could bring differing groups together.

There is a scholarly view that the Petrine role which developed during the 1st Century was largely symbolic. New Testament evidence does not support Peter as being "the actual leader" in either Jerusalem or Rome. And, with respect to succession, the scholars find no evidence that any of the twelve apostles were accorded the title of bishop as head of a group of churches; all had died before this concept even became established.

True, 3d Century writers list a line of bishops of Rome running from Peter through others to Clement at the end of the 1st Century. But the evidence is strong, as already noted, that the single-bishop concept for a group of churches in a particular community did not even emerge until early in the 2d Century and many years later in Rome. Before that, there is no evidence that Clement or anyone else at that time termed himself a bishop.

The New Jerome Biblical Commentary states flatly, "To be honest, it must be admitted that the New Testament never shows Peter or any other member of the Twelve appointing a successor." Father McBrien of Notre Dame, in "Catholicism," concludes that "we have no basis for positing a line of succession from Peter through subsequent bishops of Rome." Thus, the chain linking Peter through the bishops of Rome to the Papacy is quite simply not established by the New Testament. Challenged at the time of the Reformation, it is now found weakened to non-existence even by modern Catholic scholars.

Scholars write about the differences between what they call the "James trajectory" and the "Peter trajectory". The memory of James who advocated adherence to Jewish law while still worshipping Jesus lasted well into the 2d Century. The "trajectory" of Paul declined as the years wore on in the 1st Century and by the 2d Century, he became to some an enemy responsible for the failure of the mission to the Jews.

By the end of the 1st Century, the Petrine influence was apparently dominant in the Christian communities and Christianity itself was well on its way to becoming a separate religion, developing an independent and unique structure and organization, even though the sometimes-violent struggle for self-identification continued into the 2d Century. In a number of communities, a degree of maturity had been achieved, but there was still much turbulence among Jews, still violence stemming from Rome, still persecution from the conservative Jews.

Indeed, this rejection and violence undoubtedly hastened the consideration of Christianity as a new and separate religion. 1 Peter 2.9-10 tells Gentile Christians that they are "a chosen race, a royal priesthood, a holy nation, God's own people." It is not hard to imagine the bitterness and hostility that was aroused in traditional Jews still considering themselves to be "God's chosen people" by the teaching of I Peter which came on top of John's vitriolic attacks on Jews and the years-earlier letters of Paul rejecting the Jewish law.

Other controversies caught the attention of Christians. First was their growing recognition that the predicted end-time and "second coming" was not going to occur in their lifetimes. This and the rise of gnosticism dictated a need for a more permanent structure and organization.

This movement to centralization was also required by the practical facts of growth. Its rapidity is reflected dramatically in the letters of Pliny the Younger to Emperor Trajan describing extensive proceedings against the Christians. And in the process of growth, Christianity was increasingly forgetting its Judaistic origins and becoming even more affected by the Hellenist and Roman cultures as it became institutional-ized. It was a time of departure from what some scholars call the "prim-itive Christianity" taught by the eyewitnesses to Jesus.

The Rise of Gnosticism

There was restlessness as the Christian church grew, and this is reflected in the rise of gnosticism, so much feared and fought by Ignatius early in the 2d Century. And some scholars suggest today that the virus of gnosticism had started spreading long before then and dur-ing the 1st Century. At its core was the tradition that Jesus had imparted to a selected elite, a few of his disciples, certain "secrets" concerning his divinity and teachings. Its teaching included a mysterious separation of the soul from the body, and some strains of gnosticism even became involved in homosexuality and erotica.

The mysticism of gnosticism is, some say, akin to portions of the teachings of John and the letters of John reflect a bitter controversy, per-haps with the Gnostic movement. That controversy existed side by side with the continued persecution by the Romans. After the death of Ignatius, the very active persecution lapsed for some years, but history tells of its strong re-emergence in later years.

Gnosticism, too, was distinctly in opposition to the humanism taught by Jesus and featured in the traditions of most Christian com-munities earlier in the 1st Century. Those communities in their early years were founded on equality. Men and women, masters and slaves were treated alike, at least in the house churches, and class rigidity was frequently resisted.

The emergence of gnosticism emphasizes the view of the scholars that Christianity at the end of the century was not monolithic in its beliefs. Diversity had been at the heart of the Jesus movement from the beginning and conflicts continued on into the next century as reflected by the epistles of John.

Christianity As a Separate Religion

As Christianity formed its own image, its own doctrines, the differentiation from Judaism took form in a variety of ways. One, already noted, was the movement toward celebration of the sabbath on Sunday rather than Saturday, which began in Paul's time. There are many other departures much more substantive. Anti-Judaism, if not racial anti-Semitism, was firmly in place among Christians, keeping pace with the total rejection and sometimes derision of the traditions of Jesus and the teachings of Paul which was widespread among traditional Jews. Some writers, particularly Jewish, say that the very way in which Christianity achieved its separation, with the emphasis by Paul on opposition to Jewish law, the so-called second covenant, and condemnation of the activities of the Judaizers, inevitably planted the seeds of the virulent anti-Semitism that erupted in later years.

By the end of the century, two new "religions" had begun – Christianity and rabbinical Judaism. Both had a credal or doctrinal base, much more than just a remarkably unusual body of literature. As to Christianity, though it was yet to be formalized, it had the start of an organizational structure. And the traditions surrounding the birth, death, and resurrection of Jesus were firmly embedded throughout the then-known world.

CHAPTER THIRTEEN

The Origins of Christian Sexism

The 1st Century saw two most unfortunate developments that have bedeviled Christianity to this day – Christian anti-semitism and Christian sexism. Both began well before the end of the century; the denigration of Jews by the followers of Jesus and their relegation of women to a distinctly second-class status. The next two chapters examine how this happened.

In recent years and perhaps emphasized even more commencing in 1990, America's year of the woman, Christian churches began struggling with the place of women in church structure. Those who have striven for more equality of treatment at the leadership level have continued to run head-on into the same kind of male dominance that is featured throughout the scriptures.

Even beyond the leadership role issues there is the teaching of the books of the New Testament. Women are understandably restless, many hostile, at the put-down of women that has too often been taught in materials used by the mainline churches. Those who felt that way in the

Catholic church have for centuries had their outlet in the Mariology of that branch of Christianity, but even that is largely absent in the Protestant sects.

Many Catholics and Protestants should recognize – they cannot ignore – the New Testament facts that in the gospels it was women, not men, who stood by Jesus at the cross and that it was a woman who carried to mankind the message of the empty tomb and the resurrection of Jesus. How, therefore, say many today, can woman be denied the right to carry the Eucharistic message as priest or minister?

Certainly there are the skeptics who dispute the gospel accounts of the women at the cross and the tomb, but it defies belief that any 1st Century Palestinian wishing to build a good case for credibility of the event would have concocted female false witnesses. If it were fiction, they would have used Peter or James the brother of the Lord or even the establishment Nicodemus.

Most puzzling to women is the blatant teaching of women as second-class citizens in writings of early Christian leaders, particularly in the Pauline letters originated not too long after the death of Jesus. Embarrassment is most often the reaction when militant women ask their pastors about the submission of women to men required by the teaching of the Pauline letters, the statements that "a woman's head is her husband", and that "women were created for the sake of man". Also the adjuration that women must be "subordinate" and that "it is shameful for a woman to speak in church."

Largely ignored or dodged by most speakers from the pulpit are both the language of Paul so denigrating to women and the dramatic change in the overall Christian church attitude toward women which many say commenced with Paul and dramatically accelerated from the 1st to the 2d Centuries.

Jesus Taught Female Equality

No close reader of the gospels can doubt that Jesus taught the equal worth and dignity of women, giving them key roles in witnessing to his identity and mission. His teaching and practices, say most scholars, were astonishingly at variance with prevalent Palestinian practices. He saw a productive partnership of women with men in both home and church. Schussler Fiorenza, the female biblical scholar, calls the Jesus movement a "discipleship of equals". This is amply demonstrated by the very human and vivid gospel stories of Jesus and the women who were a vital part of his ministry – Martha, Mary of Bethany, Mary Magdalene, and the various women who were the recipients of both his frank advice and his miraculous cures. Jesus fully accepted the group of women who followed him in Galilee and to Jerusalem.

These women did not just travel with Jesus – although that by itself was a significant departure from Palestinian custom. Luke singles out women who were providing funds for Jesus out of their own resources. (Lk. 8.2-3) Mary Magdalene, Joanna, wife of Herod's steward, Chuza, Susanna, "and many others" are featured.

There was the occasion when Jesus broke the sabbath to cure a crippled woman. He shared deep theological insights with the Syro-Phoenician Gentile woman at the well, meekly accepting a lesson from her – and cured her daughter. He defended the unveiled, unbraided woman who outraged the all-male diners by anointing him in their presence. Jesus sympathized with Martha's complaint that she was being required to do all the work.

Women were prominent at the end. Women mourn the crucifixion, women watch the burial, women find the tomb, women see the risen Jesus. Mary Magdalene, prominent on all these occasions, is several times mentioned as being in the company of Joanna and Mary, mother of Jesus. In view of the rank of Joanna's husband and the status of Jesus' mother, this places Mary Magdalene at a high level among the disciples.

To Jesus, then, women were clearly not secondary. While certainly aware of the Judaistic tradition limiting religious discourse with women by religious leaders (witness the apostles' reactions to Jesus' dialogue with the woman at the well) he certainly never commanded them to be silent and subservient.

Jesus, upheld firmly the traditional Judaistic views on marriage and family and stressed monogamous marriage as a "renewal of the individual union of Adam and Eve." Women were "the bride of Yahweh." Not to be ignored on this subject is the undeniable fact that Jesus was very tough on divorce – his teaching was a radical departure from the easy-divorce teaching of the Pharisees. He was in agreement with the prevailing tenet that marriage and procreation were essential to a continuing society. Jesus' occasional remarks regarding celibacy as reflected in Matthew and Luke are consistently explained as advising preparation for the end-time. In short, no one can argue that Jesus gave anything less than totally equal status to women.

The central role of Mary, the mother of Jesus, the stature given to Anna and Elizabeth in the infancy narratives, and the stories of Mary of Bethany and Mary Magdalene contrast strangely with the later 1st Century denigration of women. So does the entrusting by Jesus of the beloved disciple to Mary, saying "Woman, here is your son." After the crucifixion, women were at the forefront of the Jesus movement. Mary, the mother of John Mark, led a house church in Jerusalem; some women even achieved the title of presbytera. Luke gives great prominence to women and even mentions the daughters of Philip as well-known prophets. Three of Luke's five persons who speak by power of the Holy Spirit or as prophets in the infancy narratives are women.

But then came Paul, who never even mentions Mary the mother of Jesus anywhere in his letters and has been criticized over the years as being a cheerleader in the denigration of women which occurred in the transition from the early churches to the more structured church of the next century. Paul is frequently named as the source of anti-sexual views emphasizing continence, virginity, celibacy and asceticism, and even the labeling of women as the ultimate source of sin. Many writers have over the centuries blamed Paul as the primary author of anti-sexual beliefs and practices of the Christian Church, culminating with acceptance of celibacy as the "true Christian way."

Before turning to the letters of Paul to examine these anti-woman charges, it is well to consider the general 1st Century attitudes towards women in the prevailing Hellenistic, Roman, and Judaistic societies and the relationship of the views of those societies to those of the Christian movement.

Prevailing Societal Views on Women

Although Athens was named after the goddess of wisdom, Socrates taught that it was divine punishment to be born a woman; his pupils Plato and Socrates agreed. The Greek world of the 1st Century promoted the superiority of men. Women were frequently portrayed as responsible for sexual temptation and sin. This is not to say, however, that women had no positive roles or failed to achieve prominence. Women functioned as magistrates and officials. And some were highly respected priestesses with huge followings – witness the chief priest of the Ephesian Artemis whose temple was one of the seven wonders of the world.

On the sexual level, total sexual renunciation was rare. There was the dualism of Greek thought – the soul is the divine, the body can be the source of all evil. Hellenistic society included the Greek cult religions that emphasized the "vital spirit" of the man's body which would be depleted by fluid emissions resulting from frequent sexual activity; progressive "loss of heat" could make a man "womanish." How prevalent this view was is just not known, but this fear of loss of "vital spirit" helped give male continence a firm place. Artemidorus told the athletes that "once they began to have sexual intercourse, they ended their careers ingloriously." And there was the Greek Quintillion's advice that to keep the male body in top condition and the voice "strong, rich, flexible and firm," men should practice abstinence from sex.

Turning to Judaism, some scholars claim that very early Judaism taught that the God of Israel was asexual, but that view, even if it existed, clearly did not last. Both ritual Judaism and folk Judaism in the 1st Century were firmly androcentric and patriarchal. God was father; man ruled in the temple and the synagogue; in contrast, though, woman was master of the home and tradition-keeper for the family, even when married at an early age (often 12 years old). Josephus taught that "the woman, says the law, is in all things inferior to the man."

Except among the lower classes, men and women were generally separated in public life; women were veiled and could not talk to men. Jewish men considered women to be not very bright and too much concerned with trivial matters. One view, later carried over into Christianity, held women to be seductive and sexual temptresses (a view shared by many in Roman and Hellenistic societies).

Philo, the renowned 1st Century Jewish philosopher of Alexandria, stressed the weakness of women. He held that a man who is "fast bound in the love lures of his wife" becomes a different man who is "passed from freedom into slavery".

Some scholars argue that women were virtually treated as property in 1st Century Judaism. They cite Jewish law requiring that if a man had sex with a woman betrothed to another man, he had to pay for making her a harlot, because in the eyes of other men he had damaged another man's goods. If caught, she was to be stoned; only if she was a virgin was he also to be stoned.

Women were present in synagogue services (Jesus healed one), but some scholars argue they were consigned unseen to balconies. They were denied full access to the temple, being relegated to an outer court yard. Of the 1426 persons given names in the Old Testament, only 111 are women. But some women held the offices of ruler or president of synagogues.

Sex was ordained and commanded when practiced within marriage, but it was for procreation, not "fun and games". Celibacy was not held in high regard. Apparently, some Jews did practice polygamy (see Deut. 12.15), but prostitution and homosexuality were universally condemned. Josephus wrote that "among us it is the custom to have many wives simultaneously." This is in dispute; most agree that monogamy was favored, although some sects may have disagreed. Certainly, as the Dead Sea scrolls show, the Essenes opposed polygamy.

Some scholars point out accurately that recognition of women as equals was more prevalent in Judaism than historians often admit. Women did hold offices in synagogues in ancient Judaism and the three daughters of Job are portrayed as speaking the language of angels. Tradition describes Beruriah as a rabbi and women as strong leaders appear in the story of Judith and the rule of Queen Salome Alexandria in Judea.

The influence of Hellenism in Palestine is argued two ways. Some researchers conclude that the influence of Hellenism eroded the respect given women; others argue that many women were respected by the Greeks and that some women could and did frequently own property, obtain divorces, and enjoy other masculine perquisites. Kathleen Corley, a respected 1st Century scholar, argues that this Hellenistic example bore fruit in the areas of Palestine where Hellenistic influence was strong. Some women could get divorces, some women could hold property, some women held positions of authority. She concludes that Jesus' teaching and practices regarding women were not, therefore, as unique as some scholars maintain.

Those holding that Judaism respected women cite Rebecca, Judith, Ruth and Esther, Deborah, and Hulduh, as well as Job's three daughters. Salome Alexandra was said to be Queen of Judea. The story of Rachel is honored throughout Judaism. Judith, it will be recalled, inherited her husband's vast estate and managed it through a woman steward. She also had the authority to summon and control the elders, even before her remarkable victory over Israel's oppressors. And, while the book of Judith is viewed as apocryphal by conservative Judaism, wide respect was given to the Judith story in the folklore of Judaism. Particularly after the destruction of Jerusalem late in the 1st Century when Romans killed or enslaved hundreds of thousands of Jews, Judaism and the rabbis stressed strength of family.

There is also the elevated position given to Sophia, the Wisdom Woman, the Wisdom Messenger, in Judaism. She was pictured as being with God from the beginning. Paul calls Jesus the "Sophia of God"; Matthew speaks of Jesus' deeds as being the deeds of Sophia. Proverbs has Sophia "teaching in public; she cries out in the street". It is difficult to totally reconcile the above-described places of respect given to certain women in Judaism with the recorded synagogue prayer, "Blessed art thou, O Lord, who has not made me a woman." And the Rabbinical Mishnah statement, attributed to the 1st Century, that "If any man teach his daughter Torah it is as though he taught her lechery."

The Jewish legend of the Sages of Palestine is in direct contrast with the Acts of Paul and Thecla which elevated asceticism. The sages captured the "beast" of disorderly sexual drive and tamed it to prohibit incest and sins against nature. But they carefully allowed the drive to continue, "for if you kill it, the world itself goes down; there will be no continuation of Israel." Thus, the married householders, parents of children, were the model Jews. Women were responsible for the perpetuation of Israel.

Women in Roman society, like their Greek sisters, were almost entirely in secondary roles. They did not have the matriarchal role in the household commanded by the Jewish wife-mother. There are some exceptions and there was some, limited "upward mobility" for women in Roman society from one class to another; the prestige achieved by some women indicates that they may have been able to do better than their sisters in Judaistic society; they could inherit wealth and power. Both Greek and Roman society taught that sex was to be controlled and passion resisted. Sexual self-discipline was a hallmark of the proper Roman household code and was deemed to be a strong pillar for the Roman empire and society. Roman men of the upper classes at least did not view their forced attentions on female slaves as being a violation of the Roman household code.

Contemporary Forces Operating on Christianity

Perhaps Paul absorbed some of the Hellenic views in his conversion travels through the Greek communities. He was, some say, enough of a child of Hellenism to rate celibacy as sometimes superior to marriage. Paul can be quoted as regarding the body as weak, under domination by concerns of the flesh, and too readily susceptible to the sins of sexual temptation – all views heavily reminiscent of the teachings of Hellenism prevalent in the cities visited by Paul.

Not only Paul but other early missionaries may have encouraged breaks from family ties. Christianity began as a movement challenging converts to break with tradition, encouraging men and women to throw in their lot with those who followed Jesus. Jesus so commanded his disciples. And in the preparation for the end-time, writings reflect a movement by the more dedicated of these converts toward abandonment of normal family concepts and practices to prepare for the end-time.

Another real-life factor was at work in the early church. After the crucifixion, the Jesus movement was in great part kept alive by the wandering prophets who ministered to the struggling churches. Like Paul, many apparently spoke "in tongues." And like the Old Testament prophets, some wandered destitute and tormented in animal skins and without wives and families. Not unlike John the Baptist. They undoubtedly preached as they practiced, emphasizing renunciation of family ties to serve God, as Jesus urged for the apostles. Citing, probably, Mt. 10.37: "whoever loves father or mother more than me is not worthy of me," Luke's advice attributed to Jesus about the need to "hate" one's family.

These preachers undoubtedly challenged converts to break with home and family and throw in their lot with the "brothers and sisters in Christ," just as Paul taught. Celibacy was urged "to clarify the soul as a prelude to the second coming." It is quite possible, as earlier noted in a different context, that the 2d Century struggle over celibacy and continence had its origins in the theme of these wandering preachers.

Some scholars even suggest a rather far-fetched argument that some early Christians opposed the Roman and Judaistic view that procreation was essential to preserve their cultures and traditions, arguing that marriage and childbirth should be brought to a halt so that organized society would crumble and the world opened to the coming of the Messiah. Such devious reasoning hardly accords with the tenets of either Jesus or the early Christians.

Perhaps Jesus' teaching of woman-equality was too much ahead of its time, too radical a departure from the prevailing Roman, Hellenistic, Judaistic norm. This could have resulted in criticism from observers in the community, and that, in turn, could have led the men to insist on a change lest Christianity be viewed as being too much out-of-step and therefore more subject to criticism and persecution.

And there is the very real possibility that some strong women took advantage of the freedom accorded to them in the early Jesus movement and carried their enthusiasm too far, to the point of offending the males who regarded themselves as necessarily holding the traditional leadership positions.

This tendency could have developed during the house-church period and, as that form of worship declined, there could have been a perceived need for correction of the pendulum swing. With the progression to a more institutionalized worship setting, where men would normally be "in charge", the men could have wished to assert themselves. At the same time, as Christians moved more into acceptable community life, the churches came more into accord with the prevailing societal rules and practices. This is clearly reflected in the Pauline Pastoral letters which at one and the same time speak to institutionalization of the church and the subordinate role of women in that church.

The frequent emphasis on, almost preoccupation with martyrdom in the early church may well have been a contributing factor. Recall the letters of Ignatius who dwelled on the prospects of being "ground into fine bits by the lions" as his ultimate sacrifice for the cause of Jesus. Martyrdom was the central theme of the legendary lives of the apostles. It became an ideal. And if the body could not be totally martyred, then giving up bodily desires could be achieved as a kind of partial, self-inflicted martyrdom, like self-flagellation or self-mutilation. Almost as preparatory exercises for the final and total act. In the apocryphal Acts of John, a young man dramatically castrates himself with a sickle, declaring, "There you have the pattern and cause of all this."

Gnostic teaching which may have developed late in the 1st Century held that sex was the root of evil. There was a suggestion that after Jesus Christ solved death, the great concern should become sexuality. Some Christian thinkers even presented it as the first cause of death. Avoidance of sexual intercourse, therefore, was not only a form of partial martyrdom, it was linked symbolically with the reestablishment of a lost human freedom and a regaining of the spirit of God. Segments of Christianity, including some gnostics and the Encratites, practiced rites of baptismal initiation that linked the beginning of a true Christian life with the perpetual renunciation of sexual activity.

The Pauline Letters

Against this societal and Christian development background come the Pauline letters, written by a man who was immersed both in Hellenism and in the Christian prophet and house church movements described above. By necessity in his missionary journeys, he must have been repeatedly exposed to all these forces.

Any evaluation of Paul's views toward women must start with his words in Galatians 3.28: "There is neither Jew nor Greek, there is neither slave nor free, there is neither male nor female, for you when baptized are all one in Jesus Christ." Hardly a sexist statement; Fiorenza calls it the "magna carta of Christian feminism." Next is the undeniable and frequent Pauline recognition of women as missionary leaders in the communities where he had his great Gentile conversion successes. The role of women in the Pauline movement was much closer to the teaching of Jesus than to the practices of contemporary Judaism. His salutations address women as equals; his praise of their leadership accomplishments is never sparing.

Paul designates Phoebe a "deacon of the church" (Romans 16.1) and a "protates" (leader) of her congregation. Lydia, a house church leader, was an independent woman of means who plied the "purple trade" in expensive purple-dyed fabrics. Philip's four daughters, prophets all, are described with obvious Pauline approval. Acts 21.8,9. Women in prominent roles abound in the Pauline letters. To already-mentioned Phoebe and Lydia, add Prisca, Aquila, Eudia, and Syntyche, all pictured as both important workers and leaders in Christian congregations. (See Philippians 4.2,3; Acts. 18.26; Romans 16.1-3) Clearly, the active leadership of women was a fact of everyday Christian life in the early Pauline churches. No one can argue that Paul saw these women as secondary or subservient.

Then there is the notable passage in Romans 16.7: "Greet Andronicus and Junia… who are outstanding among the apostles." John Chrysotom in the early centuries claimed "Junia" as a woman and applauded Paul for recognizing that a woman was deemed worthy of the title of apostle. Origen and Jerome agreed in the 4th and 5th centuries. However, others later changed the spelling to the masculine "Junias," permitting the argument that a woman could not have been an apostle. The view of Junia as a female apostle is opposed today by those who wish to deny to women the opportunity to become ministers and priests.

All of these commendations of women were consonant with the usage of house churches as the focus of early religious practice and activity. There is the Second Johannine letter written by "the elder to the elect lady and her children", who was undoubtedly the head of her house church; the "children" are thought to be the members of her church. Mary was in charge of the house church in Jerusalem frequented by her cousin Barnabas and other leaders in the early church. These women were in no way "subservient"; realistically, they must have led or at least participated actively in the churches in their homes. Why else would they have been so much featured in these early Christian writings?

But there are other portions of the Pauline letters which point in the opposite direction. The believer in both Paul and equality has great difficulty with the troublesome Pauline passages reflecting emphasis on celibacy, downgrading of marriage, and insistence on silence and subservience for women. For beginners, Paul totally ignores both Mary, the mother of Jesus, and Mary Magdalene. Paul takes the passage from Genesis describing marriage (Genesis 2.24, quoted with approval by Jesus) and shockingly applies it not to marriage but to a man's union with a prostitute. (1 Cor. 6.16) Then, Paul highly praises celibacy; while favored by some Jewish sects (notably the Essenes), it was far from a widespread practice in Judaism which put heavy emphasis on the need for marriage, stable family life and procreation.

Often cited are the strong anti-sex, anti-woman passages in Corinthians, Ephesians, and the Pastoral Letters. Citing the advice of

Paul regarding sexual abstinence, Gregory C. Jenks in his *What Did Paul Know About Jesus* concludes that "Paul sounds more like the first Puritan than a disciple of Jesus." These passages attributed to Paul have been called the "entering wedge of monasticism" because of their severe criticism of sexuality coupled with only faint praise for the advantages of marriage. Some scholars such as Peter Brown go so far as to argue that, "By his essentially negative, even alarmist strategy [regarding sex and marriage], Paul left a fatal legacy for future ages."

Paul's discourse on sex in his much-analyzed letter to the Corinthians starts off sympathetically to those favoring marriage (1 Cor 7.1-7):

You say, 'It is a good thing for a man not to have intercourse with a woman.' Rather, in the face of so much immorality, let each man have his own wife and each woman her own husband. The husband must give the wife what is due to her, and equally the wife must give the husband his due.

This is hardly a departure from then-prevalent teaching of Judaism. But, then Paul immediately makes it clear that his own view is not the same: *I say this by way of concession, not command. I should like everyone to be as I myself am.* And how was Paul? Celibate. So, Paul mentions the conventional morality as a "concession," but advocates celibacy. He goes on to say: "To the unmarried and the widows I say that it is well for them to remain single as I do." (1 Cor. 7.8)

Thus Paul found marriage to be acceptable but distinctly in second place to celibacy: *But if you do marry, you are not doing anything wrong... it is only that those who marry will have hardships to endure.* (1 Cor. 7:28) Paul's rationale for his position demonstrates his personal priorities, which clearly had nothing to do with procreation:

An unmarried man is concerned with the Lord's business; his aim is to please the Lord. But a married man is concerned with worldly affairs; his aim is to please his wife, and he is pulled in two directions. (1 Cor. 7.32-34)

Paul's conclusion is inescapable from his reasoning: *Thus he who marries his betrothed does well, and he who does not marry does better.* (1 Cor. 7.38) Further, *It is well for a man not to touch a woman.* (1 Cor. 7.1) Finally, there comes what many women today would regard as totally sexist teaching:

While every man has Christ for his head, a woman's head is man, as Christ's head is God... Man is the image of God, and the mirror of his glory, whereas a woman reflects the glory of man. For man did not originally spring from woman, but woman was made out of man; and man was not created for woman's sake, but woman for the sake of man. (1 Cor. 11.3, 7-9)

Even more specific is Ephesians 5.22-24: *Wives be subject to your husbands as to the Lord. For the husband is the head of the wife; ... let wives be subject in everything to their husbands...Just as the church is subject to Christ, so also wives ought to be in everything to their husbands.*

In language very difficult to square with the opening of 1 Corinthians which addresses the congregation to which he writes as "Chloe's people" (1 Cor. 1.11), he proceeds to put women in a totally subservient church role:

For they are not permitted to speak but should be subordinate, as even the law says. If there is anything they desire to know, let them ask their husbands at home. For it is shameful for a woman to speak in church. (1 Cor. 14.34-35)

Paul's treatment of women in his churches as reflected repeatedly in his letters is totally incongruent with the downgrading of women in the above-quoted passages. "That is just not my Paul", say some admirers of the great missionary.

Those who have difficulty with Corinthians also find hard to take the very similar denigration of women in Timothy and Titus, the so-called Pastoral Letters. For example, 1 Timothy states that women should "rule their households", but also should know their place:

> *[Women's] role is to learn, listening quietly and with due submission. I do not permit women to teach or dictate to the men; they should keep quiet"* (1 Tim. 2.11-12)

This theme of submission to husbands is echoed in Titus (Titus 2.5). It is impossible to reconcile the "women cannot teach" words of Timothy with Paul's praise for the teaching by Priscilla and Aquilla of Apollos, the distinguished Alexandrian. (Acts 18.24-26)

No wonder, in view of these passages, that George Bernard Shaw called Paul "the eternal enemy of women."

Attempts to Explain the Pauline Contradictions

The first explanation for perhaps the strongest of the put-downs of women (Ephesians, Timothy, and Titus) is quite simple: Paul didn't write the letters. Discussed in an earlier chapter was the view of most scholars that these letters are deutero-Pauline – ascribed to Paul by an unknown evangelist writing many years later (some scholars say well into the 2d Century). And some scholars even argue that the similar language in Corinthians is a later-date interpolation, possibly by the same evangelist who wrote the Pastoral Letters and wanted to be certain that the undeniably Pauline letter of Corinthians carried consistent anti-women language.

The second explanation advanced for the "Pauline contradictions" is that Paul's Greek words have been mis-translated or misinterpreted. For example, some cite the Corinthian language forbidding women to speak in church; this, they say, should have been translated as forbidding women to talk among themselves during services. A quite different and simpler theory is that "do not speak" meant "do not speak in tongues". To put it differently, Paul's words were aimed at a few women who were disrupting religious services, not to women generally.

These admonitions should also be placed, the argument runs, in the context of the letters' references to "treacherous" teachers who are "ruining whole households." (See 1 Tim. 1.7, 2 Tim. 3.2-7) This could tie to the problems being experienced in the early house churches like those at Corinth where according to 1 Clement, chaos was developing, possibly from the mystery religions and gnostic teaching which may have infected some women. The women in question may well have been stimulating veneration of powerful female deities (as in Corinth), or women adopting a gnostic view of the role of Eve who could procreate without male assistance. The offensive words could have been aimed at this type of teaching, not at all attempting to lay down a general rule.

One of the problems is the translation of the Greek word "authentein" as "to have or exercise authority over". Thus, 1 Tim. 2.11-15 in the New International Version is "I do not permit a woman to teach or have authority over a man; she must be silent." The New English Bible, on the other hand, translates the word as "domineer over," which can mean the exercise of personal absolute power. The Revised English Bible revision of NEB carries it further: "to dictate to the men." Who could criticize this criticism?

However, it must be added that all of these rationalizations based on language do not address all of the vehemently anti-women passages of Corinthians, Timothy, and Titus.

Then there is another rationale, already noted, that it became necessary late in the 1st Century to stress compliance by Christians with the normal patriarchal household code of the Greco-Romans in order to avoid having Christianity labelled and treated as akin to the Isis cult which worshipped women gods and the mystic, orgiastic cults which wove eroticism into man-woman equality. In other words, the evangelist author was saying, "Hey, Christians, let's be more respectable, traditional and patriarchal like the folks around us before we get into even more trouble with the community leaders and authorities," and used Paul's name as the author to give credibility and force to the writing.

This view is supported by the reference in 1 Timothy to the need for following the proscriptions regarding women so that "they will give the enemy no occasion for scandal." (1 Tim. 5.14), and in another of the Pastoral Letters where the author concludes his admonitions concerning women with the words, "then the gospels will not be brought into disrepute." (Titus 2.5)

Supporting this theory is another argument that the later letters deliberately presented a "domesticated Paul" who more fully endorses traditional Jewish attitudes toward marriage and family – a clear theme of the Pastoral Letters. Certainly there are marked differences between some teachings of Corinthians regarding celibacy and 1 Timothy, Hebrews and Ephesians, all of which favor loving marriages. At the turn of the century, Clement of Alexandria argued for marriage and against the ascetics who, he said, exaggerated and misunderstood Paul's teaching. Indeed, he argued that both Peter and Paul were married.

Harrington writes in "Jesus and Paul – Signs of Contradiction" that disciples of Paul after his death found a "disturbing [to them] prominence of women in the Christian movement." Some scholars even go so far as to attribute this view to Peter, arguing that his followers are responsible for twisting Paul's true views. This theory would perhaps cause the feminists of today to transfer their ire from Paul to Peter.

The Argument of the Literalists

Many of the scholars' attempts to avoid the straightforward reading of the anti-woman language in Timothy, 1 Corinthians and Ephesians run squarely into opposition by the fundamentalists. They say vehemently that if the literal reading of the books of the New Testament can be changed by arguments based on "placing in context" or "understanding the cultural situation," or simply saying that "Paul did not write it," then all of the New Testament is up for grabs and open to qualification, private interpretation or just disbelief.

The ways in which a literal reading of Paul's teaching was used (or misused, depending on the individual's view) is vividly demonstrated by The Acts of Paul and Thecla, popular in the 2d Century. In some regions, it may even have been regarded as canonical. This was a fictional account of the life of Thecla, a woman missionary who became attached to Paul and is described as becoming an apostle.

Thecla, a young virgin, after hearing Paul preaching in Iconium as she stands at a courtyard window, renounces her upbringing, her upcoming marriage, her mother, home and traditional womanhood. Cutting off her hair and donning men's clothes, she runs off to follow Paul, in love with his message of holiness in celibacy. She is attacked by her mother and the authorities for renouncing the traditional role of a woman. Paul is arrested and accused of "corrupting all the women."

Thecla is sentenced to death – to be fed alive and naked to the wild beasts. She baptizes herself in a water-filled pit and, when the beasts do not harm her, she is set free. She and Paul both escape to Antioch. A Syrian falls in love with Thecla but is rejected; Thecla adopts a life of teaching and celibacy – the perfect woman missionary and the forerunner of Catholic female orders.

The story of Thecla's continence is consistent with many of the apocryphal accounts of the lives of the apostles, who are pictured as encouraging women to renounce their pagan husband's bed and devote themselves to a life of continence. Needless to say, this outraged both the husbands and the community as much as did Thecla's actions.

A succeeding legend went further in telling the terrible story of Perpetua in Carthage who symbolized the early "convent types" of groups of secluded women. "Martyrdom of Saints Perpetua and Felicitas" describes in detail Perpetua's infatuation with death for her religious beliefs and the anguish of her pregnant co-believer, Felicitas. Both sought martyrdom in the coliseum, giving up their bodies and the unborn baby to the wild animals.

Obviously, as many scholars note, these legends did not accurately depict Paul's teaching. As one wrote, "No Saint Thecla would have heard such views floating up to her through the open windows from a neighboring courtyard, when the real Paul preached in Iconium." But, fairly or no, the leaders of the early 2d Century churches without question attributed these views to Paul.

Early in the 2d Century virginity and asceticism became increasingly ascendant in the writings of some Christians who advocated these practices as true expressions of Christian life, although undoubtedly restricted to the elite. These few, it was urged, could achieve true equality of men and women. Only as ascetics could women become "like men."

This teaching reminds some scholars of the passage in the recently discovered Gospel of Thomas which quotes Jesus as saying, "I myself shall lead Mary in order to make her male, so that she too may become a living spirit resembling you males. For every woman who will make herself male will enter the Kingdom of Heaven." Gnosticism was ambivalent; some sects elevated sexual activity, even making it into a ritual. Some saw God as a "dyad", embodying both masculine and feminine traits. Then there is the gnostic teaching portrayed in the apocryphal "Great Questions of Mary" where Jesus is with Mary Magdalene when he "brings forth a woman from his side" and has sexual intercourse with her.

The Role of Later Writers

The purity of asceticism was certainly emphasized by many 2d Century Christian writers. Tertullian downplayed marriage and endorsed virginity as the "better Christian way." He urged that "the best thing for a man is not to touch a woman." Origen considered sex a consequence of sin, "a stain on the soul;" woman was a "symbol of weakness and evil." Origen argued that women were more lustful than men and were a primary source of carnal corruption in society. Women were thought to stir up the sexual desire and jealousy that pitted males against each other.

Some scholars argue that this anti-sex theme arose from the elevation of the purity of Mary, Mother of Jesus; Mary was pure and sexless. This view of Mary gained ascendancy in 2d Century Christianity and at the same time guilt became strongly associated with sex. Bodies were evil; souls were good. This theme has been carried through the centuries and is fought out in the feminist movement today. Many female liberation fighters oppose Mariology, the worship of Mary, for this reason, even though to many women the lead role traditionally given to Mary makes up for the second-place treatment often afforded to women.

Episcopalian Bishop F.H. Borsch carries the controversy over Mary into the church treatment of women, arguing that as long as Mary is denied her full humanity, including her sexuality, women will be restrained in the roles they can play in the church.

But back to the early years of Christianity. By the 3d Century, conjugal abstinence was enjoined by the church for all persons in major religious orders. Efforts were increased to restrict the conjugal life of the clergy who at that time were still free to marry. It was not until the 4th and 5th centuries that the rules hardened with the acceptance of the abstinence teachings of Augustine that prevail to this day.

Conclusion

There is no simple answer to the question of what caused the dramatic changes in man-woman relationships and the transformation from the equality taught and practiced in the early church to the extreme anti-woman, anti-sex views that came into ascendancy during the 2d Century. Nor is it easy to discern how disapproval of sexuality and elevation of the ascetic life came to be combined with the placement of women in a decidedly subordinate role. All that we have is reconstructive speculation.

Christians today live with the fall-out. Many women are understandably puzzled, some outraged at the silence or at least ambivalence of many mainline Christian churches on this entire subject. Their ministers and pastors are troubled and frequently offer what can only be called rationalization when confronted with the blatantly sexist views embodied in some of Paul's letters.

There is a tremendous reluctance to even mention the views of highly-regarded scholars, Catholic and Protestant, who discuss the possibility (some say probability) that Paul did not even write the controversial words, that Gal. 3.28 expressed his true views as being in accordance with those of Jesus, and that Chloe, Priscilla and Junia were Paul's counterparts of Jesus' Martha, Mary of Bethany and Mary Magdalene.

Certainly it is vital that this problem continue to be discussed within the Christian churches – even more so than it now is in many of those churches. Arrival of the Third Millennium should spur Christianity to finally face up totally to the pervasive dichotomy between the today-recognized proper role of women by some but far from all Christians in the world and the traditional total male dominance and female put-down which pervades so much of the scripture, both in the Old Testament and the New, as well as in the minds and actions of far too many Christian males.

It is strange and unfortunate that the new religion in the 1st Century, Christianity, as it broke from Judaism chose to reject Jesus' teaching on the role of women and to accept Judaism's then-prevalent denigration of women. Perhaps there is still time, Jesus might say, for all Christianity to disregard this relic of 1st Century Christianity. Must Christianity always be male-dominated?

CHAPTER FOURTEEN

Christian Anti-Semitism

The Jewishness of Jesus has for centuries largely been papered over or even ignored in the teachings of Christianity. Jesus is pictured simply as the founder of Christianity, somehow disembodied from his Jewish parents and forebears, separated from the Jewish religion and culture which surrounded him throughout his childhood and adult life. Younger persons particularly think of Jesus only as a Christian, not at all as a Jew, and do not even notice the strangeness, for example, of the Gospel of John having Jesus and his disciples refer to others as "the Jews" as though they were not Jews themselves.

Judaism, the religion, is little explained in Christian bible classes and schoolrooms. The Jewish images that last are largely symbols like the temple, the Pharisees, the Sadducees and the scribes. The centuries-old majesty of the Torah and the Judaistic tradition of the Mosaic Law are seldom explained. Rarely taught is the real content and historical significance of the Jewish law. Largely unknown is the leading role played by Jewish synagogues in the spreading of Christianity in the decades after

the crucifixion. Unfairly inaccurate is the general Christian view of Old Testament Judaism as a religion of a wrathful and judgmental God, quite different from the Jesus teaching of grace and love.

In Christian literature, the leaders of Judaism are often stereotyped, almost caricatured as doubting and hypocritical Jews who did not really try to understand the unique, merciful and humble Jesus. The fact that Judaism first and persistently confronted paganism is submerged. The Old Testament is treated as little more than a road paver for Jesus, and Christians are surprised to learn that Jews do not even know it as the Old Testament.

Closely read, the New Testament does, of course, actually teach the existence and some aspects of Judaism. There are many references to the great respect with which Judaism was held not only by Jesus but by his disciples. The gospels also make it abundantly clear that Jesus lived in many respects a Torah-bound life as a Jew. He was at home in the synagogue. He was undoubtedly circumcised and bar mitzvahed; he was educated and deeply rooted in the religion and traditions of his Jewish homeland. The conclusion is inescapable that he was a pious, religious Jew.

The Catholic scholar Bernard Lee in his recent study, "The Galilean Jewishness of Jesus", attributes merit to the conclusion of Rabbi Harvey Falk that Jesus could be termed a Pharisee of the Hillel school. Jesus did, as Lee points out, frequently teach from Pharisaic principles. Scholars urge that Jesus overall, even with his more rural, down-to-earth Jewishness, comes through as more like than unlike the liberal Pharisees of his day.

One of the truest marks of Jesus' Jewish education was his automatic answer to the scribe's question in Mark, "Which commandment is the first of all?" (Mk. 12.28) Jesus' response: "The first is, 'Hear, O Israel: The Lord our God, the Lord is one; and you shall love the Lord your God with all your heart, and with all your soul, and with all your mind, and with all you strength.' The second is this, 'You shall love your neigh-

bor as yourself.' There is no other commandment greater than these." That is quite close to the response that would be expected even today of a Jewish boy at his bar mitzvah.

Theologians agree that the teachings of Jesus cannot be fully understood without knowledge of the roots and branches of Judaism. There is truth in Disraeli's exaggeration that "Christianity is completed Judaism or it is nothing." Professor Emeritus W. D. Davies of Duke University says it more colorfully: "The Ark of the New Testament floated on Jewish waters."

The Beginnings of Anti-Semitism

Regrettably, the ties that could have bound Christianity and Judaism were severed by both people and events. In the beginning, in the early years after Jesus' death, Christian Jews and non-Christian Jews lived side-by-side in communal and familial harmony. A person could be simultaneously faithful to Judaism and a disciple of Jesus. Jewish Christians attended the synagogue and temple services and a few hours later celebrated their loyalty to Jesus over the family meal. But this religious harmony ended in a few decades; Acts and the letters of Paul graphically describe the hostility that developed between Christian and non-Christian Jews.

By the end of the century, there was not only anti-Judaism but anti-Semitism, if by the latter is meant frequently irrational racial hostility. That may have existed in some circles prior to the 1st Century, but nowhere near to the extent it did after the advent of Christianity.

Actually, the term anti-Semitism itself was not known until recent centuries and has led to a blurring of racial, religious and other concepts. Here, recognizing the imprecision pointed out by some scholars, it is used as commonly understood to mean both the irrational and masked rational antipathy for Jews and things Jewish, including but not limited to their religion.

Many have found the beginnings of anti-Semitism in the crucifixion of Jesus. But even laying aside the differences in the gospel accounts, it makes no sense to blame all Jews for the reactions of the relatively few Jews who gathered before Pontius Pilate – even if they did demand an execution, which many scholars seriously doubt.

In the face of the strong perception of Jewish responsibility held by many Christians, it is probably idle to argue to many that the Jews had no power to execute, that Pilate was a known brute and bully who hated the Jews and could hardly be portrayed as compassionately seeking to spare Jesus against the demands of a hostile crowd, and that the Gospel of Mark's "Barrabas custom" of releasing a condemned killer in honor of the Passover was no custom at all but an invention of the gospel writer.

Scholars have established that the Romans could very well have perceived Jesus as a political threat. They could well have taken the same view of him that Herod did of John the Baptist who, Josephus teaches, was executed as an incipient political threat, not as a reward for Salome's erotic dancing. These scholars argue that a Roman demand for Jesus' demise as a political threat is more believable than a conclusion that the Jews desired his death because he was claiming to be God. After all, the Jews had been accustomed for centuries to false prophets.

Scholars also argue persuasively that the stories of the crucifixion, written many years after the event itself, should be placed in the context of the times. Not long after Jesus' death the conflicts among Jews and Christians escalated over events entirely separate from Pontius Pilate's trial. Perhaps that helps account for the fact that the degree of Jewish involvement in the crucifixion trial and the degree of Jewish responsibility for the ultimate verdict increased as the gospels were written separately over the years.

Gentile-Jewish hostility is emphasized in Matthew, as is hostility to the non-Christian Jews by the Christian Jews. This hostility had been played down in earlier-written Mark. Then Luke, written near the end of the century, emphasizes Pilate's desire to free Jesus and has him acquitting Jesus three times, not satisfied with the once-mentioned verdict of Mark before the crowd demands execution. The version in John, the last written, is much more condemnatory of Jews than that of Mark.

Hostility of Jews to Christians (and vice versa) was not pronounced in the years immediately following the crucifixion. After years of study, Raymond Paul is convinced that the early Christians (most of whom were, after all, Jews themselves) thought that the Romans were responsible for the crucifixion. This could explain the portrayal in Acts of the Jerusalem Jews initially accepting the Christians after the crucifixion.

The Teachings of Paul

The growth of anti-Semitism in New Testament writings goes far beyond the crucifixion accounts. First came the teachings of Paul.

For the missionary Paul, faith in Jesus replaced the Jewish law. Jews who continued to adhere to the Mosaic law, deeply honored in all Jewish communities inside and outside of Palestine, were doomed to the "yoke of slavery" (Gal. 5.2). In contrast, those who departed from the law to become Christians would enjoy "love, joy, peace, long-suffering, gentleness, goodness, faith" (Gal. 5.22-23).

Paul repeatedly taught on the doorsteps of the synagogues to all who would listen in all the cities he visited that "all who rely on works of the law are under a curse." (Gal. 5.8-10) Those within hearing were not just converts and pagans but traditional Jews visiting their place of worship. They heard him teach that those who rejected Jesus were turning back "to the weak and beggarly elemental spirits whose slaves you want to be once more." (Gal. 4.8-9) Thus, they heard him argue that the Jewish law was an instrument of sin, that whether implemented through works and deeds or not, it essentially involved the slavery of men by evil spirits.

Imagine the deep feelings of these traditional Jews when they heard themselves and their highly respected Mosaic law thus cursed by Paul, a former Pharisee. The feelings persist; Nietzsche calls Paul "a genius in hatred." Anyone who studies Acts knows full well the physical retaliation inflicted on Paul by the traditional Jews in community after community.

Even stronger and more offensive to non-Christian Jews must have been Paul's words as recorded in Philippians. Defensively describing himself as "circumcised on the eighth day, of the people of Israel, of the tribe of Benjamin, a Hebrew boy born of Hebrews," Paul strikes out viciously at the "Judaizers" who oppose his work. He calls them "dogs", a curse theretofore reserved for pagan Gentiles (Jesus so used the word, Mk 7.27; Mt. 15.26). Paul preached, "Look out for the dogs, look out for the evil workers, look out for those who mutilate the flesh" (Philippians 3.2), referring, some say, to the conservative Jews rejecting Jesus and practicing circumcision.

In 1 Thessalonians 2.14-15, Paul attacks "the Jews who killed both the Lord Jesus and the prophets."

Then there are the vitriolic words by Paul about Jews who observe Jewish law. Scholars attempt to soften these attacks by pointing to his repeatedly-expressed pride in his Jewish heritage and his personal adherence to the law (it was Paul who circumcised his disciple, Timothy, because his mother was a Jew). Paul's battle was directed in the main against those he perceived as hypocritical Jews as well as those who tried to impose the strictures of the law on Jews converted to Christianity. But the effort here is not to decide whether Jews were justified in their resentment of Paul; rather, it is to note both its existence and its depth, as well as the role it played in the growth of animosity running deeply in both directions.

Contributing to this reciprocal animosity was also the teaching of Paul concerning the "two covenant" and "double rejection" theories. The former embodies the proposition that God replaced his covenant to the Jews as "His chosen people" with a new covenant favoring the Christians. The rejection theory argues that God rejected the Jews because they rejected Jesus. Anti-Pauline scholars have argued that this teaching went beyond the express words of Jesus who never taught that Jews who did not believe in him were rejected by God.

The gospels do, however, contain the parable stories where the rejection theory can be implied. The Parable of the Pounds (Lk. 19.12-27) is one example. In that story, Jesus concludes that death is due those who rejected the leader sent by the nobleman: "But as for these enemies of mine, who did not want me to reign over them, bring them here and slay them before me." The code is explained by Professor Michael J. Cook of the Hebrew Union College:

The nobleman is Jesus, his kingdom of God, those who send an embassy seeking to thwart his accession to dominion over them are the Jews, and the execution of these rebels upon the return of the nobleman now become king is the well-merited destruction of the Jews at the second coming. Once the Jews are destroyed the only ones remaining chosen, are by default, Gentiles.

Other examples are Mt. 8.11-12 where Gentiles replace Jews ("the sons of the Kingdom") at the table of Abraham, Isaac, and Jacob (sitting at this table signifies one's having attained the status of being chosen); and Mt. 22.8-10 "those invited [who] were not worthy" refers to the Jews, while the new persons recruited are the Gentiles). Then, there are the two parables of the wicked tenants and the stone (Matt. 21.33-44) and Jesus' conclusory remarks after telling these parables: "Therefore I tell you, the Kingdom of God will be taken away from you and given to a nation producing the fruits of it." In other words, taken away from the Jews not accepting Christianity and given to those who do.

Many scholars argue that these coded allegories are inventions of the gospel writers, not actually told by Jesus, and that they, like the teachings of Paul on the "second covenant" came long after the death of Jesus when Christianity had clearly been rejected by most Jews. They point to Hebrews which most scholars agree was written long after Jesus' death. Hebrews picks up on this theme and makes it even harder on the Jews. Pointing out that a Jew who violated the law of Moses "dies without mercy", Hebrews asks "How much worse punishment do you think will be deserved by the man who has spurned the Son of God?" (Heb. 10.29) It is not hard to imagine the animosity toward Christianity that these damnation concepts generated among Jews – in the 1st Century and for many centuries thereafter.

Another contrast between Judaism and Christianity employed in the early conversion battles was the Christian concept of redemption through confession. The Jewish law was portrayed by those seeking to convert the Jews as threatening severe penalties, even death in an extreme case. On the other hand, Christianity offered confession, forgiveness and new life. Jewish leaders cannot have liked hearing this contrast used in an effort to convert Jews away from their traditional religion.

There were, of course, many who could argue that Mosaic Law was too much maligned; that there were many Pharisees who rebelled against over-strict application of the law and that many Jews simply did not follow it. But, as so often happens it is not the facts but the perception of the facts that counts. And Jews in the early centuries, going far beyond the resentful Pharisees, developed strong anti-Christian beliefs and heaped primary blame on Paul. Unfortunately, their feelings were reciprocated, particularly among those Christian Jews who were so openly despised by their traditional Jewish brethren who adhered to the strict teachings of Judaism.

The Gospels of Matthew and John

After Paul came Matthew. Here, just thirty years after the death of Jesus and about ten years after Mark, we find for the first time in the accounts of Pilate's trial of Jesus the eternal curse on the Jews (Mt. 27.25): "The whole people cried out, `Let his blood be on us and on our children.'" A curse which one writer said has echoed down the dark and bloody corridors of the history of Jewish persecution.

Also in Matthew, Jesus is portrayed as condemning the Pharisees in what has come to be called the "Seven Woes" polemic (Mt. 23) which ends as follows: "You are sons of those who murdered the prophets. Fill up, then, the measure of your fathers. You serpents, you brood of vipers, how are you to escape being sentenced to hell?"

This vitriolic language aimed at the Pharisees (and possibly only the Shammai followers among the Pharisees) has never been forgotten by Jews who call it "infamous Matthew 23". Rabbinic Judaism reminds them constantly that it was the Pharisees who led Judaism back after the slaughter and slavery of the Jews by the Romans. Little wonder, then, the persistent Jewish dislike for Matthew 23 as a foundation for anti-Judaism, even though it is delimited on its face to the Pharisees. One Jewish scholar writes that "one can only guess at how many pogroms and persecutions against Jews" were caused by Matthew 23.

Finally, there is the Fourth Gospel, written towards the end of the 1st Century, which has had an even more devastating impact on Christian-Jewish relationships. In direct contrast with its reputation of containing the most beautiful passages about love to be found in the New Testament, the verses of John contain very emotional attacks on all Jews, stronger even than Matthew 23. One scholar puts the question boldly in a recent article, "Is it true that John is the `father of anti-semitism'?"

Even the posing of the question will come as a surprise to most Christians, a shock to many. Christians are vaguely aware of some of

John's attacks on Jews but put them on a par with those of Matthew, Mark and Luke and excuse them as being aimed at the Pharisees, or the "Jewish leaders," whatever that phrase means. But John does not so qualify the attacks.

The strong feelings that are evoked among Jews by the Gospel of John are best understood by reading exactly what the author did say about all Jews:

5.42: But I know that you [Jews] have not the love of God within you.

7.1: [Jesus] would not go about in Judea, because the Jews sought to kill him.

8.23-24: He said to them [the Jews], "… I told you that you would die in your sins, for you will die in your sins unless you believe that I am he."

8.31,40: Jesus then said to the Jews… "You seek to kill me… You are of your father the devil, and your will is to do your father's desires. He was a murderer from the beginning, and has nothing to do with the truth, because there is no truth in him. When he lies, he speaks according to his own nature, for he is a liar and the father of lies."

16.2-3: They will put you [the Jewish Christians] out of the synagogues; indeed, the hour is coming when whoever kills you will think he is offering service to God. And they will do this because they have not known the Father, nor me.

Apologists for John argue that the author, in using the word "Jews" was only referring to the antagonistic leaders as Jesus did when he attacked the Pharisees in Matthew 23. It is curious, though, that the author did not so specify. And even more curious is the failure of the apologists to address the key question: Did Jesus even say those words?

Bernard Lee, a highly respected Catholic scholar, in "The Galilean Jewishness of Jesus", argues that the words reflected the feelings not of Jesus but of the Christian Jews late in the 1st Century: "Much of the bitterness we feel in the gospels [toward Jews] is the anguish of the post-70 period read back into the historical life of Jesus."

The Gospel of John is but an extreme example of the attacks on non-Christian Jews that were hallmarks of the 1st century Jesus movement. E.P. Sanders discusses the ways in which Christians falsely labeled Judaism and the non-Christian Jews. And the Jews, regrettably, reciprocated.

The Invective Did Not End With the 1st Century

This brings us to the end of the 1st Century – but the attacks on the Jews continued. St. John Chrysostom reportedly taught that synagogues should be compared to brothels.

Justin Martyr's 2nd century dialogue with Trypho describes Jesus as a magician who led people astray and refers to the story circulated in Jewish communities that the disciples of Jesus had stolen the body of Jesus from the tomb in an effort to prove the resurrection. Celsus in the 3rd century repeats the stories of a Jewish informant that Jesus was of lowly origin and invented the virgin birth to hide his mother's adultery.

The highly respected Jerome, viewed as one of the writing founders of the Christian church, describes Jewish prayers as akin to the grunting of pigs and braying of donkeys. Professor Grant, the Protestant scholar, describes in theological detail the "strained and bitter feelings which attended the separating of church from synagogue."

The Jews on the street and in social and family gatherings naturally furthered the Pharisaic dispute with Christianity. What resulted in the folklore was a parody of Jesus. The fireside stories portrayed his mother as playing the harlot with a Roman soldier named Pandira. These stories reached their culmination at some point in antiquity in the Jewish polemical biography of Jesus called "Toledot Yeshu", discussed earlier, which reached its full form in the Middle Ages when it was widely circulated throughout Europe and provided for many years for many Jews virtually all they ever knew about Jesus.

Anti-Semitism in the Middle Ages

Nurtured by stories like Toledot Yeshu and fed by the emotional fires roused by the gospel teachings regarding Jewish beliefs and Jewish law, a wholly negative, destructive attitude towards Jesus became prevalent in Jewish communities everywhere, well-developed by the time of the Middle Ages. At best, there was a cold neutrality. Christians were blamed for many evils that beset the Jews, and Jews were continually blamed by Christians for the crucifixion. Basic racial prejudices were intensified with time. Intermarriage, always one of the great prejudice kindlers for mankind, was rare and highly disapproved – it was viewed at least as disparagingly as color-combining.

In many Jewish families, a child who married a Christian was treated as dead. The same antipathy, even if not the same result, was reciprocated. On the Christian side, anti-Judaism and anti-Semitism led to and fed the physical persecution of the Jews that persisted over the centuries. Cruelty abounded in Europe and the East. Jews argue with justice that they have been the most persecuted group in the history of civilization, repeatedly massacred, tortured, burned, uprooted and totally expelled from both communities and entire countries, like England and Spain in Europe. All bloody chapters in the history of man's inhumanity to man. Time and again they were forced by torture to choose death or Christianity. Sometimes, no alternative was offered.

In the Middle Ages, Catholic liturgy for Good Friday referred openly to "the perfidious Jews" and that day became a day of fear and punishment for Jews throughout Eastern Europe. After mass, Christian bigots would frequently ride their horses on destructive rampages through the Jewish communities. Jews were repeatedly blamed for outbreaks of the

Black Death. They were charged with ritual murders of Christians and lurid tales surrounded accusations against Jews from whom, not incidentally, the authorities would enrich themselves by seizing all property. They were accused of stealing Christian children and using their blood in religious rites related to circumcision. Those charged were sometimes tortured into admissions of guilt and then executed by burning; a recent historical study shows one method where a dying Jewish man is pictured hung by his feet, upside down over an open fire, side-by-side with hungry dogs suspended by their hind legs, ravenous jaws reaching for the man's body.

Fortunately, with the Reformation came some relief for the Jews of central Europe. Even this, however, was short lived; Martin Luther gave vent to anti-Semitism in his declining years. Finally, with the French Revolution in the 18th Century, some of the governmental shackles were removed along with some of the worst forms of anti-Jewish cruelty. Not because of reversal of basic attitudes toward the Jews, unfortunately, but because freedom generally was in the air. The ensuing hundred years were marked by actions in various European countries which materially increased freedoms afforded to all people. Many European Jews did finally "escape the ghetto walls", although many remained.

Anti-Semitism in Recent Centuries

When fundamentalism became strong among Protestants in the 19th Century, it brought a strong literal interpretation of the words of the New Testament and this led to some unintended results. The vituperative language of Matthew and John haunted Christianity even in the free world. It was particularly strong in rural and southern America. Professor Grant criticizes this unfortunate by-product of fundamentalism:

One of the most tragic results of a literal interpretation of the New Testament is the support which has been derived from it for anti-Semitism, one of the blackest and most ineradicable blemishes upon the modern world." (Grant, An Introduction to New Testament Thought, p. 96.)

With the 20th Century came Hitler and Nazism. From the beginning of the Third Reich in the 1930's, Hitler used the Jews as scapegoats and passages from the New Testament to further his evil ends. Mein Kampf cites the New Testament in support of Hitler's virulent attacks on the Jewish people. Following his lead, Julius Streicher, founder of the Nazi newspaper *Der Sturmer*, castigated the Jews before 200,000 massed German youths in 1935: "Don't believe in priests so long as they defend people whom Christ called `sons of the Devil.'" Professor John Pawlowski of the Catholic Theological Union puts it bluntly: "Christian anti-Semitism served as indispensable seed bed and primary motivation for many who cooperated with the Nazi's `final solution.'" The pejorative words of John, placed in the mouth of Jesus, were cited by those who led the pogroms, Crystallnacht, and Dachau.

And the anti-Semitism was not confined to Germany. Too common in America during the 1930's and 1940's was the statement, "Hitler is wrong about a lot of things but he's sure right about the Jews." It took the full facts of the genocide, the death of six million Jews, to awaken many to the awful evil covered up by banal anti-Semitism. The holocaust did finally open the eyes of countless skeptics. As Geza Vermes puts it, "In the shadow of the chimneys of the death camps, anti-Judaism, even academic anti-Judaism, has become not only unfashionable but obscene."

Reacting, some say, to the charges of Papal silence during the holocaust years, the Roman Catholic Church in its Nostra Aetate of the 2d Vatican Council finally officially exculpated the Jews as a race from responsibility for Jesus' death and repudiated the doctrine attributed to Paul that Jews were a people rejected by God. A recent book,

Constantine's Sword (James Carroll, Houghton Mifflin, 2001), explores at great length the uneasy history of Jewish-Catholic relations.

However, there is still a feeling expressed by some critics that the Nostra Aetate did not go far enough and that the Catholic Church did not speak out strongly enough about the slaughter of Jews by Hitler's Germany. Pope John has recognized the continued existence of the problem of anti-semitism.

Despite these efforts, polls show that as many as ten percent of American Catholics still see the Jews as principally responsible for the death of Jesus and, worse, allow it to lead to a negative assessment of contemporary Jews. These Catholics are not alone; the virus of anti-Semitism remains very alive through vandalism and graffiti in cities of America. Regrettably, what Vermes called an obscenity still lurks in millions of minds.

The Winds of Change

Fortunately, anti-Semitism has become a widely condemned practice in America. Helping achieve that result has been the world-wide respect for the establishment, growth and international success of Israel. One Jewish scholar finds hope in the fact that some fundamentalists untouched even by Auschwitz have been moved by the State of Israel. The Jewish religion, too, has changed. Liberal Judaism has come to life. The Reform movement is fully established and takes its place alongside the orthodox. A middle group has emerged, particularly in America, called Conservative Judaism, neither orthodox nor reform.

And a different view of Jesus has emerged from some of the reformed Jewish sources. Some Jewish scholars have gone so far as to downplay the responsibility of Jesus for the "new covenant" and "double rejection" theories, concluding that Paul was mostly to blame. Jesus was a "Jewish rabbi" espousing "proper Jewish ethics" and was misinterpreted by his later followers. He was, in short, a laudable teacher whose benevolence, decency, philosophy and ethics should be respected.

One Jewish scholar has concluded that Jesus' ethical code, by itself, could be viewed as a "choice treasure in the literature of Israel," a view akin to that of Spinoza in the Seventeenth Century who did not accept the divinity of Jesus but placed him "first among men." Some Jewish scholars argue that Jesus should be welcomed to the ranks of Jews who have marked human history, both religious and secular, men such as Moses, King David, Maimonides, Spinoza, Freud, and Einstein.

Some Jewish scholars argue that there is no essential difference between some teachings of Jesus and strains of rabbinic Judaism, particularly the school of Hillel, existing at the time of Jesus. To reach the opposite result, they argue, requires giving undue emphasis to distortion and exaggeration of Jesus' words by the author-evangelists who wrote long after the death of Jesus.

The process of reaching these conclusions has been called the "Jewish reclamation of Jesus." However, despite this "new" Jewish scholarship, the mainstream approach to Christianity among Jewish people generally does not seem to have changed a great deal. At the other extreme, the orthodox Jews argue that the liberal view treating Jesus in a more accommodating manner amounts to "truckling" or "kowtowing" to the Christian religion. The middle ground Jews, most of whom are totally unaware of the scholarship to the right or the left, probably would for traditional reasons resist any open "reclamation of Jesus." Many remain understandably puzzled as to why, if Jews are resented for not accepting Jesus, equal feeling of hostility is not extended to all non-Christians. One answer of course is that, regrettably, anti-Semitism is far broader than the New Testament words.

Just as emotional anti-Semitism and anti-Judaism persist among many, there is still considerable criticism of Christianity in Jewish circles. Some continue to complain that the Old Testament was "stolen" from Judaism and it is more than occasionally argued that Paul,

Matthew and John "paved the way to Auschwitz." Scholars continue to take the view that Christians have misinterpreted Jesus' teachings – that he was a "rabble rouser" whose real views condemned the learned and respectable people as the true sinners.

On theological grounds, what has come to be called the two-covenant theology (the new promise to Christians following the original covenant by God to the Jews as his chosen people) continues to divide Judaism and Christianity just as it did when first enunciated by Paul in the 1st Century. The fundamentalists still espouse it. No matter how hard well-meaning theologians try to rationalize or compromise, the Jewish rejection or supersession theory stands in the way of ecumenicism.

The "one-covenant widened" approach which gives chronological primacy to Judaism still leaves Jews in a second-class status after the Christians join the broadened covenant. They still must, as with the theology of the "two parallel covenants," accept Jesus before finally entering the Kingdom of God. To use Paul's olive tree allegory, the branch remains severed; the Jews are suspended in either sinful schism or only temporary legitimacy. And Jewish religious leaders such as Rabbi Eliezer Berkowits can still say that Christian dogma continues to prevent dialogue and fuel anti-Semitism:

We reject the idea of inter-religious understanding as immoral because it is an attempt to whitewash the criminal past. (Judaism, Jan. 1966, p. 74)

A dramatic (and unlikely) answer to the ecumenical dilemma would be a frank blind-alley admission of doctrinal irreconciliation and a joint confession that the ultimate resolution by God remains a mystery, an inscrutable portion of the plans of God. This, of course, will be rejected by the conservatives of both religious persuasions. Or, equally unlikely, Christians could simply set aside the literal reading of the dual covenant texts. After all, say some few scholars, Christians have rejected the New Testament teaching with respect to acceptance of slaves and denigration of women – why not emancipate the Jews from the two covenant theory?

Probably, though, more progress toward ecumenism can be made by less controversial efforts to remove "rough spots" and harmonize relationships. Jewish scholars are breaking relatively new ground, as has been pointed out. Modern Christian scholarship is increasingly recognizing the Old Testament view of man's relationship to God and is also saying more and more that some of the most virulent anti-Jewish passages in the gospels are the product of later-date evangelists, not the words of Jesus. Why not simply say, as Professor Grant urges: "My Jesus could not have uttered those words."

More and more scholars and theologians are saying openly that recognition of the essential continuity between Judaism and Christianity is a basis for mutual respect and engagement. Some scholars suggest that troublesome roots and anti-semitism are in the over-Hellenized interpretation of the New Testament which took Christianity away from its original, natural, communal, social, ethical and egalitarian concerns shared with and derived from Judaism.

Another avenue for Christianity is utilizing New Testament footnotes and annotations explaining the context of the attacks on Jews, particularly in Matthew and John. An example is the headnote to the Gospel in the New American Bible, The New Catholic Translation (Thomas Nelson, N.Y. 1971). After explaining that the writing of the Gospel in the last decade of the 1st Century went through two stages including first one of the apostle John's disciples and then an editor, the headnote goes on (p. 1140):

The polemic between the synagogue and the church influenced Johannine language toward harshness especially by reason of the hostility toward Jesus manifested by the authorities – Pharisees and Sadducees – who are referred to frequently as "the Jews." Today, there is a very real effort by Christians and Jews to understand one another and thus to eliminate all embittered criticism.

But as earlier noted, many scholars argue that the author of John was reacting to the synagogue-Christian Jew fight, not merely the Pharisee-Sadducee leadership. The Sadducees were gone when the Jewish Christians were expelled from the synagogues after the revolt. But at least there is recognition in the headnote of the need to understand the context in which the words of John were used.

Another example of progress is the total omission in some recent Bible commentaries of the explanation involving rejection of the Jews as God's chosen people, so offensive to many Jews, and their replacement by the Gentiles. Why do not more religious leaders simply say, "Jesus did not teach that." But again, the door is at least left open for a discussion of whether these anti-Jewish themes originated with Jesus.

Obviously, much more can and needs to be done to at least expose thoughtful Christians and Jews to the results of modern scholarship. The more that message reaches practicing Christians and Jews, the better opportunity there is for the furtherance of the ecumenical spirit. Ultimately and hopefully it could become everywhere a relationship akin to that existing a few years after the crucifixion when Jews who were converted lived, loved and worked with those who were not.

Hans Küng has said it well from the Christian side of the fence: "Religions, Christianity, the Church, cannot solve or prevent all the world's conflicts, but they can begin to do away with at least the conflicts of which they themselves are the cause and for whose explosiveness they are partly to blame."

And all Americans should join in constantly emphasizing that anti-Semitism in America not only has been but is now not just dismal and humiliating but catastrophic to necessary religious understanding.

Appendix

Editions and Versions of the Bible

A Biblical scholar wrote recently that he was asked, "If God inspired the New Testament and was 'at the elbow' of the writers, why do we need so many different editions and versions?" Good question. There may be only one edition in the bible rack at each church, but there are many different versions in the bookstores, both lay and religious. Catholics and a variety of Protestant sects each claim to have the best version. And a number of entirely new editions and versions have been published in the last few years. What accounts for all of this?

Several factors, say the scholars. First, there are now 5,338 ancient Greek manuscripts containing the gospels – in whole or fragment form. None have been dated by the paleographers to the 1st Century; the earliest complete text of the gospels is mid-4th Century. And for over 1400 years, versions of the New Testament were copied by hand; scholars note that they made many, many mistakes.

Complicating the problem, certain churches have become wedded to particular manuscripts, ignoring older ones that came to light; examples are the Catholic Church's long adherence to translations from the Latin Vulgate, and the tenacious hold of the King James Version on many Protestants.

Finally, there have been dramatic steps in reconstructing old Greek texts and improving translational methods. Startling discoveries like the Dead Sea Scrolls have, while not yielding any new manuscripts of New Testament books, disclosed several long-hidden apocryphal gospels and shed tremendous light on the 1st Century usage of Greek, thereby greatly improving translation abilities of the scholars.

These are today's most widely used editions and versions:

1. **King James Authorized Version (KJAV)**, still distributed by Gideons and used in many churches in America. There is a revised version of the King James. (KJRV; 1885)

2. **Revised Standard Version (RSV) and New Revised Standard Version (NRSV; 1992)**. Historically, these developed out of the King James tradition.

3. **Revised English Bible (REB; 1989)** which replaced the New English Bible (NEB). These are the British Protestant inheritors of the King James tradition.

4. **New International Version (NIV; 1978)**. A product of evangelical scholars, it is often called the conservative alternative to the RSV and NRSV and claims to be closer to the original KJAV.

5. **New American Standard Bible (NASB; 1973)**, another conservative Protestant version more closely tied to the KJAV.

6. **New American Bible (NAB; 1987)**. New edition of the American Catholic bible.

7. **New Jerusalem Bible (NJB; 1985)**. New edition of the Catholic bible widely used in Europe.

8. **Good News Bible (also called Today's English Version; 1966)**, and **The Living Bible (a paraphrased version)**. Both are designed for popular usage, written in everyday English; variously used by both Protestants and Catholics.

Catholic traditionalists still like the Knox Bible, a 1954 translation from the Latin Vulgate. Some still use the Confraternity of Christian Doctrine version of 1960. Jehovah's Witnesses have their version – "New World Translation of the Holy Scriptures" (1961). There are several Gideon's editions based on the King James (International, New King James, and Revised Berkeley). And, finally, there are a variety of reference bibles available; for example, the New Scofield Reference Bible (1967).

What impact does this wide choice have on practicing Christians? Very little to most; the Sunday service Christian will rarely perceive the differences, even when his or her church places new versions in the bible racks. But it matters considerably to some and certainly to those who take their bible studies seriously.

Before tracing the development of these various versions and summarizing what the bible scholars say about reasons for making choices among the multitude now available, it is worthwhile to look at some samples of their many differences. Some are fascinating and arouse strong feelings; they go far beyond what could be termed trivial matters. None, however, involves any really essential questions of Christian faith.

The Brothers and Sisters of Jesus

The centuries-old controversy over the reality of Jesus' "brothers and sisters" has been discussed in an earlier chapter; pointed out there is the very strong Catholic tradition that Jesus may have had cousins, but no blood brothers and sisters. In Mark 3.32, the NRSV refers to Jesus' "mother, brothers and sisters" in describing the family. The NASB, REB, NIV and NAB editions eliminate "sisters"; the family is "mother and brothers". The Catholic Knox Bible and the King James versions all eliminate both "brothers and sisters," leaving "mother" and "brethren."

Some of the Bible commentaries explain the problem, which is caused by the Catholic doctrine of Mary's perpetual virginity —Jesus could not have either brothers or sisters. Jerome's Bible Commentary points it up by saying with respect to the Greek word which most editions interpret as "brother": "This word must be taken as kinsmen."

Rejection of Jesus by His Family

There is another controversy involving Jesus' family, together with his mental state: Whether the family disavowed him as deranged, also discussed in an earlier chapter. Mark 3 tells the story of Jesus' return home after a tumultuous reception by "great multitudes" from Galilee and Judea. Then, this is inserted (Mark 3.21; using the King James Version): "And when his friends heard of it, they went out to lay hold on him: for they said, He is beside himself."

KJAV has Jesus "friends" hearing of it and laying hold on him "for he is beside himself." NIV changes "friends" to "people" and says as to Jesus that he "lost his senses". NJV uses "relations" instead of "friends" or "people" and has Jesus "out of his mind." RSV uses "family" and "beside himself", and has Jesus "seized" by the family; NRSV changes that word to "restrain" and uses "out of his mind."

The NIV, REB, and NAB are basically the same: "When his family heard about this, they went out to take charge of him, saying, 'He is out of his mind.'" Some versions go even further, saying "He's gone mad" or was "deranged", and having his family "take him by force".

The controversial issues are whether Jesus was "seized" or "restrained" or "laid hold of" by his relations or family, or by non-family people, and whether he was deemed to be simply upset ("beside himself"), or mentally unbalanced ("gone out of his mind", "gone mad", or "deranged"). The translations implying dementia are rejected by those scholars who attribute Jesus' perceived strangeness to an "ecstatic" state of mind.

Some scholars argue that this verse supports the theory that Jesus' own family (including his mother) were not aware of his divinity; otherwise, they would not have regarded him as deranged. The King James Version totally avoids the issue by omitting any reference to the family. NIV, REB, and NAB quite definitely have the family both taking charge and evaluating Jesus' mental condition. NRSV is in the middle – it involves the family in taking charge of Jesus, but very carefully has not the family but "people" commenting on Jesus' mental condition. Particularly interesting is the change from RSV where Jesus is "beside himself" to NRSV where Jesus "has gone out of his mind."

Leading Bible commentaries (Jerome, Harper, Wycliff, Collegeville) all interpret the verse as saying that it was his family that took charge of Jesus and that, whatever the exact words, the Greek manuscripts intended to say that the family thought his mental faculties were temporarily affected.

The Mariology Controversies

There are two controversies involving Mariology. First is the salutation to Mary by the visiting angel; the second goes back to Isaiah's prophecy of the virgin birth.

First, the angel's salutation to Mary. Catholics know by heart these traditional words, "Hail Mary, full of grace, blessed are thou among women". First, there is scholarly dispute over this passage. Luke 1.28 attributes this language to the angel in the Douay version taken from the Latin Vulgate. Raymond Brown, the noted Catholic scholar, states in his work, "Mary in the New Testament", that "it would be defended by few scholars today", and that "it is almost certainly a later addition to Luke's text by a scribe."

None of the most widely-used versions of the New Testament in circulation today have the Douay statement in the angel's greeting; most of it ("blessed are you among women and blessed is the fruit of your womb") does appears in the statement of Elizabeth when Mary visits her before the birth of Jesus (Lk 1.42; see NRSV, NEB, KJAV, NAB). And there are differences, too, in the wording of the salutation as given to Mary by the angel in Lk 28. Jerome's Bible Commentary does not have it in full as quoted above. It has the greeting, "Hail, full of grace, the Lord is with you", but omits the words "Blessed are you among women", noting that they appear only in "some inferior Greek manuscripts." RSV and NSRV use the same shortened version. The versions in other editions follow:

KJV: "Hail, thou that art highly favored, the Lord is with thee; blessed are thou among women."

NASB: "Hail favored one! The Lord is with you."

NRSV: "Greetings, favored one. The Lord is with you."

REB: "Greetings, most favored one! The Lord is with you."

NAB: "Rejoice, O highly favored daughter. The Lord is with you. Blessed are you among women."

NJB: "Rejoice, you who enjoy God's favor. The Lord is with you."

NIV: "Greetings, you who are highly favored, the Lord is with you."

The Way: "Congratulations, favored lady! The Lord is with you!"

Good News Bible: "Peace be with you! The Lord is with you and has greatly blessed you."

The second Mariology controversy involves the virgin birth. The Old Testament, specifically Isaiah 7.14, was cited as the prophecy for the virgin birth: "The Lord ... will give you a sign; it is this: A virgin is with child, and she will give birth to a son and call him Immanuel." The KJAV, NIV, NAB, and NASB all use the word "virgin". REB and NRSV use "young woman", but the NRSV has a footnote stating "or virgin.

It would be hard to find other passages where the variations among various editions so dramatically illustrate the tension among three factors motivating different translations: Religious doctrine or tradition, modern translation philosophy and word-for-word literalcy.

Who Are the Blessed Poor?

One of the most beautiful and treasured portions of the New Testament is Matthew's Sermon on the Mount. (Mt. 5.1ff) It does not appear in Mark at all; Luke has it, but places the event on a "level place", leading scholars to call it the "Sermon on the Plain." (Lk. 6.17ff) For unknown reasons of their own, Matthew has Jesus addressing a small group of disciples on the mountain; Luke has Jesus giving the talk to a huge crowd assembled on the plain.

Some scholars suggest that the "sermon" was not actually delivered as a body or speech by Jesus, but that the versions in Matthew and Luke are a piecing together by the author-evangelist of separately spoken sayings or statements by Jesus.

The first of the so-called Beatitudes addressed to the disciples, whether there were many or few, whether they were on a mountain or on a plain, deals with the poor. (Mt. 5.3) The RSV has it this way: "Blessed are the poor in spirit, for theirs is the kingdom of heaven"; so does the NAB. Does "in spirit" mean spiritually? Or mentally, as in "dispirited"?

The Lucan version drops the words "in spirit". NIV and NASB have it this way: "Blessed are you who are poor, for yours is the kingdom of God." (Lk. 6.20) Here, the reference is rather clearly to the materially poor. The REB changes it a little: Blessed are you who are in need; the Kingdom of God is yours." This could refer to either spiritual or material need.

Which of these meanings did the gospel writer of either Matthew or Luke intend? Which should the translator choose? When the preacher prepares his sermon, which does he use? Clearly, the well-to-do congregation would like to hear the "in spirit" added to avoid the thought that wealth may inhibit their entry to heaven. And equally as clearly, the needy would like to hear the opposite, telling them that the Golden Gates are wide open to the poor.

Did God Reject the Jews?

Outright omission of key words extremely offensive to Jews but important to fundamentalists is involved in some versions; in the instance here discussed, it involves the popular-language translations. Paul's letters to Galatians (Gal. 6.16); has this sentence addressed to the Christians (NRSV):

"Peace be upon them, and mercy, and upon the Israel of God."

The key phrase is "Israel of God," meaning to the Jews God's chosen people. Paul in Galatians argued that Christians became the selected people of God, superseding the original chosen people, the Jews.

This is known as the "doctrine of supercession" and is, of course, highly offensive to believers in Judaism, who naturally still consider themselves to be the "Israel of God." On the other hand, there are very conservative Protestant sects who insist on emphasizing the so-called "Second Covenant" or "New Covenant", the replacement of Jews by Christians as "God's chosen people." Perhaps for this reason, the phrase is eliminated from several modern translations of Paul's words, including one ("Today's English") incorporated in The New Catholic Study Bible which carries the imprimatur of the Catholic Archbishop of Philadelphia:

Galatians 6.16 in The Way and The Living Bible:

"May God's mercy and peace be upon all of you who live by this principle and upon those everywhere who are really God's own."

In The Bible in Today's English:

"As for those who follow this rule in their lives, may peace and mercy be with them – with them and with all of God's people."

Each of these translations described God's blessing upon the Christians. But completely absent is the reference to replacement or supercession by Christians of the unbelieving Jews, as conveyed by Paul's phrase "Israel of God". Is this translation or rewriting?

Kill or Murder?

The translation problems are not limited to the New Testament. A translation difficulty in the Old Testament is the choice of a word in God's Sixth Commandment (Exodus 20.13), a word that is extremely important to pacifists and those opposed to the death penalty.

The King James, followed by RSV, NAB and NJB, reads: "Thou shalt not kill" (or "you shall not kill.") The NRSV, REB, NIV, Good News Bible, Living Bible and Knox (an interesting mix of very modern and very traditional) all substitute the word "murder" for "kill".

The Hebrew Tanakh uses "murder," not "kill," and most modern Christian Bible commentaries, Catholic and Protestant (Wycliff, Harper, Jerome, Collegeville) speak of a prohibition of "murder."

The same translation problem carries over into the New Testament in Mt. 5.21: "Ye have heard it said … `thou shalt not kill.'" This is KJAV; "kill" also appears in NKJV, NJB, and RSV. The word is changed to "murder" in NIV, NRSV, and NAB.

Obviously, there is a substantial difference between "kill" and "murder." How many times has the Sixth Commandment been cited by those opposing capital punishment and going to war? For those who believe in literalcy of every word in the Bible, which translation do they choose?

The Lord's Prayer

The ending of the Lord's prayer (Mt. 6.13) varies from Protestant to Catholic churches. In most Protestant churches, the ending is customarily, "For thine is the kingdom and the power and the glory forever. Amen." It appears this way in the KJAV and the NASB but is relegated to a footnote in the REB, NIV and NRSV, and does not appear at all in the NAB or the NJV. It is not used by Catholics as a part of the Lord's Prayer.

And even the frequently-used line from the King James and almost universally recited during services, "and lead us not into temptation but deliver us from evil", is not always the same in the various editions. NJV, NRSV, and REB, for example, have it, "And do not put us to the test [or time of trial], but save us from the evil one."

The Eucharist

Luke 22.19b-20 present the issue; here are the verses in the NRSV describing the Last Supper:

"(19b) Then he took a loaf of bread, and when he had given thanks he broke it and gave it to them, saying 'This is my body which is given for you. Do this in remembrance of me.' (20) And likewise the cup after supper, saying, 'This cup which is poured out for you is the new covenant of my blood.'"

The controversy involves the words "Do this in remembrance of me". These words in the Gospel of Luke do not appear in either the Marcan version of the Last Supper (Mk. 14.23-24), or the Matthean version (Mt. 26.26-28).

The NRSV footnotes these words in Luke with the statement, "other ancient authorities [meaning ancient manuscripts] lack, in whole or in part, verses 19b-20." So does NASB. KJAV, NJB, and NAB have all of

19b-20, including the disputed words, without any footnote. REB leaves the words out of the text but footnotes their existence in "some" manuscripts. RSV went back and forth between text and footnote in various editions. The Douay-Rheims footnotes the words "Do this for a commemoration of me", saying that this "sacrament is to be continued in the church to the end of the world."

The absence of these words in some of the ancient manuscripts of the Gospel of Luke as noted by some of today's versions together with their absence from the other two Synoptic Gospels (Mark and Matthew) leads many scholars to the conclusion that they are a post-crucifixion add-on by the early evangelists. Their appearance in Paul's 1 Cor. 11.23-26 is argued as confirming this conclusion since Paul arguably based his version of the Last Supper on his observance of the practices in the post-crucifixion house churches. But even if verses 19b-20 are to be included in the Gospel, what about the words "do this in remembrance of me" which appear only in Matthew, not in any of Mark, Luke or John? Did Jesus say them or not? Many scholars vote "no" on this question.

Another problem is the reference to the "new covenant of my blood". KJAV uses the words "new testament", a very puzzling translation; all other versions use "covenant". Some omit the word "new", possibly in deference to the controversy over whether Jesus (unlike Paul) ever espoused the so-called new covenant theory that Christians replaced Jews as the chosen people of God.

Speaking in Tongues and Handling Snakes

Mark 16.17-18 is a part of the "longer ending" which scholars agree was added long after the gospel was written. Favored (and viewed as inspired) by some fundamentalist charismatic sects which speak in "tongues" and handle serpents, it describes "signs" or "miracles" which will accompany those who believe. Versions differ as to what the "believers" do:

They will: "speak with tongues," or "speak new languages." They will: "handle snakes", "pick up snakes with their hands", or "If they pick up snakes, they will not be harmed."

As to the choice between "new languages" or "tongues", the charismatics obviously prefer "tongues." Snake handling sects want to have the snakes actually "handled" or "picked up with hands", with the added reassuring language, left out in some versions, that "they will not be harmed."

The New Testament Add-Ons

Different versions and editions do not always agree on the few portions of the New Testament that have consistently been labeled from ancient times as add-ons by unknown persons after the original text was written. These verses cause great problems for the literalists.

For example, there is the episode in John where Jesus defends the adulterous woman about to be stoned for her sins: "He that is without sin among you, let him first cast a stone at her." (Jn. 7.53-8.11) This passage has long been viewed by scholars as a later-date insertion. It appears out of place textually and is totally missing from the best Greek manuscripts relied on for the New Testament text; when and how it crept into the gospel are unknown. Some versions footnote this or insert a heading (NAB, REB, NRSV, NIV). Of course, for fundamentalists, it is canonical and inspired as part of the text as found in the King James Version.

Chapter 21 of John is an add-on made rather obvious from the text itself (or so the scholars say) and was recognized as such by 2d Century commentators. They reasoned that it was added by an editor working on a revision of the gospel before it achieved any circulation of consequence among the Christian communities. Again, few editions or versions explain this chapter as an editorial add-on; practically all do not, treating the added verses as a part of the original text.

The so-called Marcan Longer Ending (Mark 16:9-20) is similarly treated. NAB recognizes the problem but says that 9-20 "have been traditionally accepted as an inspired part of the gospel." KJAV ignores the problem. REB, NASB, NIV, NRSV call attention to the problem with footnotes stating that "most reliable" or "earliest" manuscripts do not have verses 9-20.

The "longer ending" includes the famous "go into the whole world" charge to the apostles (leading scholars to argue that it is a post-resurrection, hindsight insertion). It also includes the above-discussed controversial verses about handling snakes and drinking poisons with immunity. Vocabulary and style make it clear that the entire longer ending was written by someone other than the author of the gospel.

Jesus Riding Two Donkeys

Going from the certainly divisive and almost divine to the amusingly inconsequential variations, there is the story of the two donkeys and Jesus' celebrated entry into Jerusalem on Palm Sunday, done in a manner fulfilling an Old Testament precedent. The King James Version has the Matthean picture of Jesus sending his disciples to obtain his entry mount from a nearby farm. Matthew (21.5) first quotes from Scripture the story of the triumphant King:

"As it was written, the King cometh sitting upon an ass, and a colt, the foal of an ass."

The King James Old Testament has the same language in Zechariah 9.9. Then, Matthew describes the scene as the disciples: "brought the ass, and the colt, and put on them their clothes, and they set him [Jesus] thereon." (Mt. 21.6)

The picture is complete – although strange – of Jesus astride both a larger and a smaller animal, the colt and the ass, the same double-animal ride of the king in Zechariah.

The RSV corrects the Old Testament statement; it has only one animal in Zechariah 9.9: The king rides "on an ass, on a colt the foal of an ass." The word "and" between "ass" and "colt" is not there; the Hebrew Bible translation is the same as the RSV Old Testament. In the same RSV edition, however, the New Testament Matthew story retains the "and", keeping Jesus "mounted on an ass, and on a colt, the foal of an ass."

The silly confusion continues in other editions. NAB says, "they brought the ass and the colt and laid their cloaks on them, and he mounted. Mounted one or two? The popular language versions stay with the ambiguous, two-animal translation (Today's English Version): "They [the disciples] brought the donkey and the colt, threw their cloaks over them, and Jesus got on."

One solution is to just ignore Matthew and turn in any edition to the Palm Sunday story as told by any of Mark, Luke, or John. In each of these gospels, both Jesus and the King are clearly riding one animal: "And Jesus found a young ass and sat upon it; as it is written, `Fear not, daughter of Zion; behold your king is coming, sitting on an ass's colt.'" (Jn. 12.14-15) "And they brought the colt to Jesus, and threw their garments on it; and he sat upon it." (see Mk. 11.7, Lk. 19.35)

Noah Webster Corrected the King James

Noah Webster published a King James Version in 1833 in which he corrected about 150 words and phrases. In Matthew 23.24, for example, there was the phrase "strain at a gnat and swallow a camel." Webster identified this as a printer's error and corrected it to read "strain out a gnat." But even obvious error is not easily remedied in the King James

Version; the former language still appears in modern editions. Other versions widely circulated today go with Webster.

*   *   *

There are other anomalies; for example, the spurious King James text about the three heavenly witnesses in 1 John 5.7. It is not in any of the ancient Greek manuscripts and was apparently inserted by Erasmus in the New Testament assembled by him in the 16th Century.

And there is Deuteronomy 32.18. RSV and NIV have it "You forgot the God who gave you birth." The words about God giving birth raise the controversy; feminists point to the Hebrew bible where the words "gave you birth" are, literally, "writhing in labor", and wonder at the NJV translation to "fathered you" and the KJAV, "God formed thee." The New Jerusalem Bible Commentary supports the feminists, saying "God gave birth, a maternal attribution."

Once more, the question remains – what difference do all of the above-discussed variances in editions and versions really make? To all, the humorous confusion in Matthew over the animals which Jesus rode is non-consequential. To the casual Christian, none of these variances matter. But, taking some of the variations individually, there are some who care deeply. For example, to the believers in Mary's perpetual virginity, to the zealous Mariology followers, to particular narrow sects, to the pacifists, to the missionaries, some of the differences discussed above can be exceedingly important, going to the very heart of their individual beliefs.

Overall, none of these variations can be placed in context without understanding the development of the English language versions of the New Testament.

Development of English Language Bibles

The Gutenberg bible of 1456, the first one printed, contained the Latin Vulgate version used for centuries by Catholics and originally translated from Greek to Latin by Jerome in the 4th Century. The first English Bible was John Wycliff's word-for-word translation in 1384 of the Latin Vulgate into English, largely written while he was in prison. Called heresy by the Catholic Church, the translation led to his body being exhumed and burned in 1428.

Then, William Tyndale, a partisan of Luther, produced in 1526 Tyndale's Bible, the first printed English version, a direct translation from the original Greek relying not on Jerome's Latin but on the work of Erasmus of Rotterdam who in 1516 printed the New Testament from selected Greek manuscripts. Tyndale's version also angered the Catholic Church. It was burned by the Bishop of London and in 1536 Tyndale was publicly executed, burned at the stake. However, his work was used by Coverdale in the so-called Great Bible of 1539.

The Elizabethan era produced the Geneva Bible of 1560 and the Bishops Bible in 1568, both translations from the original Greek. The Geneva Bible became the most popular Bible of the 16th Century; it was the Bible of Shakespeare, Bunyan, the Puritans and Oliver Cromwell and its wide popularity continued for many years. To the pilgrims who had used the Geneva Bible, the later King James version was "a fond thing lately invented."

The King James Version, commonly called the Authorized Version of 1611 (KJAV), was 9/10ths taken from Tyndale's Bible and was the first to win Crown approval. Designed to replace existing competing versions in all church services, it has become sacrosanct for many Protestants and is widely used and revered for its beauty and artistry to this day. Termed a "literary masterpiece" and "the noblest monument to English prose," it has supplied many quotations for English music, literature, and politicians. Sayings from its text are imbedded in the English language.

The KJAV is treated as "inspired" by many fundamentalists who love the resonance of "thou," "thy," and other archaic language used in that version. Many Christians will never depart emotionally from the familiar old English; a good example is the 23rd Psalm, which to many "just doesn't sound right" as it appears in modern versions. The King James Version led to a veritable explosion in the circulation of the bible in the 18th Century.

However, substantial defects in the King James version became very apparent in the 19th Century. Some related only to language, particularly words and phrases that became obsolete and hard to understand. Much more serious concerns about the King James were later raised by scholars. Better and almost complete Greek manuscripts were discovered (the best are called Sinaiticus and Vaticanus); they differed in material respects from the inferior Byzantine texts used for both the Tyndale and King James versions. Sinaiticus and Vaticanus are dated to the middle of the 4th Century and are the oldest manuscripts which contain the complete text of all four gospels. They rendered some portions of the text of the King James Version rather hopelessly out of date.

These problems did not, however, affect usage of the King James; many conservatives favor it to this day. In the 19th Century the Gideons put the KJAV in hotel and hospital rooms throughout America. Many Jews in English-speaking countries have continued until very recently to use the King James version of the Old Testament as the printed source for their scripture.

Because of the problems with the King James version, the Church of England sponsored a Revised Version late in the 19th Century. Its American counterpart was the American Standard Version of 1901. Both tried to stay as true as possible to the King James Authorized Version but removed archaic language and made improvements in translation. Despite this, or perhaps because of this, the ASV was not a success in America.

The English effort to produce an up-to-date version of the King James resulted in the New English Bible, which more recently became the Revised English Bible of 1989. In America, in 1952, the Revised Standard Version combined new translations from ancient Greek manuscripts with an effort to preserve basic content from the King James version and endeavored to eliminate archaic forms of expression.

The RSV (now replaced by the NRSV) finally became established as one of the best modern English versions, receiving both widespread Protestant and considerable Catholic acceptance; many scholars favored it. However, traditional and conservative Protestants disliked it intensely, finding it "unfaithful" to the revered King James. Some conservative Protestants sought a Bible of their own and this effort culminated in first the New American Standard Bible (NASB) of 1971 and then the New International Version (NIV) of 1978.

Catholic scholars for centuries used their own English language version, based, like Wycliff's Bible, on the Latin Vulgate. The New Testament was published in Rheims in 1582 and the Old Testament in Douay in 1609. This became the Douay-Rheims version which with revisions, notably by Challoner in the 18th Century, held undisputed sway among Catholics for many years.

Catholics finally produced a new English version after Pope Pius XII approved departure from the Latin. The 1970 result was the New American Bible (NAB), a translation from the best available Greek manuscripts. A 1987 edition of the NAB is based on a totally new translation from the original Greek manuscripts. Many Catholics, however, particularly in England, like the New Jerusalem Bible (NJB), originally based on a French language predecessor, "La Bible d' Jerusalem". A later (1985) edition of the New Jerusalem (NJRV) has used the oldest Greek manuscripts for a new translation.

As Catholics know, while the Vatican has permitted English language versions to be used in the mass, the Latin Vulgate version is still preserved for some liturgical purposes. The 1941 Confraternity Revision of the New Testament and the Knox Bible of 1950 are both based on the Latin Vulgate.

Translation Problems

The most exciting biblical find of the 19th Century was at Oxyrhynthus, Egypt, in 1896-1897; 200 volumes of ancient papyri were discovered. Then, in the first half of the 20th Century, a series of ancient fragments containing portions of New Testament books in Greek were uncovered – for example, the Chester Beatty papyri (fragments of Mark and Acts and much of the Pauline letters); the Bodmer Papyri (portions of John and Luke, with some of the epistles); and the famous Rylands Papyri (about seventy verses of the Book of John).

All these were fragments (about 88 in all) and carefully carbon dated by paleographic experts back to the 2d and 3d centuries. Perhaps their greatest significance was the 2d Century corroboration they provided for the 4th Century Vaticanus and Sinaiticus Greek manuscripts called the Great Codices. Scholars still labor over the ancient manuscripts; the International Greek New Testament Project has been at it for about 40 years and much remains to be done.

The 1940's brought exciting new finds. First was the ancient library found at Nag Hammadi, Egypt, in 1945. Twelve ancient codices stored in an earthen jar lifted the veil on the world of the gnostics. Then came the fabulous 1947 Qumran Dead Sea Scrolls found by Bedouins chasing a straying goat. They consist of many thousands of fragments and it will take years for the translation process to be completed. Many of the Qumran manuscripts have been dated by paleographic experts to the 1st Centuries BC and AD and include texts of the Hebrew Bible. No

New Testament books were found at either Nag Hammadi or Qumran, but the former yielded Coptic texts of the apocryphal Gospel of Thomas and Gospel of Philip.

A number of these discoveries shed startling new light on the usage of Greek at the time the New Testament books were written. The writings included hundreds of official reports, letters and business documents. Studying them, scholars realized for the first time that much of the Greek used by the 1st Century writers of the New Testament books was in reality Koine or ordinary, common, street-usage Greek, influenced by both the Semitic and Latin language and quite different from classic Greek. Before this, the New Testament Greek had been perceived as so different that scholars often called it "bad Greek" or "Holy Ghost Greek". Many Greek words in the New Testament were unknown in the classical literature. And even words in classical Greek have now become better understood.

This knowledge has produced results on two linguistic levels – better understanding of the Greek language used in the books of the New Testament, and better translations into English. Scholars have a new grasp of the word choices, idioms, nuances of meaning, grammar, and common phrasing. All of this work has helped stimulate many of the new editions and versions of the New Testament discussed at the beginning of this chapter.

The problems of translation cannot be minimized. Professor C. H. Dodd, director of the committee supervising the translation for the New English Bible, went so far as to characterize it as an "impossible art." W. D. Davies, Professor Emeritus at Duke University and Co-Editor of the Cambridge History of Judaism, says "every translation is only an approximation."

Basically, there are two schools of translation utilized by those producing modern Bibles. "Formal correspondence" is the more traditional method, favored by the conservatives. It endeavors to use intelligible, modern English but takes less initiative in trying to make current the formal meaning of the words. There is more emphasis on literal word-by-word translation. The other school is called "dynamic equivalence" and involves restructuring the original message into modern forms and patterns of speech for easier reading and understanding. Original author's meaning is frequently emphasized over formal translation of each separate word.

A modern example using a different language makes this translation dilemma understandable to everyone. Mexicans use the word "mañana" to mean roughly "at some time in the near future". Should it be translated that way or literally as "tomorrow"?

And there is another problem involving translation that the scholars have yet to face: the difficult issue of "sexism" –practically all the language of all Bible editions is heavily masculine oriented. Already some feminists (and some theologians, recently Carl Jung) are raising this issue, even going so far as to ask, "Must God be a man?"

Translation differences lead many people to stoutly maintain that this or that version is "tainted," "corrupted" or "unfaithful." One of the problems that translators and many readers share is that they seek a "majesty and beauty" in the Bible which the original Greek simply does not supply; direct, literal translation from the Greek rarely yields any inspiring text. The King James version, for many people, still meets this need.

Conclusion

Hopefully, this analysis will enable the reader to better understand how the major editions and versions were developed and how to choose from the many now available. Perhaps it will help promote decisions based on something other than emotion, if such a decision is desired. Here are a few guidelines.

Those readers who prefer the closest readable English approximation of a literal word-by-word translation using the "formal correspondence" school may choose New American Standard Bible or the New International Version, both favored by conservative Protestants.

The Good News/Today's English Version, and The Living Bible all have a very relaxed style and make for easy reading. Their liberality of language is, however, not accepted by many traditionalists; these versions carry "dynamic equivalence" translation to an extreme. Catholics desiring one of the easy-to-read versions can find it in the Catholic Study Bible; Protestants can find the same in the Today's English Version. Or either can read The Way or The Living Bible.

A more conservative "dynamic equivalence" translation is found in the NEB. In the middle are the RSV, NRSV, and NAB. American Catholics often favor the NAB. The RSV, widely respected among Protestants, has also gained acceptance among a number of Catholics and scholars. The NRSV has some text changes based on recent scholarly work and, with the headings and larger type available in some editions, is even more readable.

A final warning: these classifications have all the dangers of generalizations. And to the more casual Christian, the choice of version or edition usually makes little difference. What really matters to these Christians is both the basic story and the direct messages of Jesus, the events of his ministry, the passion story, and the resurrection. This is sufficient to support his or her basic needs and beliefs. The preference for these Christians is usually for texts made familiar by church attendance. The Bible in the rack, the family Bible at home – these meet their needs. Neither in living nor in religious practice, is there much patience for the differences in various versions of the Bible; they are largely meaningless.

But if a Christian desires to pursue Bible reading seriously or studiously, then the scholars and many religious leaders are correct in saying that the choice of which edition or version to use can assume more importance. Christians taking this approach should certainly be as fully aware (if not more so) of the different facets of their religious product as they are of the appliance or automobile that is selected for family usage.

About the Author

Daniel Walker is a retired attorney and author. His career preparation for writing this meticulously researched, plain-language account of First Century turbulence and the birth of Christianity included a stint as Law Clerk to the U.S.Supreme Court Chief Justice, years of trial law practice and authorship of the million-copy selling report on the violence at the 1968 Democratic National Convention. To the dismay of Mayor Richard Daley, Walker called it a "police riot" and entitled his book "Rights in Conflict" (Bantam Publ., 1968).

The author served as Governor of Illinois (1972-1976). He has written widely for legal audiences.

Walker is now retired to his original home in San Diego, California, enjoying his wife Lily, seven children, 22 grandchildren and one great grandchild.

Printed in the United States
2707